The Family Handyman Contents

Vol. 18, No. 7

Publisher
Jim Scheikofer
The Family Handyman®

Director, Publication Services
Sue Baalman-Pohlman
HDA, Inc. (Home Design Alternatives)

Editor
Kimberly King
HDA, Inc. (Home Design Alternatives)

Newsstand Sales
David Algire
Reader's Digest Association, Inc.

Marketing Manager
Andrea Vecchio
The Family Handyman

Production Manager
Judy Rodriguez
The Family Handyman®

Plans Administrator
Curtis Cadenhead
HDA, Inc. (Home Design Alternatives)

Copyright 2004 by
Home Service Publications, Inc.,
publishers of
The Family Handyman Magazine,
2915 Commers Drive, Suite 700,
Eagan, MN 55121.
Plan copyrights held by home
designer/architect.

Featured Homes

Plan #710-053D-0017 is featured on page 164.
Photo courtesy of HDA, Inc., St. Louis, MO

Plan #710-026D-0122 is featured on page 255.
Photo courtesy of Design Basics, Inc.

Sections

The Family Handyman magazine and HDA, Inc. (Home Design Alternatives) are pleased to join together to bring you this collection of best-selling home plans with many different styles for many different budgets from some of the nation's leading designers and architects.

Technical Specifications - At the time the construction drawings were prepared, every effort was made to ensure that these plans and speci-fications meet nationally recognized building codes (BOCA, Southern Building Code Congress and others). Because national building codes change or vary from area to area some drawing modifications and/or the assistance of a professional designer or architect may be necessary to comply with your local codes or to accommodate specific building conditions. We advise you to consult with your local building official for information regarding codes governing your area.

On The Cover...

Rear View

Plan #710-072D-0005 is featured on page 116.
Photo courtesy of Bloodgood Plan Service, photographer; Mark Englund

Reader's Digest

Quaint Exterior, Full Front Porch   Plan #710-053D-0030

1,657 total square feet of living area   **Price Code B**

Special features

- Stylish pass-through between living and dining areas
- Master bedroom is secluded from living area for privacy
- Large windows in breakfast and dining areas
- 3 bedrooms, 2 1/2 baths, 2-car drive under garage
- Basement foundation

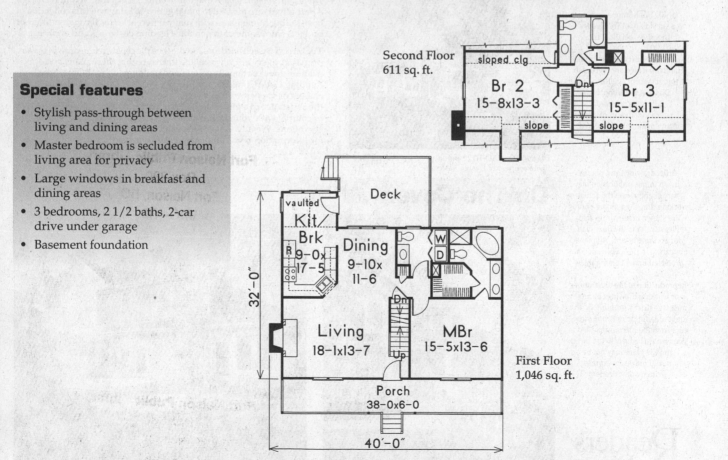

Second Floor
611 sq. ft.

sloped clg

Br 2
15-8x13-3

Br 3
15-5x11-1

slope   slope

First Floor
1,046 sq. ft.

vaulted

Deck

Kit/
Brk
9-0x
17-5

Dining
9-10x
11-6

Living
18-1x13-7

MBr
15-5x13-6

32'-0"

Porch
38-0x6-0

40'-0"

TO ORDER BLUEPRINTS USE THE FORM ON PAGE 15 OR CALL TOLL-FREE 1-877-671-6036
View thousands more home plans online at www.familyhandyman.com/homeplans

NEW! Power Sand®

THE ULTIMATE ABRASIVE BLOCK.

IT SANDS WOOD!
4X FASTER THAN SANDPAPER*

IT STRIPS PAINT!
NEVER CLOGS OR GOES DULL.

IT REMOVES RUST!
ONE BLOCK EQUALS UP TO
25 SHEETS OF SANDPAPER*

TRY ME FREE!

REVOLUTIONARY, NEW POWERSAND®
IS THE NEXT GENERATION IN ABRASIVES

TACKLE TOUGH SURFACE PREP WITH POWERSAND SUPER STRIPPING BLOCKS. EACH BLOCK WORKS
FOUR TIMES FASTER THAN SANDPAPER AND LASTS AS LONG AS TWENTY-FIVE SHEETS*. POWERSAND
WILL NOT CLOG, TEAR OR GO DULL AND ELIMINATES THE NEED FOR CHEMICAL STRIPPERS.

* When compared to 60-grit sandpaper on latex paint.

Luxury Home Filled With Extras   Plan #710-047D-0056

3,426 total square feet of living area   **Price Code F**

Special features

- Enormous master bath features double walk-in closets and an enormous whirlpool tub under a bay window
- Angled walls throughout add interest to every room
- Open and airy kitchen looks into a cozy breakfast nook as well as the casual family room
- Future space on the second floor has an additional 515 square feet of living area
- 5 bedrooms, 4 baths, 3-car side entry garage
- Slab foundation

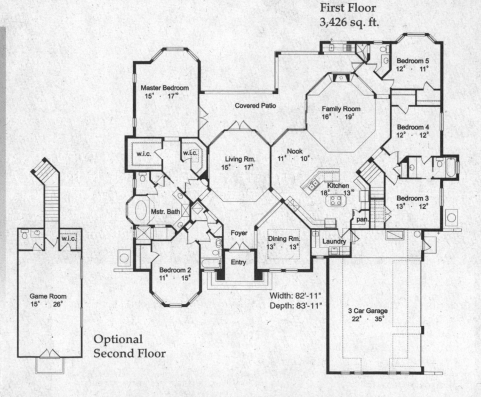

First Floor
3,426 sq. ft.

Optional
Second Floor

Width: 82'-11"
Depth: 83'-11"

4

TO ORDER BLUEPRINTS USE THE FORM ON PAGE 15 OR CALL TOLL-FREE 1-877-671-6036
View thousands more home plans online at www.familyhandyman.com/homeplans

DON'T LET YOUR **Santa Fe Sky** GET CLOUDY.

Priming with KILZ® before you paint stops old colors and stains from bleeding through to the topcoat, and gives your new paint a smoother, more even finish. To learn more about why you should prime with KILZ every time you paint, go to **www.KILZ.com/prime**.

Keep Colors Honest – Prime Every Time With KILZ.

Towering Stone Entry

Plan #710-011D-0015

1,893 total square feet of living area

Price Code D

Special features

- Two-story home delivers comfort and beauty
- Handsome open staircase adds interest
- Master suite includes walk-in closet and a private bath with twin sinks, oversized tub and a shower
- 3 bedrooms, 2 1/2 baths, 3-car garage
- Crawl space foundation

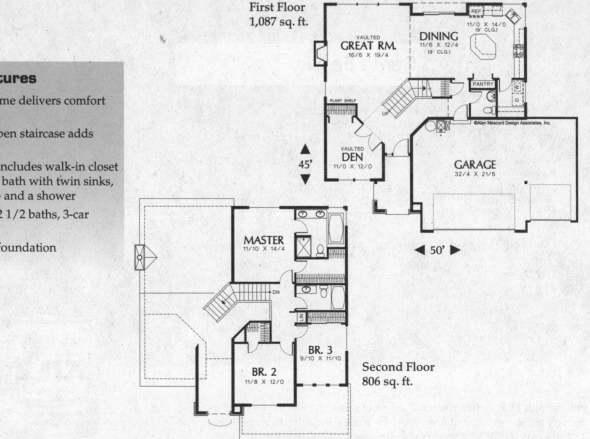

First Floor
1,087 sq. ft.

VAULTED
GREAT RM.
16/6 X 19/4

DINING
11/6 X 12/4
(9' CLG.)

11/0 X 14/0
(9' CLG.)

REF

PLANT SHELF

PANTRY

UP

W

D

©Alan Mascord Design Associates, Inc.

VAULTED
DEN
11/0 X 12/0

GARAGE
32/4 X 21/6

45'

50'

MASTER
11/10 X 14/4

DN

LIN

BR. 3
9/10 X 11/10

BR. 2
11/8 X 12/0

Second Floor
806 sq. ft.

Popular T-Stair

Plan #710-007D-0005

2,336 total square feet of living area

Price Code D

Special features

- Stately sunken living room with partially vaulted ceiling and classic arched transom windows
- Family room features plenty of windows and a fireplace with flanking bookshelves
- 4 bedrooms, 2 1/2 baths, 2-car garage
- Basement foundation

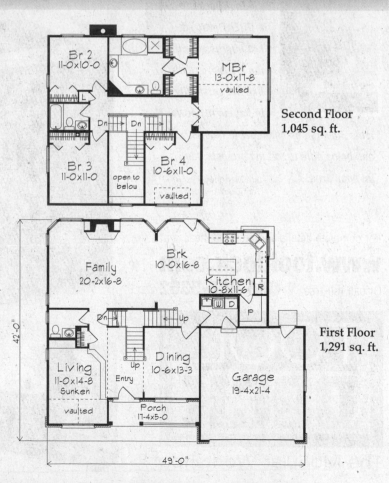

Second Floor
1,045 sq. ft.

Br 2
11-0x10-0

MBr
13-0x17-8
vaulted

Dn   Dn

Br 3
11-0x11-0

open to below

Br 4
10-6x11-0

vaulted

First Floor
1,291 sq. ft.

Family
20-2x16-8

Brk
10-0x16-8

Kitchen
10-8x11-6

Dn   Up

Living
11-0x14-8
Sunken

vaulted

Entry

Up

Dining
10-6x13-3

Garage
19-4x21-4

Porch
17-4x5-0

42'-0"

49'-0"

8

TO ORDER BLUEPRINTS USE THE FORM ON PAGE 15 OR CALL TOLL-FREE 1-877-671-6036
View thousands more home plans online at www.familyhandyman.com/homeplans

Attractive Exterior

Plan #710-055D-0030

2,107 total square feet of living area

Price Code C

Special features

- Master bedroom is separate from other bedrooms for privacy
- Spacious breakfast room and kitchen include center island with eating space
- Centralized great room has fireplace and easy access to any area in the home
- 4 bedrooms, 2 1/2 baths, 2-car garage
- Crawl space, basement, walk-out basement or slab foundation, please specify when ordering

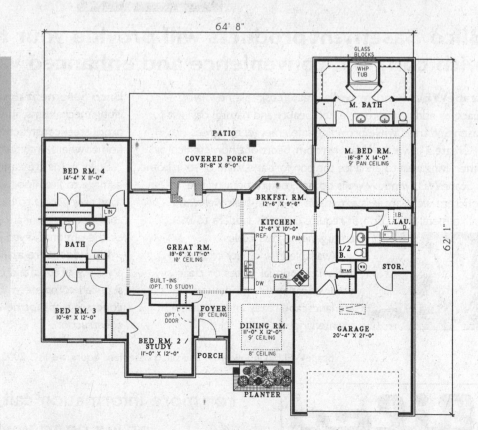

TO ORDER BLUEPRINTS USE THE FORM ON PAGE 15 OR CALL TOLL-FREE 1-877-671-6036
View thousands more home plans online at www.familyhandyman.com/homeplans

Our Blueprint Packages Offer...

Quality plans for building your future, with extras that provide unsurpassed value, ensure good construction and long-term enjoyment.

A quality home - one that looks good, functions well, and provides years of enjoyment - is a product of many things - design, materials, craftsmanship.

But it's also the result of outstanding blueprints - the actual plans and specifications that tell the builder exactly how to build your home.

And with our BLUEPRINT PACKAGES you get the absolute best. A complete set of blueprints is available for every design in this book. These "working drawings," are highly detailed, resulting in two key benefits:

☐ Better understanding by the contractor of how to build your home and...

☐ More accurate construction estimates.

When you purchase one of our designs, you'll receive all of the BLUEPRINT components shown here - elevations, foundation plan, floor plans, sections, and/or details. Other helpful building aids are also available to help make your dream home a reality.

Cover Sheet

The cover sheet is the artist's rendering of the exterior of the home. It will give you an idea of how your home will look when completed and landscaped.

Interior Elevations

Interior elevations provide views of special interior elements such as fireplaces, kitchen cabinets, built-in units and other features of the home.

Foundation Plan

The foundation plan shows the layout of the basement, crawl space, slab or pier foundation. All necessary notations and dimensions are included. See plan page for the foundation types included. If the home plan you choose does not have your desired foundation type, our Customer Service Representatives can advise you on how to customize your foundation to suit your specific needs or site conditions.

Details

Details show how to construct certain components of your home, such as the roof system, stairs, deck, etc.

Sections

Sections show detail views of the home or portions of the home as if it were sliced from the roof to the foundation. This sheet shows important areas such as load-bearing walls, stairs, joists, trusses and other structural elements, which are critical for proper construction.

Floor Plans

The floor plans show the placement of walls, doors, closets, plumbing fixtures, electrical outlets, columns, and beams for each level of the home.

Exterior Elevations

Exterior elevations illustrate the front, rear and both sides of the house, with all details of exterior materials and the required dimensions.

What Kind Of Plan Package Do You Need?

Now that you've found the home you've been looking for, here are some suggestions on how to make your Dream Home a reality. To get started, order the type of plans that fit your particular situation.

YOUR CHOICES

- **THE 1-SET STUDY PACKAGE -** We offer a 1-set plan package so you can study your home in detail. This one set is considered a study set and is marked "not for construction." It is a copyright violation to reproduce blueprints.

- **THE MINIMUM 5-SET PACKAGE -** If you're ready to start the construction process, this 5-set package is the minimum number of blueprint sets you will need. It will require keeping close track of each set so they can be used by multiple subcontractors and tradespeople.

- **THE STANDARD 8-SET PACKAGE -** For best results in terms of cost, schedule and quality of construction, we recommend you order eight (or more) sets of blueprints. Besides one set for yourself, additional sets of blueprints will be required by your mortgage lender, local building department, general contractor and all subcontractors working on foundation, electrical, plumbing, heating/air conditioning, carpentry work, etc.

- **REPRODUCIBLE MASTERS -** If you wish to make some minor design changes, you'll want to order reproducible masters. These drawings contain the same information as the blueprints but are printed on erasable and reproducible paper which clearly indicates your right to copy or reproduce. This will allow your builder or a local design professional to make the necessary drawing changes without the major expense of redrawing the plans. This package also allows you to print copies of the modified plans as needed. The right of building only one structure from these plans is licensed exclusively to the buyer. You may not use this design to build a second or multiple dwelling(s) without purchasing another blueprint. Each violation of the Copyright Law is punishable in a fine.

- **MIRROR REVERSE SETS -** Plans can be printed in mirror reverse. These plans are useful when the house would fit your site better if all the rooms were on the opposite side than shown. They are simply a mirror image of the original drawings causing the lettering and dimensions to read backwards. Therefore, when ordering mirror reverse drawings, you must purchase at least one set of right-reading plans.

Other Helpful Building Aids...

Your Blueprint Package will contain the necessary construction information to build your home. We also offer the following products and services to save you time and money in the building process.

- **MATERIAL LIST -** Material lists are available for many of the plans in this book. Each list gives you the quantity, dimensions and description of the building materials necessary to construct your home. You'll get faster and more accurate bids from your contractor while saving money by paying for only the materials you need. See the Home Plans Index on page 14 for availability and pricing.

- **DETAIL PLAN PACKAGES -** Framing, Plumbing & Electrical Plan Packages: Three separate packages offer homebuilders details for constructing various foundations; numerous floor, wall and roof framing techniques; simple to complex residential wiring; sump and water softener hookups; plumbing connection methods; installation of septic systems and more. Each package includes three-dimensional illustrations and a glossary of terms. Purchase one or all three. Cost: $20.00 each or all three for $40.00. Note: These drawings do not pertain to a specific home plan.

- **THE LEGAL KIT™ -** Our Legal Kit provides contracts and legal forms to help protect you from the potential pitfalls inherent in the building process. The Kit supplies commonly used forms and contracts suitable for homeowners and builders. It can save you a considerable amount of time and help protect you and your assets during and after construction. Cost: $35.00

- **EXPRESS DELIVERY -** Most orders are processed within 24 hours of receipt. Please allow 7-10 business days for delivery. If you need to place a rush order, please call us by 11:00 a.m. Monday-Friday CST and ask for express service (allow 1-2 business days).

- **TECHNICAL ASSISTANCE -** If you have questions, call our technical support line at 1-314-770-2228 between 8:00 a.m. and 5:00 p.m. Monday-Friday CST. Whether it involves design modifications or field assistance, our designers are extremely familiar with all of our designs and will be happy to help you. We want your home to be everything you expect it to be.

HOME DESIGN ALTERNATIVES, INC.

QUICK AND EASY CUSTOMIZING
MAKE CHANGES TO YOUR HOME PLAN IN 4 STEPS

HERE'S AN AFFORDABLE AND EFFICIENT WAY TO MAKE CHANGES TO YOUR PLAN.

1 Select the house plan that most closely meets your needs. Purchase of a reproducible master is necessary in order to make changes to a plan.

2 Call 1-877-671-6036 to place your order. Tell the sales representative you're interested in customizing a plan. A $50 refundable consultation fee will be charged. You will then be instructed to complete a customization checklist indicating all the changes you wish to make to your plan. You may attach sketches if necessary. <u>If you proceed with the custom changes the $50 will be credited to the total amount charged.</u>

3 FAX the completed customization checklist to our design consultant at 1-866-477-5173 or e-mail **custom@drummonddesigns.com.** Within *24-48 business hours you will be provided with a written cost estimate to modify your plan. Our design consultant will contact you by phone if you wish to discuss any of your changes in greater detail.

4 Once you approve the estimate, a 75% retainer fee is collected and customization work gets underway. Preliminary drawings can usually be completed within *5-10 business days. Following approval of the preliminary drawings your design changes are completed within *5-10 business days. Your remaining 25% balance due is collected prior to shipment of your completed drawings. You will be shipped five sets of revised blueprints or a reproducible master, plus a customized materials list if required.

*Terms are subject to change without notice.

16

BEFORE
Plan 2829

Customized Version of Plan 2829

AFTER

Sample Modification Pricing Guide

The average prices specified below are provided as examples only. They refer to the most commonly requested changes, and are subject to change without notice. Prices for changes will vary or differ, from the prices below, depending on the number of modifications requested, the plan size, style, quality of original plan, format provided to us (originally drawn by hand or computer), and method of design used by the original designer. To obtain a detailed cost estimate or to get more information, please contact us.

Sample Modification Pricing Guide	*Average Cost
Adding or removing living space	Quote required
Adding or removing a garage	Starting at $400
Garage: Front entry to side load or vice versa	Starting at $300
Adding a screened porch	Starting at $280
Adding a bonus room in the attic	Starting at $450
Changing full basement to crawl space or vice versa	Starting at $220
Changing full basement to slab or vice versa	Starting at $260
Changing exterior building material	Starting at $200
Changing roof lines	Starting at $360
Adjusting ceiling height	Starting at $280
Adding, moving or removing an exterior opening	$65 per opening
Adding or removing a fireplace	Starting at $90
Modifying a non-bearing wall or room	$65 per room
Changing exterior walls from 2"x4" to 2"x6"	Starting at $200
Redesigning a bathroom or a kitchen	Starting at $120
Reverse plan right reading	Quote required
Adapting plans for local building code requirements	Quote required
Engineering and Architectural stamping and services	Quote required
Adjust plan for handicapped accessibility	Quote required
Interactive Illustrations (choices of exterior materials)	Quote required
Metric conversion of home plan	Starting at $400

*Prices and Terms are subject to change without notice.

The Family Handyman

Dramatic Curved Stairway   Plan #710-026D-0119

3,775 total square feet of living area

Price Code F

Special features

- Screened porch off living and dining areas brings the outdoors in
- Bookshelves flank each side of the fireplace in the family room
- Built-in bookshelves in den
- Second floor master bedroom has a bayed sitting area and a wonderful bath
- 4 bedrooms, 3 1/2 baths, 3-car side entry garage
- Basement foundation

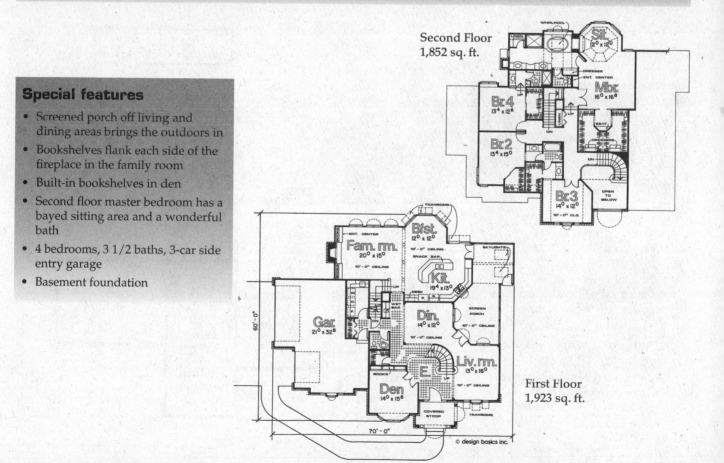

Second Floor
1,852 sq. ft.

First Floor
1,923 sq. ft.

TO ORDER BLUEPRINTS USE THE FORM ON PAGE 15 OR CALL TOLL-FREE 1-877-671-6036
View thousands more home plans online at www.familyhandyman.com/homeplans

17

OPEN Living Areas
Plan #710-021D-0007

1,868 total square feet of living area

Price Code D

Special features

- Luxurious master bath is impressive with an angled quarter-circle tub, separate vanities and large walk-in closet
- Energy efficient home with 2" x 6" exterior walls
- Dining room is surrounded by a series of arched openings which complement the open feeling of this design
- Living room has a 12' ceiling accented by skylights and a large fireplace flanked by sliding doors
- Large storage areas
- 3 bedrooms, 2 baths, 2-car side entry garage
- Slab foundation, drawings also include crawl space foundation

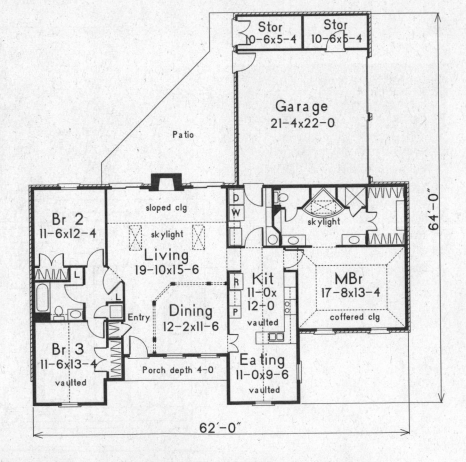

TO ORDER BLUEPRINTS USE THE FORM ON PAGE 15 OR CALL TOLL-FREE 1-877-671-6036
View thousands more home plans online at www.familyhandyman.com/homeplans

18

Cozy Covered Front Porch

Plan #710-035D-0045

1,749 total square feet of living area

Price Code B

Special features

- Tray ceiling in master bedroom
- Breakfast bar overlooks vaulted great room
- Additional bedrooms are located away from master suite for privacy
- Optional bonus room above the garage has an additional 308 square feet of living area
- 3 bedrooms, 2 baths, 2-car garage
- Walk-out basement, slab or crawl space foundation, please specify when ordering

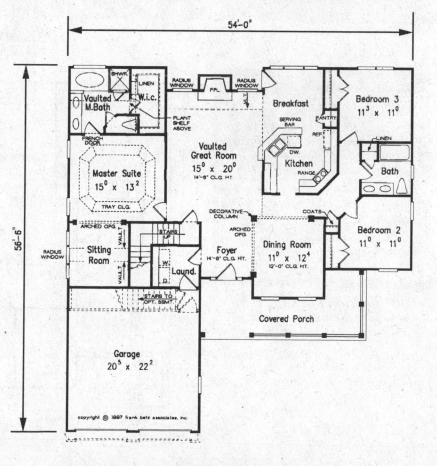

TO ORDER BLUEPRINTS USE THE FORM ON PAGE 15 OR CALL TOLL-FREE 1-877-671-6036
View thousands more home plans online at www.familyhandyman.com/homeplans

19

2,665 total square feet of living area

Price Code E

Special features

- 9' ceilings on first floor
- Spacious kitchen features many cabinets, center island cooktop and breakfast room with bay window, adjacent to laundry room
- Second floor bedrooms boast walk-in closets, dressing areas and share a bath
- Twin patio doors and fireplace grace living room
- 4 bedrooms, 3 baths, 2-car rear entry garage
- Slab foundation, drawings also include crawl space foundation

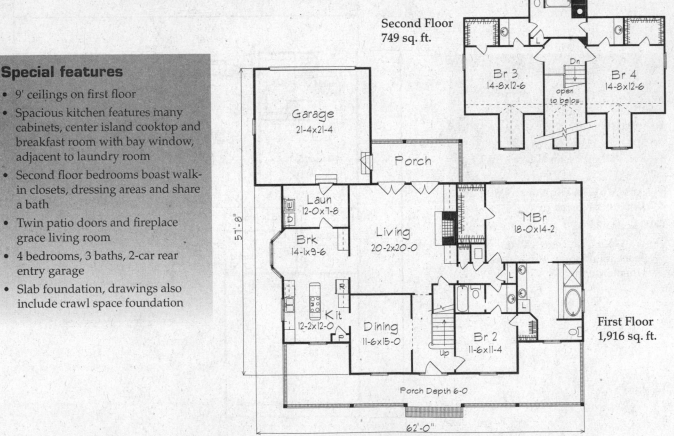

Second Floor
749 sq. ft.

Br 3
14-8x12-6

open
to below

Dn

Br 4
14-8x12-6

Garage
21-4x21-4

Porch

Laun
12-0x7-8

Brk
14-1x9-6

Living
20-2x20-0

MBr
18-0x14-2

Kit
12-2x12-0

Dining
11-6x15-0

Br 2
11-6x11-4

Up

First Floor
1,916 sq. ft.

51'-8"

Porch Depth 6-0

62'-0"

TO ORDER BLUEPRINTS USE THE FORM ON PAGE 15 OR CALL TOLL-FREE 1-877-671-6036
View thousands more home plans online at www.familyhandyman.com/homeplans

20

THE Family Handyman

Bay Window In Master Bedroom   Plan #710-053D-0002

1,668 total square feet of living area

Price Code C

Special features

- Large bay windows in breakfast area, master bedroom and dining room
- Extensive walk-in closets and storage spaces throughout the home
- Handy covered entry porch
- Large living room has fireplace, built-in bookshelves and sloped ceiling
- 3 bedrooms, 2 baths, 2-car drive under garage
- Basement foundation

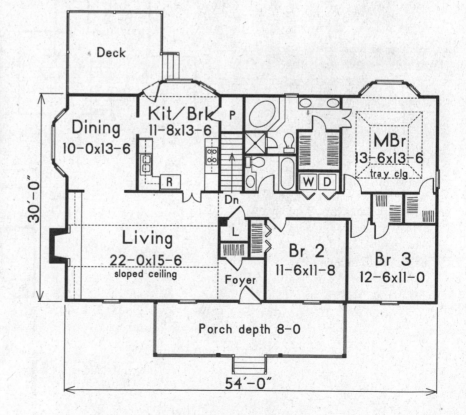

Deck

Dining
10-0x13-6

Kit/Brk
11-8x13-6

P

MBr
13-6x13-6
tray clg

Dn

W   D

Living
22-0x15-6
sloped ceiling

L

Br 2
11-6x11-8

Br 3
12-6x11-0

Foyer

30'-0"

Porch depth 8-0

54'-0"

TO ORDER BLUEPRINTS USE THE FORM ON PAGE 15 OR CALL TOLL-FREE 1-877-671-6036
View thousands more home plans online at www.familyhandyman.com/homeplans

21

Surrounding Porch For Views — Plan #710-058D-0020

1,428 total square feet of living area

Price Code A

Special features

- Large vaulted family room opens to dining area and kitchen with breakfast bar
- First floor master bedroom offers large bath, walk-in closet and nearby laundry facilities
- A spacious loft/bedroom #3 overlooking family room and an additional bedroom and bath conclude the second floor
- 3 bedrooms, 2 baths
- Basement foundation

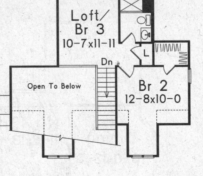

Loft/Br 3
10-7x11-11

Open To Below

Dn

Br 2
12-8x10-0

Second Floor
415 sq. ft.

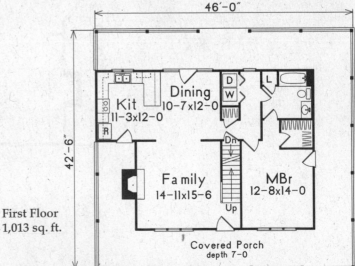

46'-0"

42'-6"

Kit
11-3x12-0

Dining
10-7x12-0

Family
14-11x15-6

MBr
12-8x14-0

Dn

Up

First Floor
1,013 sq. ft.

Covered Porch
depth 7-0

Angled Den With Built-Ins — Plan #710-043D-0001

3,158 total square feet of living area

Price Code E

Special features

- Coffered ceiling in entry
- Vaulted ceilings in living room, master bedroom and family room
- Interior columns accent the entry, living and dining areas
- Kitchen island has eating bar adding extra seating
- Master bath has garden tub and a separate shower
- 3 bedrooms, 2 1/2 baths, 3-car garage
- Crawl space foundation

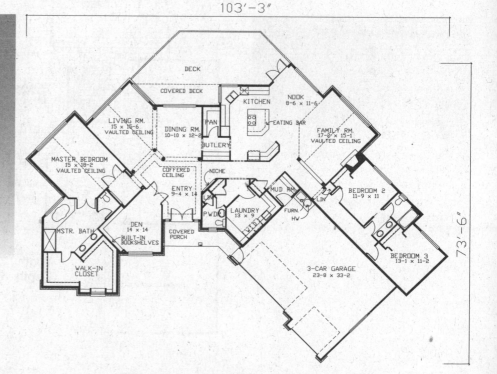

103'-3"

73'-6"

DECK

COVERED DECK

KITCHEN

NOOK
8-6 x 11-6

LIVING RM.
15 x 16-6
VAULTED CEILING

DINING RM.
10-10 x 12-2

PAN

EATING BAR

FAMILY RM.
17-2 x 15-1
VAULTED CEILING

BUTLERY

MASTER BEDROOM
15 x 18-2
VAULTED CEILING

COFFERED
CEILING

NICHE

MUD RM.

BEDROOM 2
11-9 x 11

ENTRY
9-4 x 14

LIN

FURN.
HW

LAUNDRY
13 x 9

PWDR

LIN

MSTR. BATH

DEN
14 x 14
BUILT-IN
BOOKSHELVES

COVERED
PORCH

BEDROOM 3
13-1 x 11-2

3-CAR GARAGE
23-8 x 33-2

WALK-IN
CLOSET

TO ORDER BLUEPRINTS USE THE FORM ON PAGE 15 OR CALL TOLL-FREE 1-877-671-6036
View thousands more home plans online at www.familyhandyman.com/homeplans

23

The Family Handyman

Second Floor Bonus Space   Plan #710-047D-0045

2,551 total square feet of living area   **Price Code D**

Special features

- Archway joins formal living and family rooms
- Master suite has private bath and access to a covered patio
- Breakfast nook overlooks family room with cozy corner fireplace
- Future space on the second floor has an additional 287 square feet of living area
- 3 bedrooms, 3 baths, 2-car side entry garage
- Slab foundation

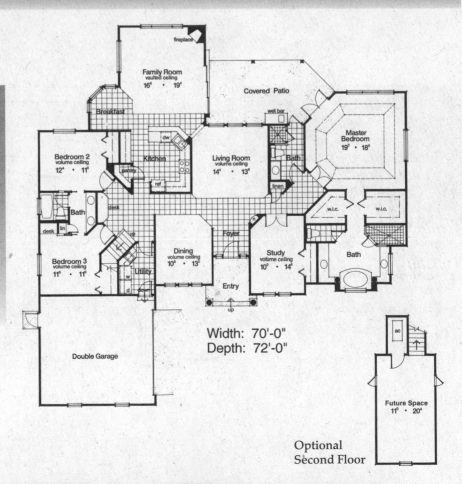

Width: 70'-0"
Depth: 72'-0"

Optional
Second Floor

TO ORDER BLUEPRINTS USE THE FORM ON PAGE 15 OR CALL TOLL-FREE 1-877-671-6036
View thousands more home plans online at www.familyhandyman.com/homeplans

Charming Covered Entry

Plan #710-033D-0014

2,013 total square feet of living area

Price Code D

Special features

- Sliding doors in dinette allow convenient access outdoors
- Family room includes cozy fireplace for informal gathering
- All bedrooms located on second floor for privacy
- Master bath includes dressing area, walk-in closet and separate tub and shower
- 4 bedrooms, 2 1/2 baths, 2-car garage
- Basement foundation

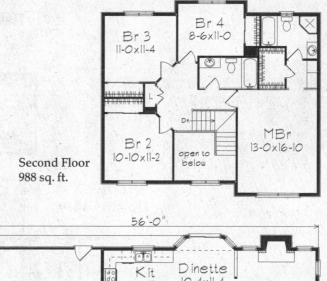

Second Floor
988 sq. ft.

Br 3
11-0x11-4

Br 4
8-6x11-0

Br 2
10-10x11-2

MBr
13-0x16-10

open to below

Dn

L

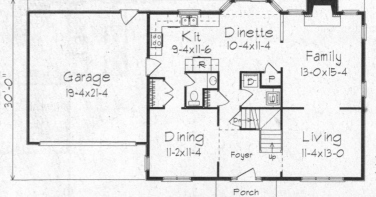

56'-0"

30'-0"

Garage
19-4x21-4

Kit
9-4x11-6

Dinette
10-4x11-4

Family
13-0x15-4

Dining
11-2x11-4

Living
11-4x13-0

Foyer

up

Dn

Porch

First Floor
1,025 sq. ft.

TO ORDER BLUEPRINTS USE THE FORM ON PAGE 15 OR CALL TOLL-FREE 1-877-671-6036
View thousands more home plans online at www.familyhandyman.com/HOMEPLANS

25

BRIGHT AND CHEERY SUN ROOM   Plan #710-034D-0024

2,211 total square feet of living area

Price Code D

M. MAXON

Special features

- Spacious sun room has three walls of windows and access outdoors
- Family room has open view into kitchen and dining area
- Large master bedroom has private luxurious bath with step-up tub
- Bonus room has an additional 241 square feet of living area
- 4 bedrooms, 2 1/2 baths, 2-car garage
- Basement foundation

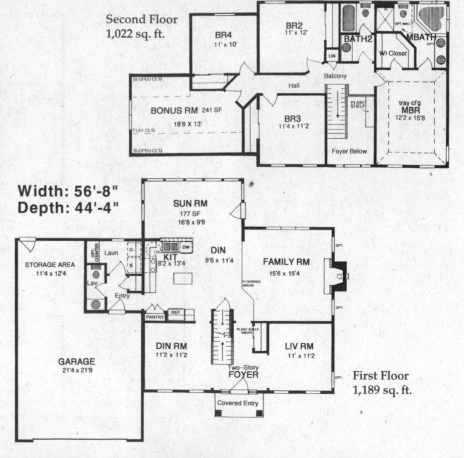

Second Floor
1,022 sq. ft.

BR4
11' x 10'

BR2
11' x 12'

BATH2

MBATH

WI Closet

OPT. WALL

LIN

SLOPED CL'G

Balcony

BONUS RM 241 SF
18'8 X 13'

FLAT CL'G

Hall

BR3
11'4 x 11'2

PLANT SHELF

tray cl'g
MBR
12'2 x 15'8

SLOPED CL'G

Foyer Below

Width: 56'-8"
Depth: 44'-4"

SUN RM
177 SF
16'8 x 9'8

STORAGE AREA
11'4 x 12'4

OPT. COUNTER

Laun

KIT
8'2 x 13'4

DW

DIN
8'6 x 11'4

FAMILY RM
15'6 x 15'4

Lav

Entry

FLOORING BREAK

PANTRY

REF

GARAGE
21'4 x 21'8

DIN RM
11'2 x 11'2

PLANT SHELF ABOVE

Two-Story
FOYER

LIV RM
11' x 11'2

First Floor
1,189 sq. ft.

Covered Entry

Study Off Main Entrance

Plan #710-036D-0060

1,760 total square feet of living area

Price Code B

Special features

- Stone and brick exterior has old world charm
- Master bedroom includes a sitting area and is situated away from other bedrooms for privacy
- Kitchen and dinette access the outdoors
- Great room includes fireplace, built-in bookshelves and an entertainment center
- 3 bedrooms, 2 baths, 2-car side entry garage
- Slab foundation

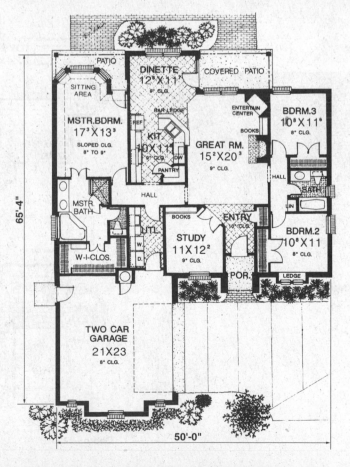

TO ORDER BLUEPRINTS USE THE FORM ON PAGE 15 OR CALL TOLL-FREE 1-877-671-6036
View thousands more home plans online at www.familyhandyman.com/homeplans

27

RICH WITH Victorian Details

Plan #710-062D-0046

2,632 total square feet of living area

Price Code E

Special features

- Energy efficient home with 2" x 6" exterior walls
- Master bedroom has a cheerful octagon-shaped sitting area
- Arched entrances create a distinctive living room with a lovely tray ceiling and help define the dining room
- 4 bedrooms, 2 1/2 baths, 2-car garage
- Basement or crawl space foundation, please specify when ordering

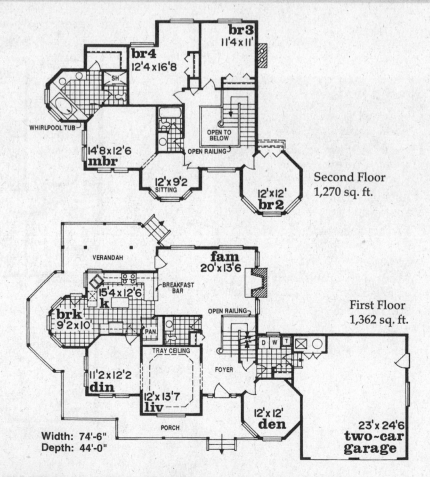

br3
11'4 x 11'

br4
12'4 x 16'8

SH

WHIRLPOOL TUB

OPEN TO BELOW

OPEN RAILING

14'8 x 12'6
mbr

12' x 9'2
SITTING

12' x 12'
br 2

Second Floor
1,270 sq. ft.

VERANDAH

fam
20' x 13'6

BREAKFAST BAR

15'4 x 12'6
k

brk
9'2 x 10'

PAN

OPEN RAILING

TRAY CEILING

FOYER

D W T

11'2 x 12'2
din

12' x 13'7
liv

12' x 12'
den

23' x 24'6
two-car garage

PORCH

First Floor
1,362 sq. ft.

Width: 74'-6"
Depth: 44'-0"

28

TO ORDER BLUEPRINTS USE THE FORM ON PAGE 15 OR CALL TOLL-FREE 1-877-671-6036
View thousands more home plans online at www.familyhandyman.com/homeplans

Family Handyman

COPYRIGHT LARRY E. BELK

2,586 total square feet of living area

Price Code D

Special features

- Great room has an impressive tray ceiling and see-through fireplace into bayed breakfast room
- Master bedroom has walk-in closet and private bath
- 4 bedrooms, 3 baths, 2-car side entry garage
- Basement, crawl space or slab foundation, please specify when ordering

WIDTH 64'-10"

DEPTH 61'-0"

First Floor
2,028 sq. ft.

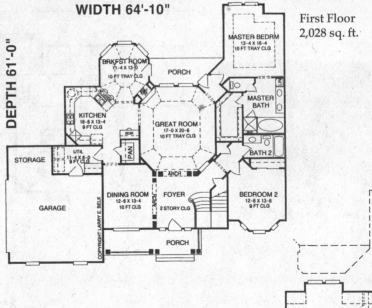

MASTER BEDRM
13-4 X 16-4
10 FT TRAY CLG

BRKFST ROOM
11-4 X 13-0
10 FT TRAY CLG

PORCH

KITCHEN
16-6 X 13-4
9 FT CLG

GREAT ROOM
17-0 X 20-6
10 FT TRAY CLG

MASTER BATH

BATH 2

STORAGE

UTIL
11-4 X 8-0
9 FT CLG

PAN

GARAGE

DINING ROOM
12-6 X 13-4
10 FT CLG

ARCH

FOYER
2 STORY CLG

BEDROOM 2
12-6 X 13-6
9 FT CLG

PORCH

COPYRIGHT LARRY E. BELK

BEDROOM 4
13-4 X 10-4

EXPANDABLE AREA
17-4 X 18-0

ATTIC

BATH 3

OPEN TO
FOYER BELOW

BEDROOM 3
13-0 X 11-6

PLANT LEDGE

Second Floor
558 sq. ft.

TO ORDER BLUEPRINTS USE THE FORM ON PAGE 15 OR CALL TOLL-FREE 1-877-671-6036
View thousands more home plans online at www.familyhandyman.com/homeplans

29

Seaside, Lake Or Mountain Views   Plan #710-032D-0019

1,995 total square feet of living area

Price Code C

Special features

- First floor solarium creates a sunny atmosphere
- Second floor office is tucked away from traffic areas for privacy
- Energy efficient home with 2" x 6" exterior walls
- Bonus room above the garage provides an additional 285 square feet of living area
- 3 bedrooms, 2 1/2 baths, 2-car side entry garage
- Basement foundation

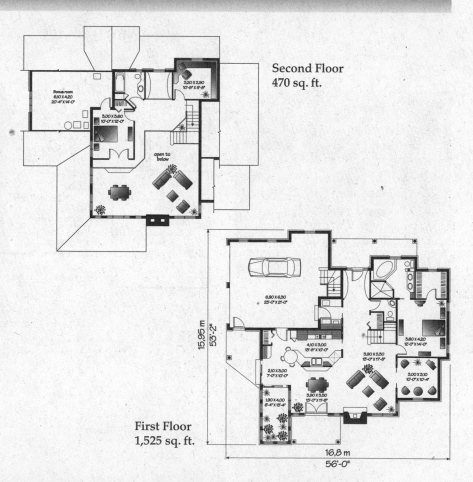

Second Floor
470 sq. ft.

First Floor
1,525 sq. ft.

Covered Breezeway To Garage — Plan #710-039D-0004

1,406 total square feet of living area

Price Code A

Special features

- Master bedroom has a sloped ceiling
- Kitchen and dining area merge becoming a gathering place
- Enter family room from charming covered front porch to find a fireplace and lots of windows
- 3 bedrooms, 2 baths, 2-car detached garage
- Slab or crawl space foundation, please specify when ordering

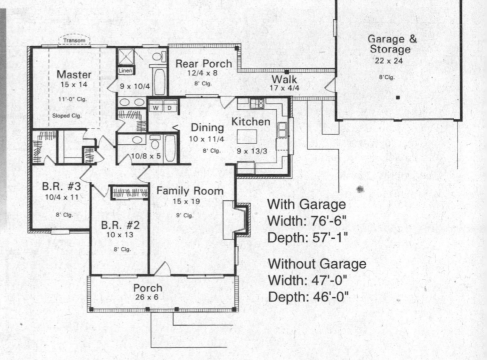

With Garage
Width: 76'-6"
Depth: 57'-1"

Without Garage
Width: 47'-0"
Depth: 46'-0"

TO ORDER BLUEPRINTS USE THE FORM ON PAGE 15 OR CALL TOLL-FREE 1-877-671-6036
View thousands more home plans online at www.familyhandyman.com/homeplans

31

Ranch-Style With Many Extras   Plan #710-049D-0012

1,295 total square feet of living area

Price Code A

Special features

- Wrap-around porch is a lovely place for dining
- A fireplace gives a stunning focal point to the great room that is heightened with a sloped ceiling
- The master suite is full of luxurious touches such as a walk-in closet and a lush private bath
- 2 bedrooms, 2 baths, 2-car garage
- Basement foundation

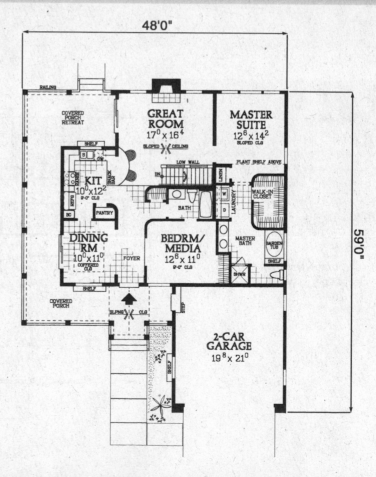

48'0"

59'0"

COVERED PORCH RETREAT

GREAT ROOM
17⁰ x 16⁴
sloped ceiling

MASTER SUITE
12⁶ x 14²
sloped clg

KIT
10⁰ x 12²

LOW WALL

PLANT SHELF ABOVE

LINEN

WALK-IN CLOSET

LAUNDRY

PANTRY

BATH

MASTER BATH

BARDEN TUB

DINING RM
10⁰ x 11⁰

FOYER

BEDRM/MEDIA
12⁶ x 11⁰

SHWR

COVERED PORCH

2-CAR GARAGE
19⁸ x 21⁰

Rooflines Add Interest

Plan #710-020D-0007

1,828 total square feet of living area
Price Code C

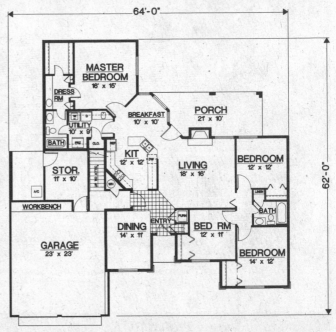

Special features

- Energy efficient home with 2" x 6" exterior walls
- Master bath features a giant walk-in closet, built-in linen storage with convenient access to utility room
- Kitchen has a unique design that is elegant and practical
- 4 bedrooms, 2 baths, 2-car garage
- Slab, crawl space or basement foundation, please specify when ordering

Economical To Build

Plan #710-038D-0018

1,792 total square feet of living area
Price Code B

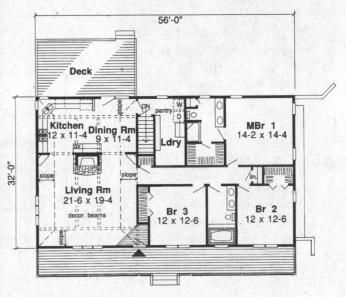

Special features

- Master bedroom has a private bath and large walk-in closet
- A central stone fireplace and windows on two walls are focal points in the living room
- Decorative beams and sloped ceilings add interest to the kitchen, living and dining rooms
- 3 bedrooms, 2 baths, 2-car drive under garage
- Basement foundation

TO ORDER BLUEPRINTS USE THE FORM ON PAGE 15 OR CALL TOLL-FREE 1-877-671-6036
View thousands more home plans online at www.familyhandyman.com/homeplans

33

Terrific Master Bedroom

Plan #710-018D-0003

2,517 total square feet of living area

Price Code D

Special features

- Energy efficient home with 2" x 6" exterior walls
- Central living room with large windows and attractive transoms
- Varied ceiling heights throughout home
- Secluded master bedroom features double-door entry, luxurious bath with separate shower, step-up whirlpool tub, double vanities and walk-in closets
- Kitchen with walk-in pantry overlooks large family room with fireplace and unique octagon-shaped breakfast room
- 4 bedrooms, 2 1/2 baths, 2-car garage
- Slab foundation, drawings also include crawl space foundation

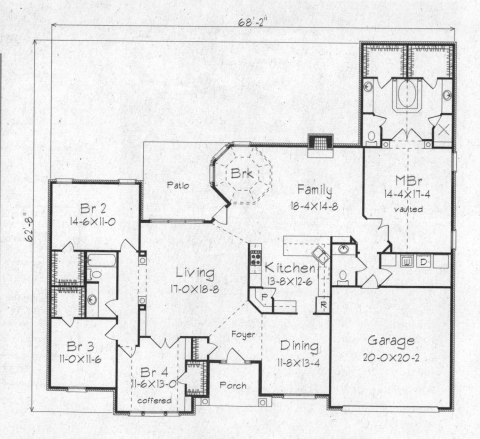

Luxurious Ranch

Plan #710-051D-0033

2,196 total square feet of living area

Price Code C

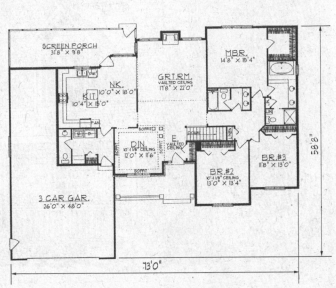

Special features

- Covered front porch leads to the vaulted foyer which invites guests into the great room
- Master bedroom features walk-in closet, private bath with double vanity, spa tub and linen closet
- Large open kitchen
- 3 bedrooms, 2 1/2 baths, 3-car garage
- Basement foundation

Pillared Front Porch

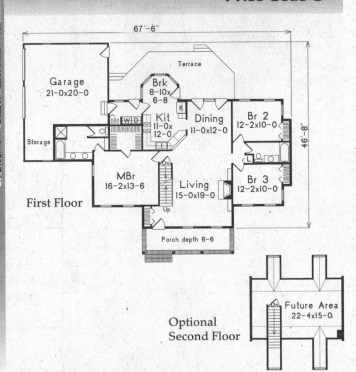

Plan #710-017D-0007

1,567 total square feet of living area

Price Code C

Special features

- Living room flows into dining room shaped by an angled pass-through into the kitchen
- Future area available on the second floor has an additional 338 square feet of living area
- Master bedroom is separated from other bedrooms for privacy
- 3 bedrooms, 2 baths, 2-car side entry garage
- Basement foundation, drawings also include slab foundation

TO ORDER BLUEPRINTS USE THE FORM ON PAGE 15 OR CALL TOLL-FREE 1-877-671-6036
View thousands more home plans online at www.familyhandyman.com/homeplans

35

THE Family Handyman

Year-Round Or Weekend Getaway   Plan #710-058D-0006

1,339 total square feet of living area

Price Code A

Special features

- Full-length covered porch enhances front facade
- Vaulted ceiling and stone fireplace add drama to family room
- Walk-in closets in bedrooms provide ample storage space
- Combined kitchen/dining area adjoins family room for perfect entertaining space
- 3 bedrooms, 2 1/2 baths
- Crawl space foundation

Second Floor
415 sq. ft.

Loft/
Br 3
10-7x11-11

Open To Below

Dn

L

Br 2
12-8x10-0

32'-0"

28'-6"

R

Kit/Din
14-11x12-0

D W F

Family
14-11x15-6
vaulted clg

Up

MBr
12-8x14-1

First Floor
924 sq. ft.

Covered Porch depth 7-0

TO ORDER BLUEPRINTS USE THE FORM ON PAGE 15 OR CALL TOLL-FREE 1-877-671-6036
View thousands more home plans online at www.familyhandyman.com/homeplans

Arch Windows Added Bonus

Plan #710-026D-0082

1,636 total square feet of living area

Price Code B

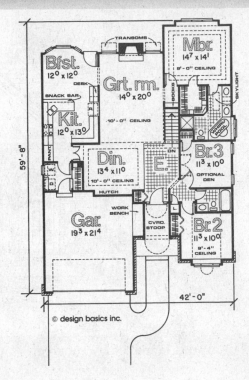

© design basics inc.

Special features

- Narrow front facade fits most unique lots
- Soaring front entrance invites guests
- Formal master bedroom and bath feature tray ceiling and whirlpool tub
- 3 bedrooms, 2 baths, 2-car garage
- Basement foundation

Classic Atrium Ranch

Plan #710-007D-0077

1,977 total square feet of living area

Price Code C

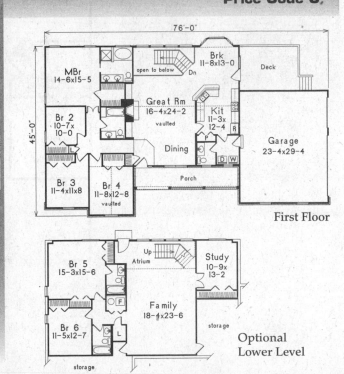

First Floor

Optional
Lower Level

Special features

- Classic traditional exterior always in style
- Spacious great room boasts a vaulted ceiling, dining area, atrium with elegant staircase and feature windows
- Atrium open to 1,416 square feet of optional living area below which consists of an optional family room, two bedrooms, two baths and a study
- 4 bedrooms, 2 1/2 baths, 3-car side entry garage
- Walk-out basement foundation

TO ORDER BLUEPRINTS USE THE FORM ON PAGE 15 OR CALL TOLL-FREE 1-877-671-6036
View thousands more home plans online at www.familyhandyman.com/homeplans

37

PLENTY OF DETAIL

Plan #710-035D-0011

1,945 total square feet of living area

Price Code C

Special features

- Master suite separated from other bedrooms for privacy
- Vaulted breakfast room is directly off great room
- Kitchen includes a built-in desk area
- Elegant dining room has an arched window
- 4 bedrooms, 2 baths, 2-car side entry garage
- Walk-out basement, crawl space or slab foundation, please specify when ordering

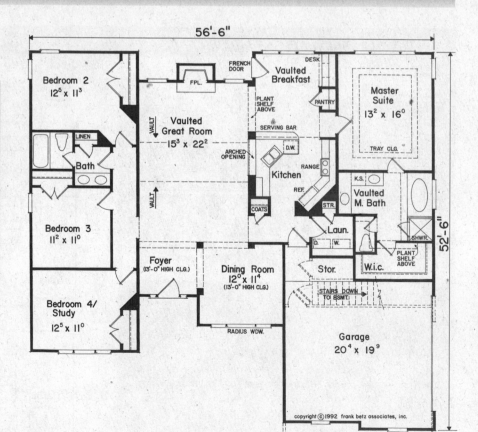

56'-6"

52'-6"

Bedroom 2
12⁵ x 11³

Bedroom 3
11² x 11⁰

Bedroom 4/
Study
12⁵ x 11⁰

LINEN

Bath

Foyer
(13'-0" HIGH CLG.)

FPL.

FRENCH DOOR

Vaulted Great Room
15³ x 22²

VAULT

VAULT

ARCHED OPENING

Kitchen

COATS

Dining Room
12⁰ x 11⁴
(13'-0" HIGH CLG.)

RADIUS WDW.

DESK

Vaulted Breakfast

PLANT SHELF ABOVE

PANTRY

SERVING BAR

D.W.

RANGE

REF.

STR.

Master Suite
13² x 16⁰

TRAY CLG.

K.S.

Vaulted M. Bath

Laun.

D. W.

Stor.

W.i.c.

SHWR.

PLANT SHELF ABOVE

STAIRS DOWN TO BSMT.

Garage
20⁴ x 19⁹

copyright © 1992 frank betz associates, inc.

Master Suite Has Media Center

Plan #710-030D-0002

1,429 total square feet of living area

Price Code A

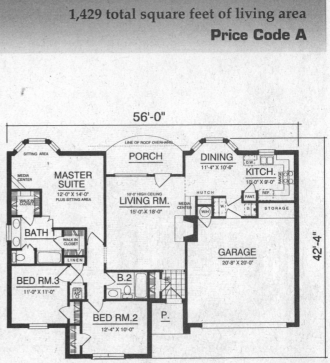

Special features

- Master suite with sitting area and private bath includes double walk-in closets
- Kitchen and dining area overlook living room
- Living room has fireplace, media center and access to covered porch
- 3 bedrooms, 2 baths, 2-car garage
- Slab or crawl space foundation, please specify when ordering

Dormers Accent Country Home

Plan #710-053D-0058

1,818 total square feet of living area

Price Code C

Second Floor
686 sq. ft.

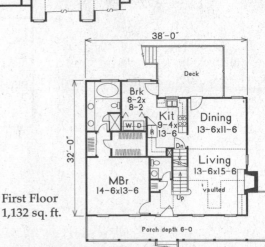

First Floor
1,132 sq. ft.

Special features

- Breakfast room is tucked behind the kitchen and has laundry closet and deck access
- Living and dining areas share vaulted ceiling and fireplace
- Master bedroom has two closets, large double-bowl vanity, separate tub and shower
- Large front porch wraps around home
- 4 bedrooms, 2 1/2 baths, 2-car drive under garage
- Basement foundation

TO ORDER BLUEPRINTS USE THE FORM ON PAGE 15 OR CALL TOLL-FREE 1-877-671-6036
View thousands more home plans online at www.familyhandyman.com/homeplans

39

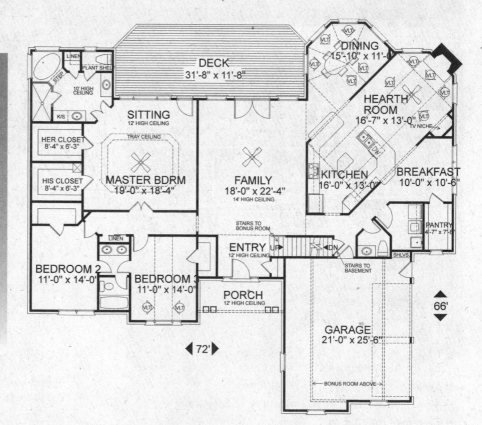

GRAND ARCHED ENTRY

Plan #710-013D-0037

2,564 total square feet of living area

Price Code D

Special features

- Hearth room is surrounded by kitchen, dining and breakfast rooms making it the focal point of the living areas

- Escape to the master bedroom which has a luxurious private bath and a sitting area leading to the deck outdoors

- The secondary bedrooms share a Jack and Jill bath and both have walk-in closets

- 3 bedrooms, 2 1/2 baths, 2-car side entry garage

- Basement, crawl space or slab foundation, please specify when ordering

40

TO ORDER BLUEPRINTS USE THE FORM ON PAGE 15 OR CALL TOLL-FREE 1-877-671-6036
View thousands more home plans online at www.familyhandyman.com/homeplans

Small And Cozy Cabin

Plan #710-058D-0010

676 total square feet of living area

Price Code AAA

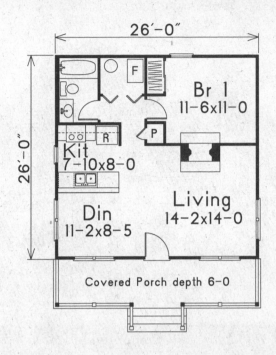

Special features

- See-through fireplace between bedroom and living area adds character
- Combined dining and living areas create an open feeling
- Full-length front covered porch is perfect for enjoying the outdoors
- Additional storage available in utility room
- 1 bedroom, 1 bath
- Crawl space foundation

Wrap-Around Porch

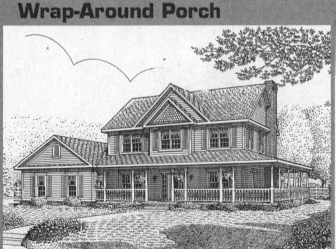

Plan #710-068D-0002

2,266 total square feet of living area

Price Code D

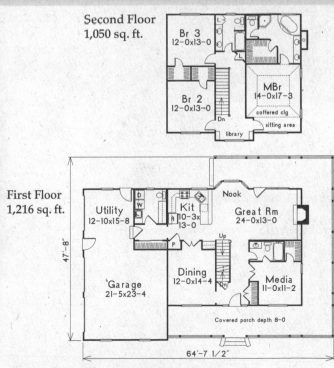

Special features

- Great room includes fireplace flanked by built-in bookshelves and dining nook with bay window
- Unique media room includes double-door entrance, walk-in closet and access to full bath
- Master bedroom has lovely sitting area, walk-in closet and a private bath with step-up tub and double vanity
- 3 bedrooms, 3 baths, 2-car side entry garage
- Basement foundation, drawings also include crawl space foundation

1,393 total square feet of living area

Price Code B

Special features

- L-shaped kitchen features walk-in pantry, island cooktop and is convenient to laundry room and dining area
- Master bedroom features large walk-in closet and private bath with separate tub and shower
- Convenient storage/coat closet in hall
- View to the patio from the dining area
- 3 bedrooms, 2 baths, 2-car detached garage
- Crawl space foundation, drawings also include slab foundation

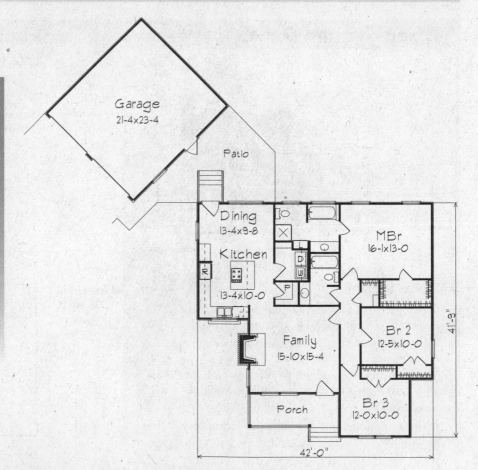

Garage
21-4x23-4

Patio

Dining
13-4x9-8

Kitchen
13-4x10-0

MBr
16-1x13-0

Family
15-10x15-4

Br 2
12-5x10-0

Br 3
12-0x10-0

Porch

41'-9"

42'-0"

Master Bedroom With Sitting Area — Plan #710-026D-0142

2,188 total square feet of living area

Price Code C

Special features

- Master bedroom includes a private covered porch, sitting area and two large walk-in closets
- Spacious kitchen has center island, snack bar and laundry access
- Great room has a 10' ceiling and a dramatic corner fireplace
- 3 bedrooms, 2 baths, 3-car side entry garage
- Basement foundation

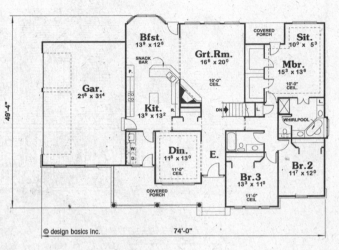

© design basics inc.

Ranch Style With Many Extras — Plan #710-035D-0050

1,342 total square feet of living area

Price Code A

Special features

- 9' ceilings throughout home
- Master suite has tray ceiling and wall of windows that overlook backyard
- Dining room includes serving bar connecting it to the kitchen and sliding glass doors that lead outdoors
- Optional second floor has an additional 350 square feet of living area
- 3 bedrooms, 2 baths, 2-car garage
- Slab, walk-out basement or crawl space foundation, please specify when ordering

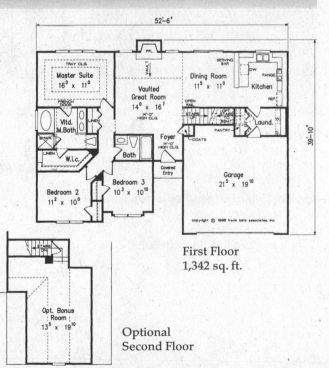

First Floor
1,342 sq. ft.

copyright © 1998 frank betz associates, inc.

Optional
Second Floor

TO ORDER BLUEPRINTS USE THE FORM ON PAGE 15 OR CALL TOLL-FREE 1-877-671-6036
View thousands more home plans online at www.familyhandyman.com/homeplans

43

Impressive Gallery

Plan #710-036D-0059

2,674 total square feet of living area

Price Code E

Special features

- First floor master bedroom has convenient location

- Kitchen and breakfast area have island and access to covered front porch

- Second floor bedrooms have dormer window seats for added charm

- Optional future rooms on the second floor have an additional 520 square feet of living area

- 4 bedrooms, 3 baths, 3-car side entry garage

- Basement or slab foundation, please specify when ordering

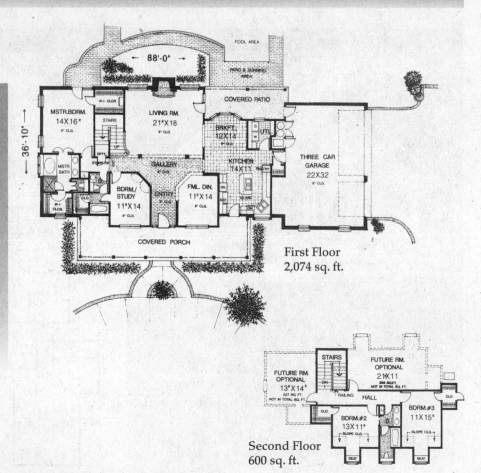

First Floor
2,074 sq. ft.

Second Floor
600 sq. ft.

TO ORDER BLUEPRINTS USE THE FORM ON PAGE 15 OR CALL TOLL-FREE 1-877-671-6036
View thousands more home plans online at www.familyhandyman.com/homeplans

Traditional Elegance

Plan #710-060D-0006

1,945 total square feet of living area

Price Code C

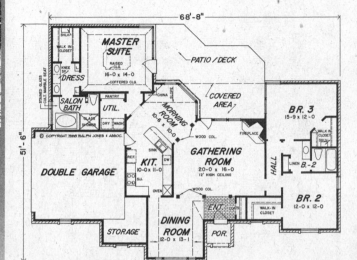

Special features

- Large gathering room with corner fireplace and 12' ceiling
- Master suite has a coffered ceiling and French door leading to the patio/deck
- Master bath has a cultured marble seat, separate shower and tub
- All bedrooms have walk-in closets
- 3 bedrooms, 2 baths, 2-car side entry garage
- Slab or crawl space foundation, please specify when ordering

Atrium Ranch With True Pizzazz

Plan #710-007D-0098

2,397 total square feet of living area

Price Code D

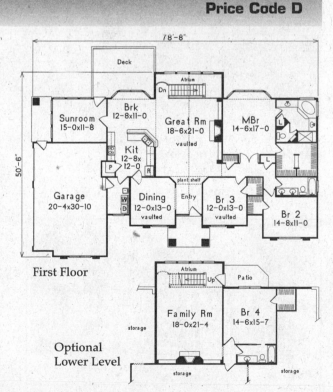

Special features

- Grand entry porch leads to a dramatic vaulted foyer
- The great room has a 12' vaulted ceiling, atrium featuring 2 1/2 story windows and a fireplace with flanking bookshelves
- Conveniently located sunroom and side porch
- 898 square feet of optional living area on the lower level with family room, bedroom #4 and bath
- 3 bedrooms, 2 baths, 3-car side entry garage
- Walk-out basement foundation

The Family Handyman

GRACIOUS ATRIUM RANCH

Plan #710-007D-0065

2,218 total square feet of living area

Price Code D

Special features

- Vaulted great room has an arched colonnade entry, bay windowed atrium with staircase and a fireplace
- Vaulted kitchen enjoys bay doors to deck, pass-through breakfast bar and walk-in pantry
- Breakfast room offers bay window and snack bar open to kitchen with laundry nearby
- Atrium open to 1,217 square feet of optional living area below
- 4 bedrooms, 2 baths, 2-car garage
- Walk-out basement foundation

Rear View

First Floor

56'-0"

58'-8"

Deck

MBr 14-4x17-8 vaulted clg

Atrium below

Dn

Brkfst 13-6x14-0 vaulted clg

Great Rm 18-7x17-8 vaulted clg

Kit 13-0x 13-0

Br 2/ Sitting 10-7x10-0

Dining 13-0x11-6 tray clg

Utility

Br 3 11-0x11-6

Br 4 11-8x13-4

Porch depth 6-0

Garage 19-4x21-4

Optional Lower Level

Up Atrium

Br 6 14-9x15-2

Family Rm 18-7x24-5

Br 5 12-4x15-2

Up

Wet Bar

Unfinished Area

TO ORDER BLUEPRINTS USE THE FORM ON PAGE 15 OR CALL TOLL-FREE 1-877-671-6036
View thousands more home plans online at www.familyhandyman.com/homeplans

Inviting Covered Verandas

Special features

- Inviting covered verandas in the front and rear of the home
- Great room has fireplace and cathedral ceiling
- Handy service porch allows easy access
- Master bedroom has vaulted ceiling and private bath
- 3 bedrooms, 2 baths, 3-car side entry garage
- Basement, crawl space or slab foundation, please specify when ordering

Plan #710-036D-0048

1,830 total square feet of living area

Price Code C

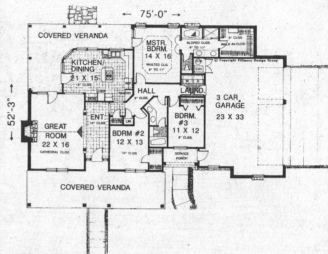

Private Bedroom Area

Special features

- Wrap-around front porch is an ideal gathering place
- Handy snack bar is positioned so kitchen flows into family room
- Master bedroom has many amenities
- 3 bedrooms, 2 baths, 2-car detached side entry garage
- Slab or crawl space foundation, please specify when ordering

Plan #710-039D-0007

1,550 total square feet of living area

Price Code B

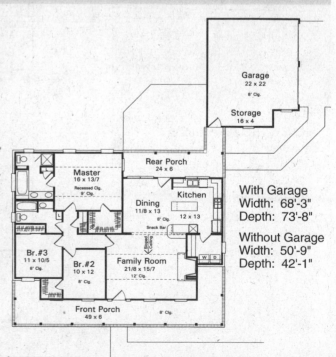

With Garage
Width: 68'-3"
Depth: 73'-8"

Without Garage
Width: 50'-9"
Depth: 42'-1"

TO ORDER BLUEPRINTS USE THE FORM ON PAGE 15 OR CALL TOLL-FREE 1-877-671-6036
View thousands more home plans online at www.familyhandyman.com/homeplans

47

THE Family Handyman

Outdoor Exposure Front And Back   Plan #710-045D-0007

2,685 total square feet of living area

Price Code E

Special features

- 9' ceilings throughout first floor
- Vaulted master bedroom, isolated for privacy, boasts magnificent bath with garden tub, separate shower and two closets
- Laundry area near bedrooms
- Screened porch and morning room both located off well-planned kitchen
- 4 bedrooms, 2 1/2 baths, 3-car garage
- Basement foundation

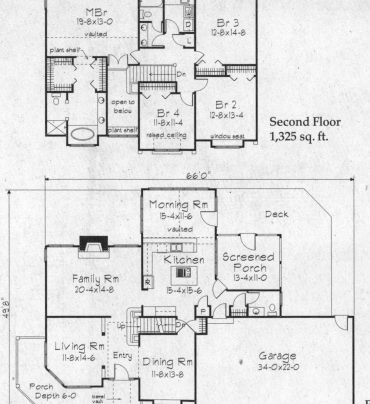

Second Floor
1,325 sq. ft.

First Floor
1,360 sq. ft.

48

TO ORDER BLUEPRINTS USE THE FORM ON PAGE 15 OR CALL TOLL-FREE 1-877-671-6036
View thousands more home plans online at www.familyhandyman.com/homeplans

Striking Plant Shelf

Plan #710-011D-0005

1,467 total square feet of living area

Price Code C

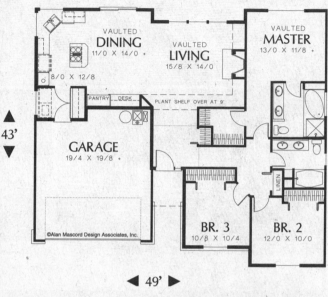

Special features

- Vaulted ceilings, an open floor plan and a wealth of windows create an inviting atmosphere
- Efficiently arranged kitchen has an island with built-in cooktop and a snack counter
- Plentiful storage and closetspace throughout this home
- 3 bedrooms, 2 baths, 2-car garage
- Crawl space foundation

Country Charm

Plan #710-045D-0017

954 total square feet of living area

Price Code AA

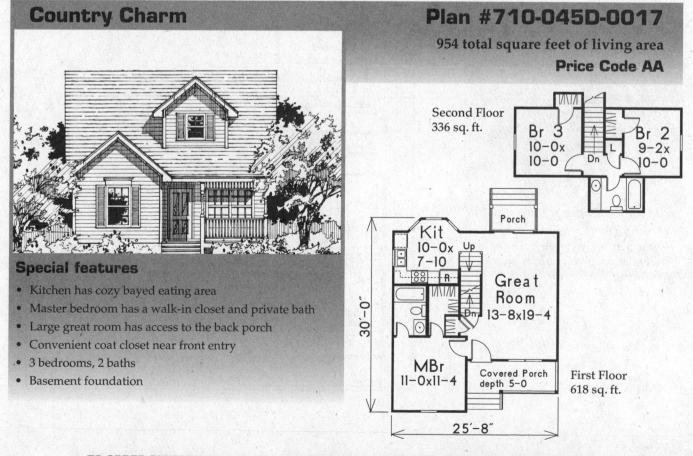

Special features

- Kitchen has cozy bayed eating area
- Master bedroom has a walk-in closet and private bath
- Large great room has access to the back porch
- Convenient coat closet near front entry
- 3 bedrooms, 2 baths
- Basement foundation

TO ORDER BLUEPRINTS USE THE FORM ON PAGE 15 OR CALL TOLL-FREE 1-877-671-6036
View thousands more home plans online at www.familyhandyman.com/homeplans

49

Award Winning Style

Plan #710-028D-0008

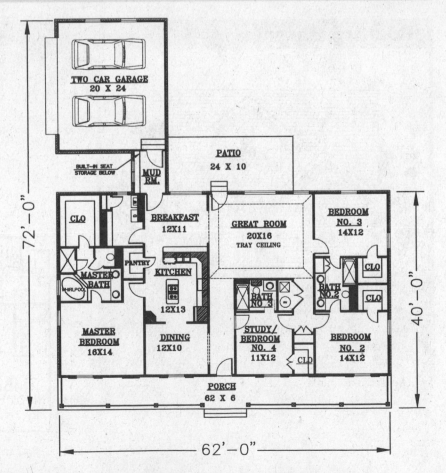

2,156 total square feet of living area

Price Code C

Special features

- Secluded master bedroom has spa-style bath with corner whirlpool tub, large shower, double sinks and a walk-in closet
- Kitchen overlooks rear patio
- Plenty of windows add an open, airy feel to the great room
- 3 bedrooms, 3 baths, 2-car side entry garage
- Basement, crawl space or slab foundation, please specify when ordering

TWO CAR GARAGE
20 X 24

BUILT—IN SEAT
STORAGE BELOW

MUD
RM.

PATIO
24 X 10

72'-0"

40'-0"

CLO

MASTER
BATH

WHIRLPOOL

BREAKFAST
12X11

PANTRY

KITCHEN
12X13

GREAT ROOM
20X16
TRAY CEILING

BEDROOM
NO. 3
14X12

CLO

BATH
NO. 3

BATH
NO.2

CLO

CLO

MASTER
BEDROOM
16X14

DINING
12X10

STUDY/
BEDROOM
NO. 4
11X12

CLO

BEDROOM
NO. 2
14X12

PORCH
62 X 6

62'-0"

TO ORDER BLUEPRINTS USE THE FORM ON PAGE 15 OR CALL TOLL-FREE 1-877-671-6036
View thousands more home plans online at www.familyhandyman.com/homeplans

50

Wonderful Great Room

Plan #710-048D-0001

1,865 total square feet of living area

Price Code D

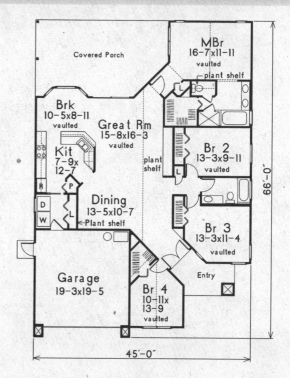

Special features

- Large foyer opens into expansive dining area and great room
- Home features vaulted ceilings throughout
- Master bedroom features an angled entry, vaulted ceiling, plant shelf and bathroom with double vanity, tub and shower
- 4 bedrooms, 2 baths, 2-car garage
- Slab foundation, drawings also include crawl space foundation

Private Master Bedroom

Plan #710-047D-0019

1,783 total square feet of living area

Price Code B

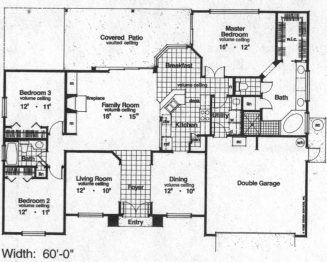

Special features

- Grand foyer leads to family room
- Walk-in pantry in kitchen
- Master bath has a step-down doorless shower, huge vanity and a large walk-in closet
- 3 bedrooms, 2 baths, 2-car garage
- Slab foundation

Width: 60'-0"
Depth: 45'-0"

TO ORDER BLUEPRINTS USE THE FORM ON PAGE 15 OR CALL TOLL-FREE 1-877-671-6036
View thousands more home plans online at www.familyhandyman.com/homeplans

51

Impressive Two-Story Grand Room   Plan #710-056D-0016

2,499 total square feet of living area   **Price Code D**

Special features

- Brick traditional with covered front porch
- Master bedroom has private bath and a sitting room with extra storage
- Impressive two-story foyer
- Kitchen and breakfast room are spacious and have laundry room nearby
- 4 bedrooms, 2 1/2 baths, 2-car garage
- Basement foundation

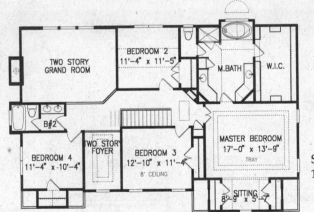

Second Floor
1,242 sq. ft.

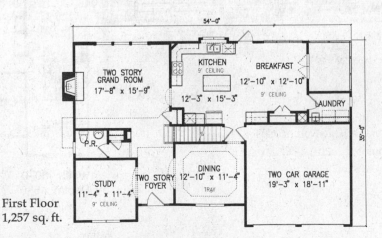

First Floor
1,257 sq. ft.

TO ORDER BLUEPRINTS USE THE FORM ON PAGE 15 OR CALL TOLL-FREE 1-877-671-6036
View thousands more home plans online at www.familyhandyman.com/homeplans

Simple And Cozy

Plan #710-026D-0154

1,392 total square feet of living area

Price Code A

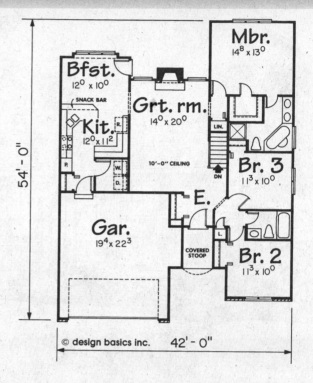

54'-0"

42'-0"

© design basics inc.

Mbr. 14⁸ x 13⁰

Bfst. 12⁰ x 10⁰

SNACK BAR

Grt. rm. 14⁰ x 20⁰

LIN.

Kit. 12⁰ x 11²

10'-0" CEILING

Br. 3 11³ x 10⁰

DN

Gar. 19⁴ x 22³

E.

COVERED STOOP

L

Br. 2 11³ x 10⁰

Special features

- Centralized great room welcomes guests with a warm fireplace
- Master bedroom has a separate entrance for added privacy
- Kitchen includes breakfast room, snack counter and laundry area
- 3 bedrooms, 2 baths, 2-car garage
- Basement foundation

Spacious Living Area

Plan #710-001D-0043

1,104 total square feet of living area

Price Code AA

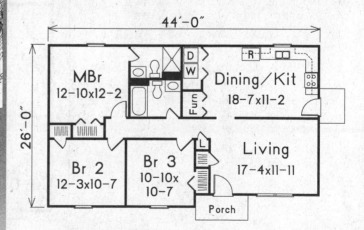

44'-0"

26'-0"

MBr 12-10x12-2

D W

Dining/Kit 18-7x11-2

R

Fun

Br 2 12-3x10-7

Br 3 10-10x 10-7

L

Living 17-4x11-11

Porch

Special features

- Master bedroom includes private bath
- Convenient side entrance to dining area/kitchen
- Laundry area located near kitchen
- Large living area creates a comfortable atmosphere
- 3 bedrooms, 2 baths
- Crawl space foundation, drawings also include basement and slab foundations

TO ORDER BLUEPRINTS USE THE FORM ON PAGE 15 OR CALL TOLL-FREE 1-877-671-6036
View thousands more home plans online at www.familyhandyman.com/homeplans

53

Enchanting Country Cottage   Plan #710-007D-0030

1,140 total square feet of living area   Price Code AA

Special features

- Open and spacious living and dining areas for family gatherings
- Well-organized kitchen with an abundance of cabinetry and a built-in pantry
- Roomy master bath features double-bowl vanity
- 3 bedrooms, 2 baths, 2-car drive under garage
- Basement foundation

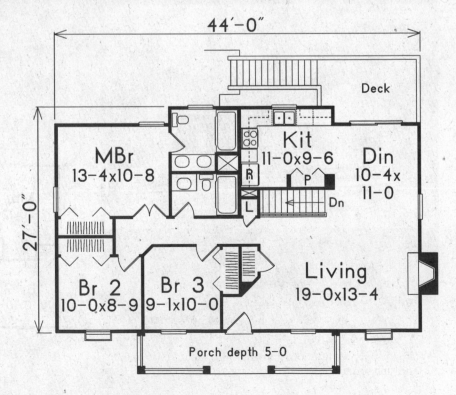

44'-0"

27'-0"

Deck

MBr
13-4x10-8

Kit
11-0x9-6

Din
10-4x11-0

R

P

Dn

L

Br 2
10-0x8-9

Br 3
9-1x10-0

Living
19-0x13-4

Porch depth 5-0

TO ORDER BLUEPRINTS USE THE FORM ON PAGE 15 OR CALL TOLL-FREE 1-877-671-6036
View thousands more home plans online at www.familyhandyman.com/homeplans

54

Dramatic Cathedral Ceilings

Plan #710-034D-0001

1,436 total square feet of living area

Price Code A

Special features

- Covered entry is inviting
- Kitchen has handy breakfast bar which overlooks great room and dining room
- Private master bedroom with bath and walk-in closet is separate from other bedrooms
- 3 bedrooms, 2 baths, 2-car garage
- Basement foundation

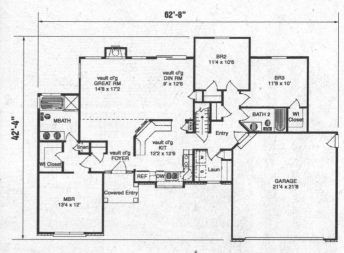

Quaint Country Home Is Ideal

Plan #710-040D-0029

1,028 total square feet of living area

Price Code AA

Special features

- Well-designed bath contains laundry facilities
- L-shaped kitchen has a handy pantry
- Tall windows flank family room fireplace
- Cozy covered porch provides unique angled entry into home
- 3 bedrooms, 1 bath
- Crawl space foundation

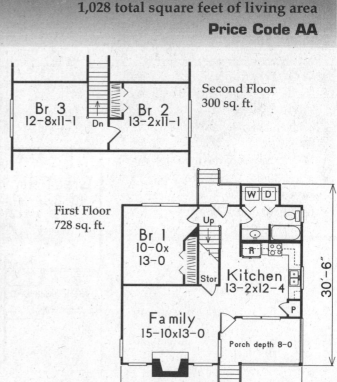

TO ORDER BLUEPRINTS USE THE FORM ON PAGE 15 OR CALL TOLL-FREE 1-877-671-6036
View thousands more home plans online at www.familyhandyman.com/homeplans

55

Spacious Vaulted Great Room   Plan #710-041D-0006

1,189 total square feet of living area   **Price Code AA**

Special features

- All bedrooms are located on the second floor
- Dining room and kitchen both have views of the patio
- Convenient half bath located near the kitchen
- Master bedroom has a private bath
- 3 bedrooms, 2 1/2 baths, 2-car garage
- Basement foundation

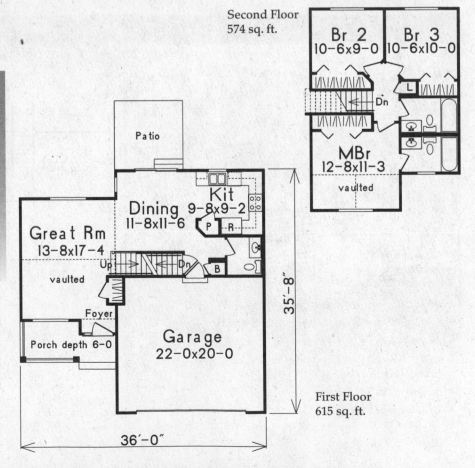

Second Floor
574 sq. ft.

Br 2
10-6x9-0

Br 3
10-6x10-0

MBr
12-8x11-3
vaulted

Patio

Kit
9-8x9-2

Dining
11-8x11-6

Great Rm
13-8x17-4
vaulted

Foyer

Porch depth 6-0

Garage
22-0x20-0

35'-8"

36'-0"

First Floor
615 sq. ft.

TO ORDER BLUEPRINTS USE THE FORM ON PAGE 15 OR CALL TOLL-FREE 1-877-671-6036
View thousands more home plans online at www.familyhandyman.com/homeplans

Luxurious Master Suite

Special features

- Secondary bedrooms separate from master suite allowing privacy
- Compact kitchen is well-organized
- Conveniently located laundry closet
- 3 bedrooms, 2 baths, 2-car garage
- Walk-out basement or crawl space foundation, please specify when ordering

Plan #710-035D-0046

1,080 total square feet of living area

Price Code AA

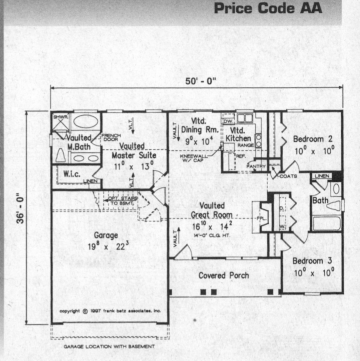

Outdoor Living Area

Special features

- Spacious living area with corner fireplace offers a cheerful atmosphere with large windows
- Second floor gathering room is great for kid's play area
- Secluded master bedroom has separate porch entrances and a large master bath with walk-in closet
- 3 bedrooms, 2 1/2 baths, 1-car garage
- Basement foundation, drawings also include crawl space foundation

Plan #710-068D-0003

1,784 total square feet of living area

Price Code B

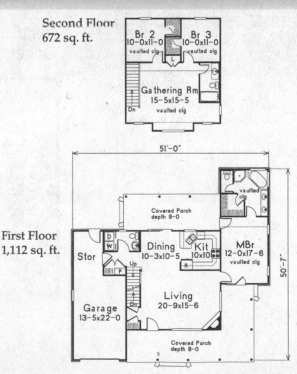

TO ORDER BLUEPRINTS USE THE FORM ON PAGE 15 OR CALL TOLL-FREE 1-877-671-6036
View thousands more home plans online at www.familyhandyman.com/homeplans

57

Enormous Master Bath
Plan #710-047D-0059

3,556 total square feet of living area

Price Code F

Special features

- Curved portico welcomes guests
- Master suite has see-through fireplace, wet bar, private bath and sitting area opening to covered patio
- Cozy family room with fireplace has adjacent summer kitchen outdoors on patio
- 4 bedrooms, 3 1/2 baths, 3-car side entry garage
- Slab foundation

Width: 85'-0"
Depth: 85'-0"

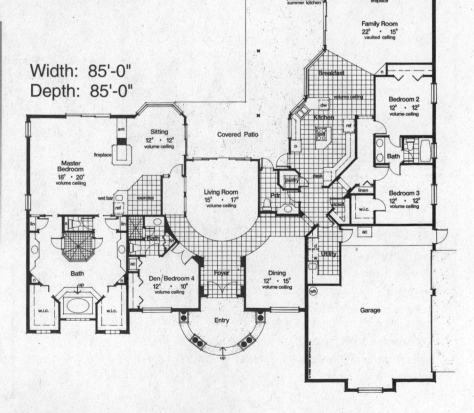

TO ORDER BLUEPRINTS USE THE FORM ON PAGE 15 OR CALL TOLL-FREE 1-877-671-6036
View thousands more home plans online at www.familyhandyman.com/homeplans

A Touch Of Old World Charm

Special features

- From the foyer, there is a panoramic view of the dramatic great room and formal dining room
- A butler's pantry is strategically placed between the formal dining room and kitchen and breakfast room
- French doors add light and style to the breakfast room
- 4 bedrooms, 2 1/2 baths, 2-car garage
- Basement foundation

Plan #710-065D-0008

2,320 total square feet of living area

Price Code D

Second Floor 725 sq. ft.

First Floor 1,595 sq. ft.

Third Floor All Purpose Room

Special features

- Energy efficient home with 2" x 6" exterior walls
- Large all-purpose room and bath on third floor
- Efficient U-shaped kitchen includes a pantry and adjacent planning desk
- 4 bedrooms, 3 1/2 baths, 2-car side entry garage
- Basement foundation, drawings also include slab foundation

Plan #710-017D-0006

3,006 total square feet of living area

Price Code E

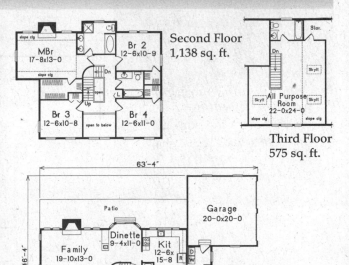

Second Floor 1,138 sq. ft.

Third Floor 575 sq. ft.

First Floor 1,293 sq. ft.

TO ORDER BLUEPRINTS USE THE FORM ON PAGE 15 OR CALL TOLL-FREE 1-877-671-6036
View thousands more home plans online at www.familyhandyman.com/homeplans

59

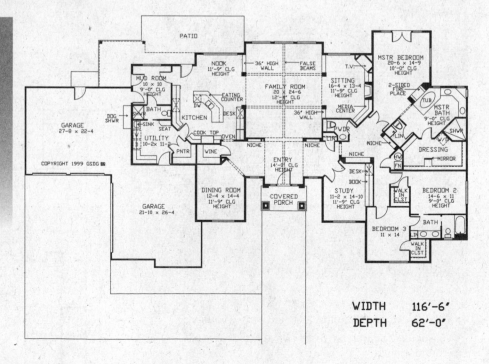

The Family Handyman

Expansive Family Room

Plan #710-043D-0002

3,671 total square feet of living area

Price Code F

Special features

- 14' ceiling in entry with display niches
- 11'-9" ceilings in nook, den, dining and sitting rooms
- Kitchen has island eating counter, pantry and built-in desk
- Fireplace in master bedroom
- 3 bedrooms, 2 full baths, 2 half baths, 4-car garage
- Crawl space foundation

WIDTH 116'-6'
DEPTH 62'-0'

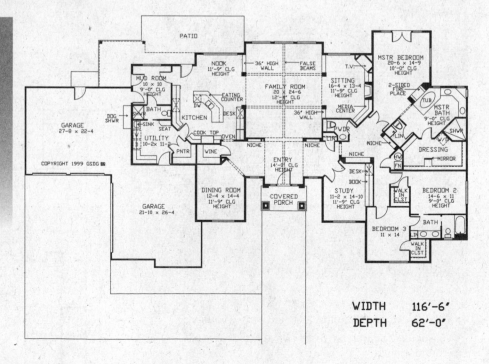

Traditional Brick Home

Special features

- Master bedroom enjoys privacy at the rear of this home
- Kitchen has an angled bar that overlooks great room and breakfast area
- Living areas combine to create a greater sense of spaciousness
- Great room has a cozy fireplace
- 3 bedrooms, 2 baths, 2-car garage
- Slab foundation

Plan #710-010D-0006

1,170 total square feet of living area

Price Code AA

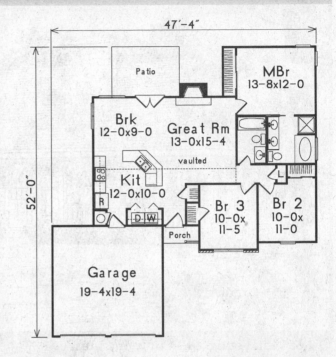

Private Master Bedroom

Special features

- Formal dining room off kitchen
- Enormous master bedroom has private bath and walk-in closet
- Optional second floor has an additional 926 square feet of living area
- 3 bedrooms, 2 1/2 baths, 2-car side entry garage
- Slab or crawl space foundation, please specify when ordering

Plan #710-020D-0012

2,684 total square feet of living area

Price Code E

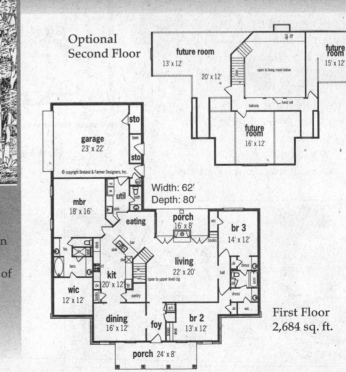

TO ORDER BLUEPRINTS USE THE FORM ON PAGE 15 OR CALL TOLL-FREE 1-877-671-6036
View thousands more home plans online at www.familyhandyman.com/homeplans

61

Tranquility Of An Atrium Cottage   Plan #710-007D-0068

1,384 total square feet of living area

Price Code B

Special features

- Wrap-around country porch for peaceful evenings
- Vaulted great room enjoys a large bay window, stone fireplace, pass-through kitchen and awesome rear views through atrium window wall
- Master bedroom features double entry doors, walk-in closet and a fabulous bath
- Atrium opens to 611 square feet of optional living area below
- 2 bedrooms, 2 baths, 1-car side entry garage
- Walk-out basement foundation

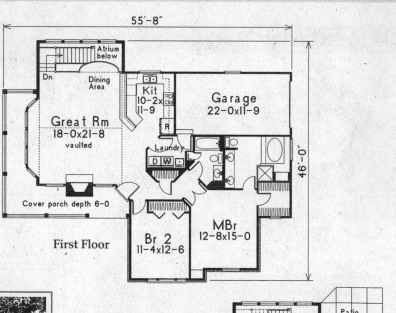

55'-8"

46'-0"

Dn

Atrium below

Dining Area

Kit 10-2x 11-9

Garage 22-0x11-9

Great Rm 18-0x21-8 vaulted

R

Laundry

D W

Cover porch depth 6-0

First Floor

Br 2 11-4x12-6

MBr 12-8x15-0

Up

Patio

Family Rm 25-0x21-4

Unexcavated

Optional Lower Level

Unfinished Basement

Rear View

TO ORDER BLUEPRINTS USE THE FORM ON PAGE 15 OR CALL TOLL-FREE 1-877-671-6036
View thousands more home plans online at www.familyhandyman.com/homeplans

Large Corner Deck

Plan #710-022D-0019

1,283 total square feet of living area

Price Code A

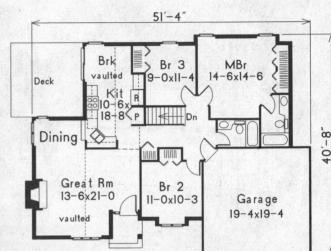

Special features

- Vaulted breakfast room has sliding doors that open onto deck
- Kitchen features convenient corner sink and pass-through to dining room
- Open living atmosphere in dining area and great room
- Vaulted great room features a fireplace
- 3 bedrooms, 2 baths, 2-car garage
- Basement foundation

Inviting Arched Windows

Plan #710-069D-0014

1,680 total square feet of living area

Price Code B

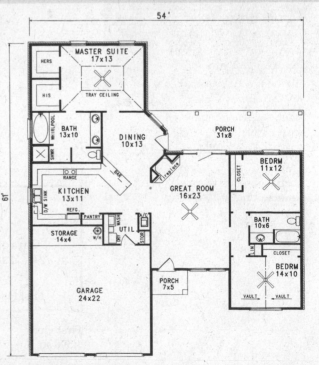

Special features

- Master suite has two walk-in closets and a private bath
- Kitchen has snack bar that overlooks into an angled dining area
- A covered porch extends the living area to the outdoors
- Extra storage in garage
- 3 bedrooms, 2 baths, 2-car garage
- Slab or crawl space foundation, please specify when ordering

TO ORDER BLUEPRINTS USE THE FORM ON PAGE 15 OR CALL TOLL-FREE 1-877-671-6036
View thousands more home plans online at www.familyhandyman.com/homeplans

63

CLASSIC Rural Farmhouse

Plan #710-014D-0012

2,363 total square feet of living area

Price Code D

Special features

- Covered porches provide outdoor seating areas
- Corner fireplace becomes focal point of family room
- Kitchen features island cooktop and adjoining nook
- Energy efficient home with 2" x 6" exterior walls
- 3 bedrooms, 2 1/2 baths, 2-car garage
- Partial basement/crawl space foundation

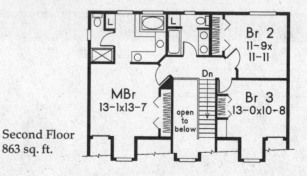

Br 2
11-9x
11-11

MBr
13-1x13-7

Dn

open to below

Br 3
13-0x10-8

Second Floor
863 sq. ft.

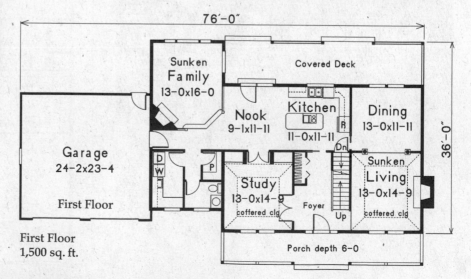

76'-0"

Sunken Family
13-0x16-0

Covered Deck

Nook
9-1x11-11

Kitchen
11-0x11-11

Dining
13-0x11-11

Garage
24-2x23-4

First Floor

DW

P

Dn

Study
13-0x14-9
coffered cld

Foyer

Up

Sunken Living
13-0x14-9
coffered cld

36'-0"

First Floor
1,500 sq. ft.

Porch depth 6-0

TO ORDER BLUEPRINTS USE THE FORM ON PAGE 15 OR CALL TOLL-FREE 1-877-671-6036
View thousands more home plans online at www.familyhandyman.com/homeplans

Outdoor Living Indoors

Plan #710-36D-0054

2,793 total square feet of living area

Price Code E

Special features

- Beautiful curved staircase invites guests into home
- Large great room stretches from the front to the back of the first floor
- Master bedroom has many amenities
- Future play room above the garage has an additional 285 square feet of living area
- 4 bedrooms, 3 1/2 baths, 3-car rear entry garage
- Crawl space or slab foundation, please specify when ordering

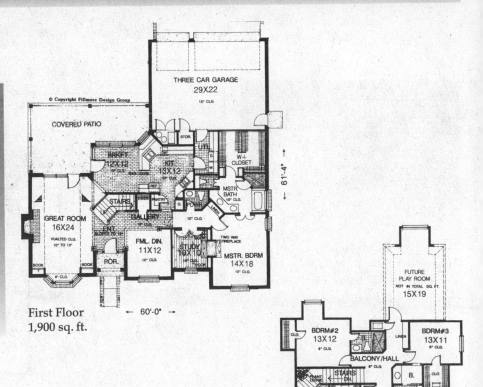

© Copyright Fillmore Design Group

THREE CAR GARAGE
29X22
10" CLG.

COVERED PATIO

BRKFT
12X12
10" CLG.

KIT
13X12
10" CLG.

STOR.

UTIL.

W-I-CLOSET

MSTR
BATH
10" CLG.

STAIRS

GALLERY
10" CLG.

GREAT ROOM
16X24
VUALTED CLG.
10" TO 13"

BOOK

FML. DIN.
11X12
10" CLG.

STUDY
10X10
10" CLG.

POWD.

TWO WAY
FIREPLACE

MSTR. BDRM
14X18
10" CLG.

POR.

BOOK

61'-4"

60'-0"

First Floor
1,900 sq. ft.

FUTURE
PLAY ROOM
NOT IN TOTAL SQ. FT.
15X19

BDRM#2
13X12
8" CLG.

BDRM#3
13X11
8" CLG.

LINEN

BALCONY/HALL
8" CLG.

STAIRS
DN

B.

ENTRY
BELOW

BDRM#4
12X13
SLOPED CLG.
8" TO 10"

B.

DECK

Second Floor
893 sq. ft.

The Family Handyman

Covered Porch Adds Charm — Plan #710-040D-0015

1,655 total square feet of living area

Price Code B

Special features

- Master bedroom features a 9' ceiling, walk-in closet and bath with dressing area
- Oversized family room includes 10' ceiling and masonry see-through fireplace
- Island kitchen with convenient access to laundry room
- Handy covered walkway from garage to kitchen and dining area
- 3 bedrooms, 2 baths, 2-car garage
- Crawl space foundation

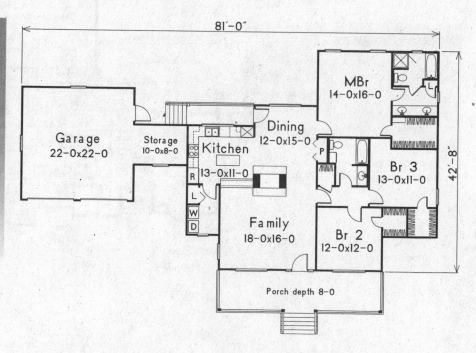

Amenity Full Ranch

Plan #710-051D-0057

2,229 total square feet of living area

Price Code D

Special features

- Welcoming and expansive front porch
- Dining room has tray ceiling
- Sunny nook with arched soffit creates an inviting entry into this eating space
- 3 bedrooms, 2 baths, 2-car side entry garage
- Basement foundation

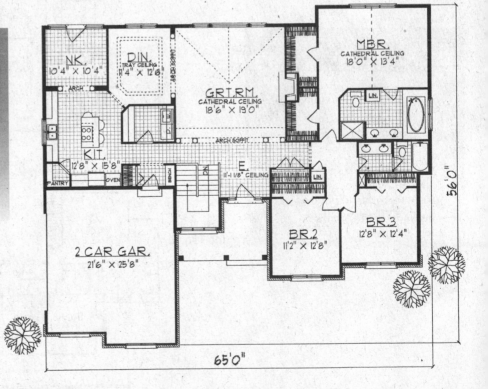

TO ORDER BLUEPRINTS USE THE FORM ON PAGE 15 OR CALL TOLL-FREE 1-877-671-6036
View thousands more home plans online at www.familyhandyman.com/homeplans

67

Fireplaces Add Warm Cozy Feeling   Plan #710-037D-0014

2,932 total square feet of living area

Price Code F

Special features

- 9' ceilings throughout home
- Rear stairs create convenient access to second floor from living area
- Spacious kitchen has pass-through to the family room, a convenient island and pantry
- Cozy built-in table in breakfast area
- Secluded master bedroom has a luxurious bath and patio access
- 4 bedrooms, 3 1/2 baths, 2-car side entry garage
- Slab foundation

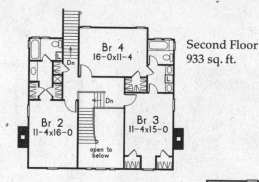

Second Floor
933 sq. ft.

Br 4
16-0x11-4

Br 2
11-4x16-0

Br 3
11-4x15-0

open to below

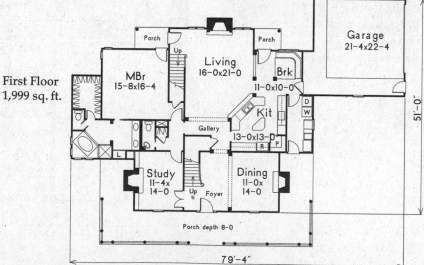

First Floor
1,999 sq. ft.

Garage
21-4x22-4

Porch   Living
16-0x21-0   Porch

MBr
15-8x16-4   Brk
11-0x10-0

Kit
13-0x13-0

Gallery

Study
11-4x
14-0   Dining
11-0x
14-0

Foyer

Porch depth 8-0

51'-0"

79'-4"

Quaint Country Home

Plan #710-024D-0010

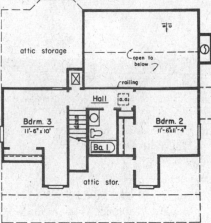

1,737 total square feet of living area

Price Code B

Special features

- U-shaped kitchen, sunny bayed breakfast room and living area become one large gathering area
- Living area has sloped ceilings and a balcony overlook from second floor
- Second floor includes lots of storage area
- 3 bedrooms, 2 1/2 baths
- Slab or crawl space foundation, please specify when ordering

**Second Floor
499 sq. ft.**

attic storage

open to below

railing

Hall

Bdrm. 3
11'-6" x 10'

Ba. 1

Bdrm. 2
11'-6"x11'-4"

attic stor.

**Width: 36'-0"
Depth: 49'-0"**

Patio

Util.

Brkfst.
9' x 11'

Living
20'-6" x 14'

Kit.
11'-6" x 10'-8"

1/2 Ba.

Dr.

Ba. 1

Dining
11'-6" x 13'

Bdrm. 1
16'-6" x 13'-6"

Foyer

**First Floor
1,238 sq. ft.**

Porch
36'x5'

TO ORDER BLUEPRINTS USE THE FORM ON PAGE 15 OR CALL TOLL-FREE 1-877-671-6036
View thousands more home plans online at www.familyhandyman.com/homeplans

69

Built-In Computer Desk

Plan #710-055D-0017

1,525 total square feet of living area

Price Code B

Special features

- Corner fireplace is highlighted in the great room
- Unique glass block window over whirlpool tub in master bath brightens interior
- Open bar overlooks both the kitchen and great room
- Breakfast room leads to an outdoor grilling and covered porch
- 3 bedrooms, 2 baths, 2-car garage
- Basement, walk-out basement, crawl space or slab foundation, please specify when ordering

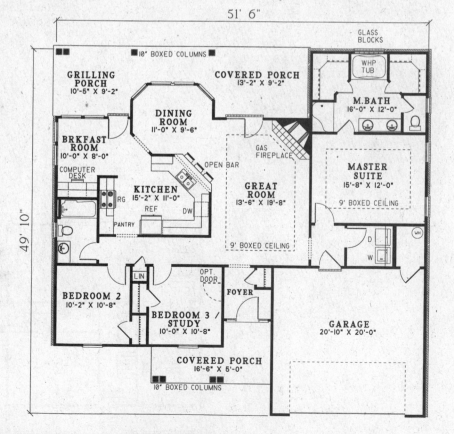

TO ORDER BLUEPRINTS USE THE FORM ON PAGE 15 OR CALL TOLL-FREE 1-877-671-6036
View thousands more home plans online at www.familyhandyman.com/homeplans

Vaulted Ceilings Add Dimension   Plan #710-048D-0011

1,550 total square feet of living area   Price Code B

Special features

- Cozy corner fireplace provides focal point in family room
- Master bedroom features large walk-in closet, skylight and separate tub and shower
- Convenient laundry closet
- Kitchen with pantry and breakfast bar connects to family room
- Family room and master bedroom access covered patio
- 3 bedrooms, 2 baths, 2-car garage
- Slab foundation

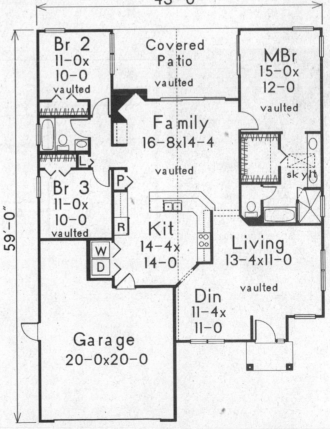

TO ORDER BLUEPRINTS USE THE FORM ON PAGE 15 OR CALL TOLL-FREE 1-877-671-6036
View thousands more home plans online at www.familyhandyman.com/homeplans

71

Lovely Arched Touches

Plan #710-069D-0012

1,594 total square feet of living area

Price Code B

Special features

- Corner fireplace in the great room creates a cozy feel
- Spacious kitchen combines with the dining room creating a terrific gathering place
- A handy family and guest entrance is a casual and convenient way to enter the home
- 3 bedrooms, 2 baths, 2-car garage
- Slab or crawl space foundation, please specify when ordering

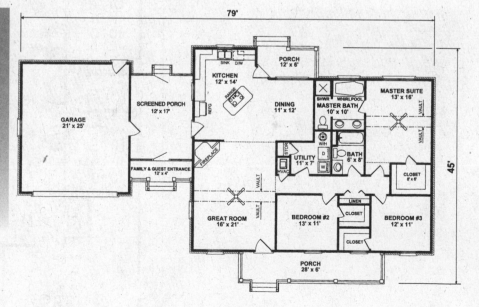

Porches Bring In The Outdoors

Plan #710-021D-0021

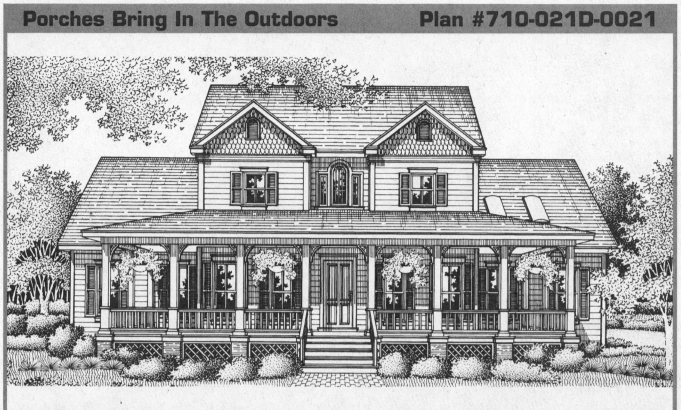

3,153 total square feet of living area

Price Code E

Special features

- Energy efficient home with 2" x 6" exterior walls
- Master bedroom has full amenities
- Covered breezeway and front and rear porches
- Full-sized workshop and storage with garage below is a unique combination
- 4 bedrooms, 3 1/2 baths, 2-car drive under garage
- Basement foundation, drawings also include crawl space and slab foundations

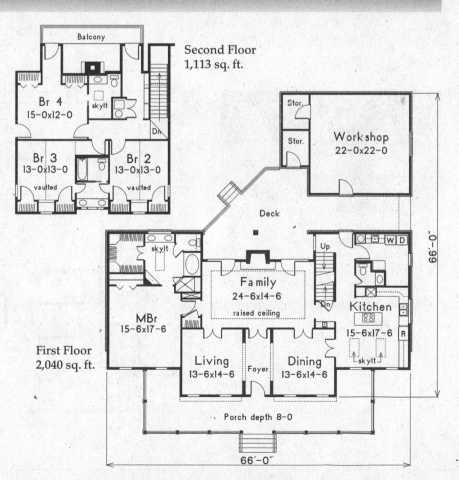

Second Floor
1,113 sq. ft.

Balcony

Br 4
15-0x12-0

skylt

Br 3
13-0x13-0
vaulted

Br 2
13-0x13-0
vaulted

Stor.

Stor.

Workshop
22-0x22-0

Deck

First Floor
2,040 sq. ft.

skylt

Up

W D

MBr
15-6x17-6

Family
24-6x14-6
raised ceiling

Dn

Kitchen
15-6x17-6

R

Living
13-6x14-6

Foyer

Dining
13-6x14-6

skylt

Porch depth 8-0

66'-0"

66'-0"

TO ORDER BLUEPRINTS USE THE FORM ON PAGE 15 OR CALL TOLL-FREE 1-877-671-6036
View thousands more home plans online at www.familyhandyman.com/homeplans

73

Symmetry Dominates Design

Plan #710-007D-0046

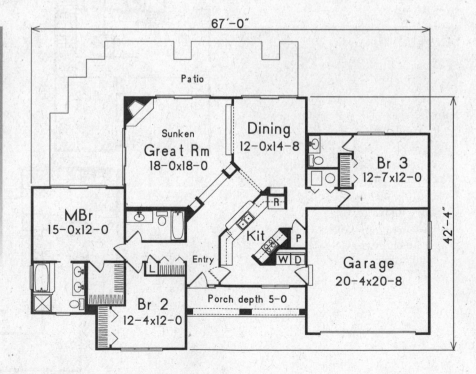

KURT KAUSS
ORLANDO

1,712 total square feet of living area

Price Code B

Special features

- Stylish stucco exterior enhances curb appeal
- Sunken great room offers corner fireplace flanked by 9' wide patio doors
- Well-designed kitchen features ideal view of great room and fireplace through breakfast bar opening
- 3 bedrooms, 2 1/2 baths, 2-car garage
- Crawl space foundation

67'-0"

42'-4"

Patio

Sunken
Great Rm
18-0x18-0

Dining
12-0x14-8

Br 3
12-7x12-0

MBr
15-0x12-0

Kit

R

P

W/D

Garage
20-4x20-8

Entry

L

Br 2
12-4x12-0

Porch depth 5-0

SOARING COVERED PORTICO

Plan #710-048D-0009

2,056 total square feet of living area

Price Code C

R. BRADSHAW

Special features

- Columned foyer projects past living and dining rooms into family room
- Kitchen conveniently accesses dining room and breakfast area
- Master bedroom features double-doors to patio and pocket door to master bath with walk-in closet, double-bowl vanity and tub
- 4 bedrooms, 2 baths, 2-car garage
- Slab foundation, drawings also include crawl space foundation

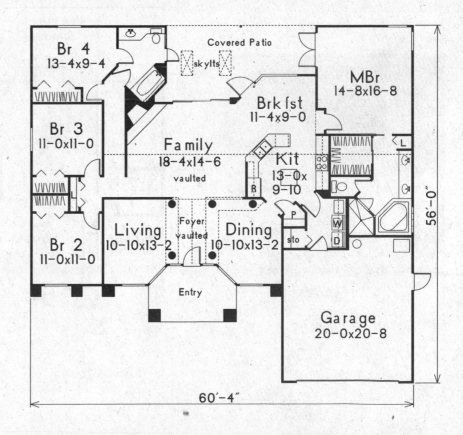

Br 4
13-4x9-4

Covered Patio

skylts

MBr
14-8x16-8

Br 3
11-0x11-0

Family
18-4x14-6
vaulted

Brk fst
11-4x9-0

Kit
13-0x
9-10

Living
10-10x13-2

Foyer
vaulted

Dining
10-10x13-2

Br 2
11-0x11-0

sto

Entry

56'-0"

60'-4"

Garage
20-0x20-8

TO ORDER BLUEPRINTS USE THE FORM ON PAGE 15 OR CALL TOLL-FREE 1-877-671-6036
View thousands more home plans online at www.familyhandyman.com/homeplans

75

Perfect Family-Sized Ranch — Plan #710-052D-0046

1,869 total square feet of living area

Price Code C

Special features

- Kitchen counter overlooks breakfast and living rooms creating a feeling of openness
- Dining room features columns separating it from the other spaces in a unique and formal way
- A sunny spa tub is featured in the master bath
- 3 bedrooms, 2 baths, 2-car side entry garage
- Basement, crawl space or slab foundation, please specify when ordering

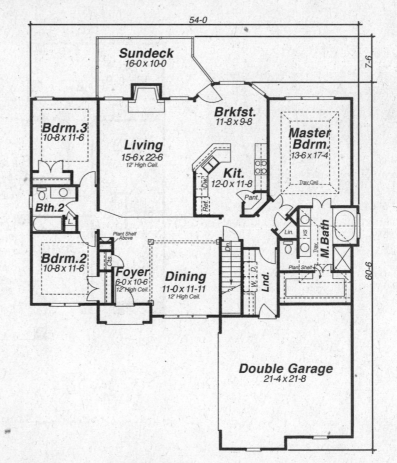

Second Floor Overlook

Plan #710-035D-0040

2,126 total square feet of living area

Price Code C

Special features

- Kitchen overlooks vaulted family room with a handy serving bar
- Two-story foyer creates an airy feeling
- Second floor includes an optional bonus room with an additional 251 square feet of living area
- 4 bedrooms, 3 baths, 2-car side entry garage
- Walk-out basement, crawl space or slab foundation, please specify when ordering

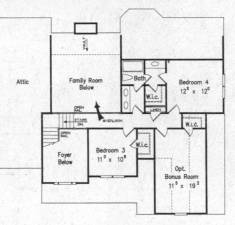

Second Floor
543 sq. ft.

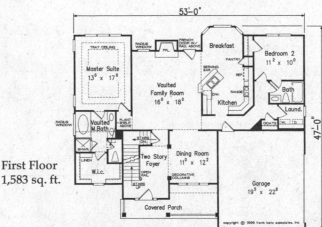

First Floor
1,583 sq. ft.

TO ORDER BLUEPRINTS USE THE FORM ON PAGE 15 OR CALL TOLL-FREE 1-877-671-6036
View thousands more home plans online at www.familyhandyman.com/homeplans

77

A Spectacular Showplace

Plan #710-007D-0058

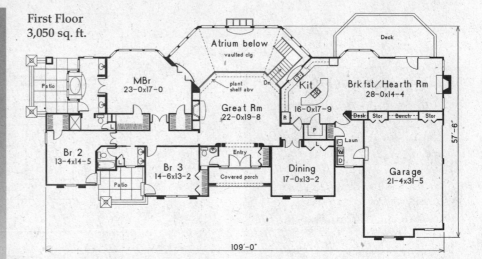

4,826 total square feet of living area

Price Code G

Special features

- Brightly lit entry connects to great room with balcony and massive bay-shaped atrium

- Kitchen has island/snack bar, walk-in pantry, computer area and an atrium overlook

- Master bedroom has sitting area, walk-in closets, atrium overlook and luxury bath with private courtyard

- Family room/atrium, home theater area with wet bar, game room and guest bedroom comprise the lower level

- 4 bedrooms, 3 1/2 baths, 3-car side entry garage

- Walk-out basement foundation with lawn and garden workroom

First Floor
3,050 sq. ft.

Deck

Atrium below
vaulted clg

MBr
23-0x17-0

Kit
16-0x17-9

Brkfst/Hearth Rm
28-0x14-4

plant shelf abv

Great Rm
22-0x19-8

Patio

Br 2
13-4x14-5

Desk Stor Bench Stor

Dining
17-0x13-2

Garage
21-4x31-5

Br 3
14-6x13-2

Entry

Covered porch

Patio

57'-6"

109'-0"

Great Room/Atrium
Interior View

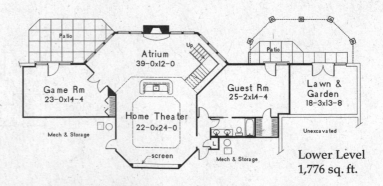

Patio

Atrium
39-0x12-0

Up

Patio

Game Rm
23-0x14-4

Guest Rm
25-2x14-4

Lawn & Garden
18-3x13-8

Home Theater
22-0x24-0

Mech & Storage

Mech & Storage

Unexcavated

screen

Lower Level
1,776 sq. ft.

COUNTRY HOME WITH UNIQUE LOFT   Plan #710-049D-0009

1,673 total square feet of living area   **Price Code B**

Special features

- Great room flows into the breakfast nook with outdoor access and beyond to an efficient kitchen
- Master bedroom on second floor has access to loft/study, private balcony and bath
- Covered porch surrounds the entire home for outdoor living area
- 3 bedrooms, 2 baths
- Crawl space foundation

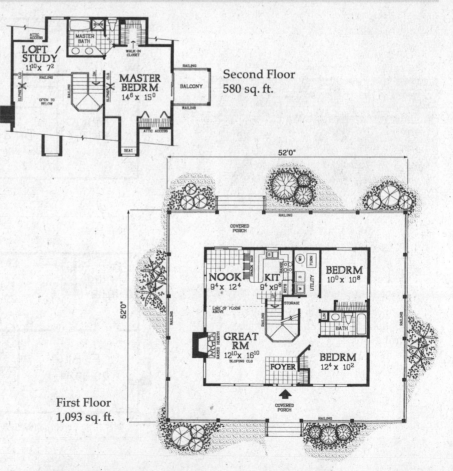

Second Floor
580 sq. ft.

First Floor
1,093 sq. ft.

TO ORDER BLUEPRINTS USE THE FORM ON PAGE 15 OR CALL TOLL-FREE 1-877-671-6036
View thousands more home plans online at www.familyhandyman.com/homeplans

79

Home Has Large Living Areas   Plan #710-001D-0025

1,998 total square feet of living area   **Price Code D**

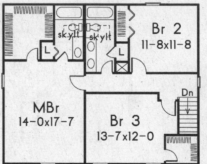

Second Floor
938 sq. ft.

Br 2
11-8x11-8

MBr
14-0x17-7

Br 3
13-7x12-0

Dn

Special features

- Large family room features fireplace and access to kitchen and dining area
- Skylights add daylight to second floor baths
- Utility room conveniently located near garage and kitchen
- Kitchen/breakfast area includes pantry, island workspace and easy access to the patio
- 3 bedrooms, 2 1/2 baths, 2-car side entry garage
- Basement foundation, drawings also include crawl space and slab foundations

58'-0"

Patio

Dining
10-10x13-0

Kit/Brk
22-5x13-0

Util
7-5x
10-4

Family
20-10x14-1

Garage
23-5x21-5

Dn

Up

32'-8"

First Floor
1,060 sq. ft.

Porch depth 5-0

Uncommon Style With This Ranch
Plan #710-013D-0015

1,787 total square feet of living area

Price Code B

Special features

- Skylights brighten screened porch which connects to family room and deck outdoors
- Master bedroom features a comfortable sitting area, large private bath and direct access to screened porch
- Kitchen has serving bar which extends dining into family room
- 3 bedrooms, 2 baths, 2-car side entry garage
- Basement, crawl space or slab foundation, please specify when ordering

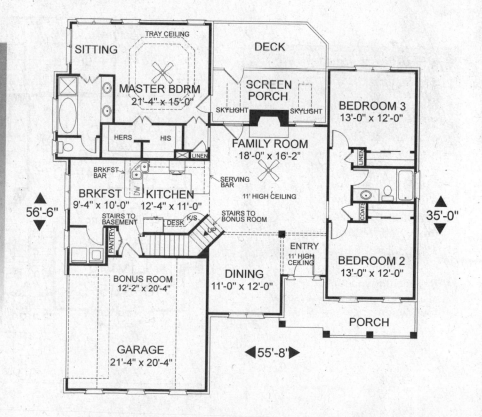

TO ORDER BLUEPRINTS USE THE FORM ON PAGE 15 OR CALL TOLL-FREE 1-877-671-6036
View thousands more home plans online at www.familyhandyman.com/homeplans

81

CHARMING And Functional Home   Plan #710-053D-0032

1,404 total square feet of living area

Price Code A

Special features

- Split foyer entrance
- Bayed living area features unique vaulted ceiling and fireplace
- Wrap-around kitchen has corner windows for added sunlight and a bar that overlooks dining area
- Master bath features a garden tub with separate shower
- Rear deck provides handy access to dining room and kitchen
- 3 bedrooms, 2 baths, 2-car drive under garage
- Basement foundation, drawings also include partial crawl space foundation

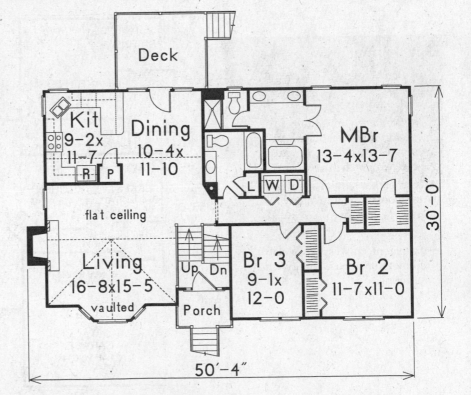

Deck

Kit
9-2x
11-7

Dining
10-4x
11-10

MBr
13-4x13-7

flat ceiling

Living
16-8x15-5
vaulted

Up Dn

Br 3
9-1x
12-0

Br 2
11-7x11-0

Porch

30'-0"

50'-4"

Circle-Top Details

Plan #710-019D-0013

1,932 total square feet of living area

Price Code C

Special features

- Double arches form entrance to this elegantly styled home
- Two palladian windows add distinction to facade
- Kitchen has an angled eating bar opening to the breakfast and living rooms
- 3 bedrooms, 2 baths, 2-car side entry garage
- Crawl space or slab foundation, please specify when ordering

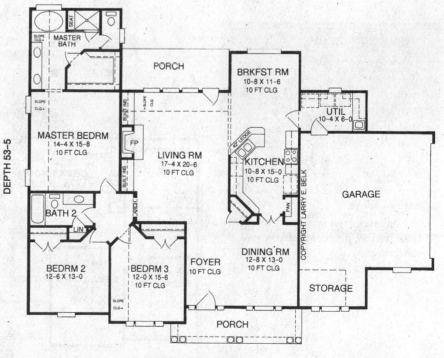

TO ORDER BLUEPRINTS USE THE FORM ON PAGE 15 OR CALL TOLL-FREE 1-877-671-6036
View thousands more home plans online at www.familyhandyman.com/homeplans

83

ARCHED CORNICES ADD ELEGANCE   Plan #710-025D-0025

2,154 total square feet of living area   **Price Code C**

Special features

- Large breakfast room is an ideal family gathering place
- Formal dining room is graced with a corner decorative column
- Separate vanities, an oversized tub and a spacious glass shower are a just a few of the amenities in the master bath
- 4 bedrooms, 2 1/2 baths, 2-car side entry garage
- Basement, crawl space or slab foundation, please specify when ordering

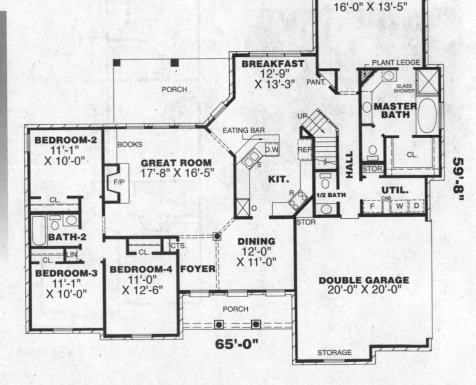

Magnificent Manor Home
Plan #710-027D-0004

3,160 total square feet of living area

Price Code E

Special features

- Covered entry porch leads into magnificent two-story foyer which accesses formal rooms on either side
- Main floor master bedroom features two walk-in closets and large master bath
- Kitchen designed for efficiency includes island cooktop and pass-through to breakfast room
- 4 bedrooms, 3 1/2 baths, 3-car side entry garage
- Basement foundation

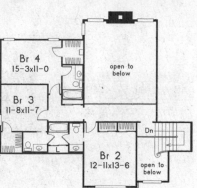

Second Floor
939 sq. ft.

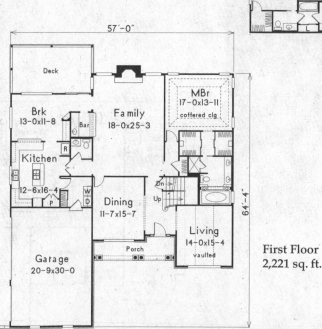

First Floor
2,221 sq. ft.

TO ORDER BLUEPRINTS USE THE FORM ON PAGE 15 OR CALL TOLL-FREE 1-877-671-6036
View thousands more home plans online at www.familyhandyman.com/homeplans

85

Striking Turret

Plan #710-035D-0056

2,246 total square feet of living area

Price Code D

Special features

- Two-story foyer
- Master suite has sitting area with bay window
- Breakfast area near kitchen
- Bedroom #4 easily converts to an office
- Optional bonus room has an additional 269 square feet of living area
- 4 bedrooms, 3 baths, 2-car side entry garage
- Walk-out basement, slab or crawl space foundation; please specify when ordering

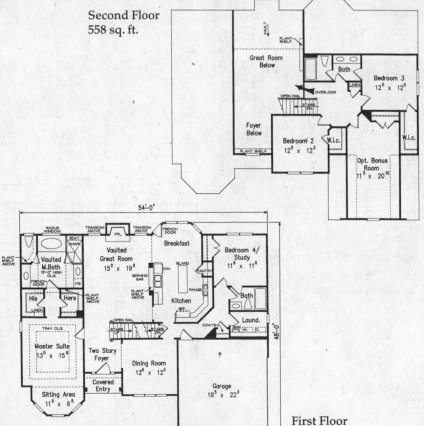

Second Floor
558 sq. ft.

First Floor
1,688 sq. ft.

TO ORDER BLUEPRINTS USE THE FORM ON PAGE 15 OR CALL TOLL-FREE 1-877-671-6036
View thousands more home plans online at www.familyhandyman.com/homeplans

The Family Handyman

1,996 total square feet of living area

Price Code C

Special features

- Dining area features octagon-shaped coffered ceiling and built-in china cabinet
- Both the master bath and second floor bath have cheerful skylights
- Family room includes wet bar and fireplace flanked by attractive quarter round windows
- 9' ceilings throughout first floor with plant shelving in foyer and dining area
- 3 bedrooms, 2 1/2 baths, 2-car side entry garage
- Basement foundation, drawings also include crawl space and slab foundations

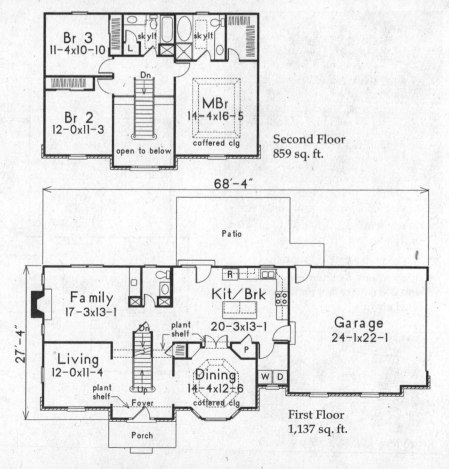

Second Floor
859 sq. ft.

First Floor
1,137 sq. ft.

TO ORDER BLUEPRINTS USE THE FORM ON PAGE 15 OR CALL TOLL-FREE 1-877-671-6036
View thousands more home plans online at www.familyhandyman.com/homeplans

87

Ultimate Atrium For A Sloping Lot Plan #710-007D-0002

3,814 total square feet of living area

Price Code G

Special features

- Massive sunken great room with vaulted ceiling includes exciting balcony overlook of towering atrium window wall
- Breakfast bar adjoins open "California" kitchen
- Seven vaulted rooms for drama and four fireplaces for warmth
- Master bath complemented by colonnade and fireplace surrounding sunken tub and deck
- 3 bedrooms, 2 1/2 baths, 3-car side entry garage
- Walk-out basement foundation
- 3,566 square feet on the first floor and 248 square feet on the lower level atrium

Rear View

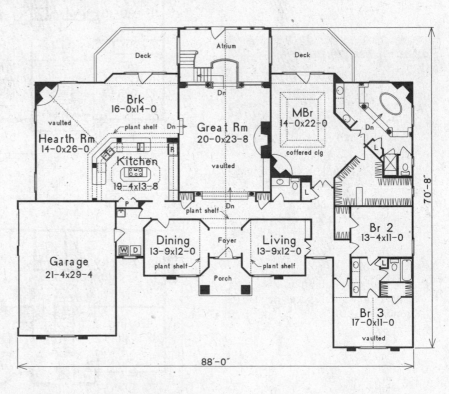

The Family Handyman

2,487 total square feet of living area

Price Code D

Special features

- Three second floor bedrooms and a convenient study loft share a hall bath
- Dining and living rooms feature French doors leading to a covered wrap-around porch
- First floor living spaces offer formal dining as well as a casual nook and kitchen with eating bar and pantry
- 4 bedrooms, 2 1/2 baths, 2-car side entry garage
- Basement foundation

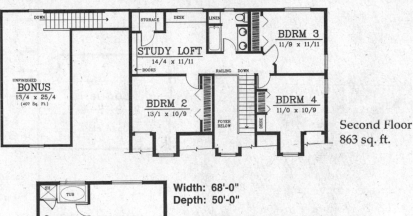

Second Floor
863 sq. ft.

STUDY LOFT 14/4 x 11/11
BDRM 3 11/9 x 11/11
UNFINISHED BONUS 13/4 x 25/4 (407 Sq. Ft.)
BDRM 2 13/1 x 10/9
BDRM 4 11/0 x 10/9

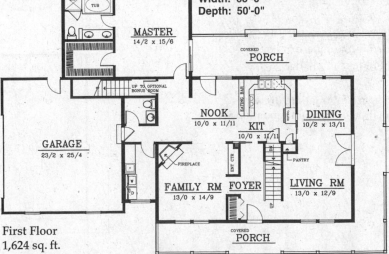

Width: 68'-0"
Depth: 50'-0"

MASTER 14/2 x 15/6
COVERED PORCH
NOOK 10/0 x 11/11
KIT 10/0 x 11/11
DINING 10/2 x 13/11
GARAGE 23/2 x 25/4
FAMILY RM 13/0 x 14/9
FOYER
LIVING RM 13/0 x 12/9
COVERED PORCH

First Floor
1,624 sq. ft.

TO ORDER BLUEPRINTS USE THE FORM ON PAGE 15 OR CALL TOLL-FREE 1-877-671-6036
View thousands more home plans online at www.familyhandyman.com/homeplans

89

Double Bay Enhances Front Entry   Plan #710-053D-0003

1,992 total square feet of living area

Price Code C

Special features

- Distinct living, dining and breakfast areas
- Master bedroom boasts full end bay window and a cathedral ceiling
- Storage and laundry area located adjacent to the garage
- Bonus room over the garage for future office or playroom is included in the square footage
- 3 bedrooms, 2 1/2 baths, 2-car garage
- Crawl space foundation, drawings also include basement foundation

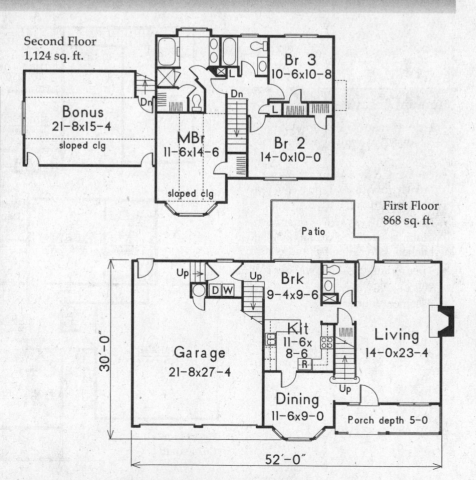

Second Floor
1,124 sq. ft.

Bonus
21-8x15-4
sloped clg

Dn

MBr
11-6x14-6
sloped clg

Br 3
10-6x10-8

Dn

Br 2
14-0x10-0

First Floor
868 sq. ft.

Patio

Up   Up   Brk
9-4x9-6

DW

Garage
21-8x27-4

Kit
11-6x
8-6

R

Living
14-0x23-4

Up

Dining
11-6x9-0

Porch depth 5-0

30'-0"

52'-0"

Three-Level Design Has It All

Plan #710-038D-0035

1,562 total square feet of living area

Price Code B

Special features

- Two sets of double-doors in great room and dining area fill home with sunlight
- Kitchen with breakfast bar allows for additional dining space
- Unique second floor loft is open to first floor and has a private covered deck
- Optional lower level has an additional 678 square feet of living area
- 3 bedrooms, 2 baths
- Basement foundation

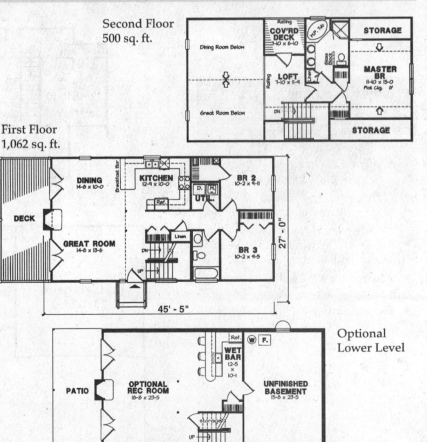

Second Floor
500 sq. ft.

First Floor
1,062 sq. ft.

Optional
Lower Level

TO ORDER BLUEPRINTS USE THE FORM ON PAGE 15 OR CALL TOLL-FREE 1-877-671-6036
View thousands more home plans online at www.familyhandyman.com/homeplans

91

Home Arranged For Open Living   Plan #710-023D-0016

1,609 total square feet of living area

Price Code B

Special features

- Kitchen captures full use of space with pantry, ample cabinets and workspace
- Master bedroom is well-secluded with walk-in closet and private bath
- Large utility room includes sink and extra storage
- Attractive bay window in dining area provides light
- 3 bedrooms, 2 1/2 baths, 2-car garage
- Slab foundation

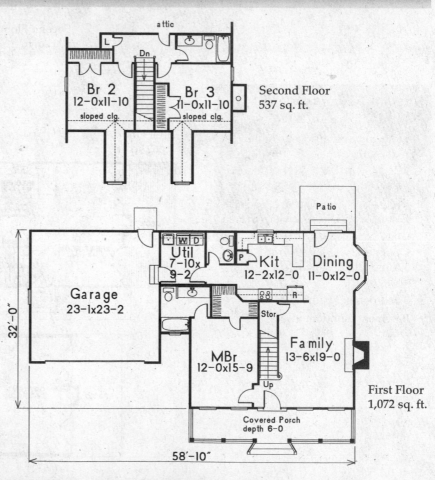

attic

Br 2
12-0x11-10
sloped clg.

Br 3
11-0x11-10
sloped clg.

Second Floor
537 sq. ft.

Patio

Util
7-10x
9-2

Kit
12-2x12-0

Dining
11-0x12-0

Garage
23-1x23-2

Stor

32'-0"

MBr
12-0x15-9

Family
13-6x19-0

Up

First Floor
1,072 sq. ft.

Covered Porch
depth 6-0

58'-10"

Exterior Accents Add Charm

Plan #710-022D-0004

1,359 total square feet of living area

Price Code A

Special features

- Covered porch, stone chimney and abundant windows lend an outdoor appeal
- Spacious, bright kitchen has pass-through to formal dining room
- Large walk-in closets in all bedrooms
- Extensive deck expands dining and entertaining areas
- 3 bedrooms, 2 1/2 baths, 2-car garage
- Basement foundation

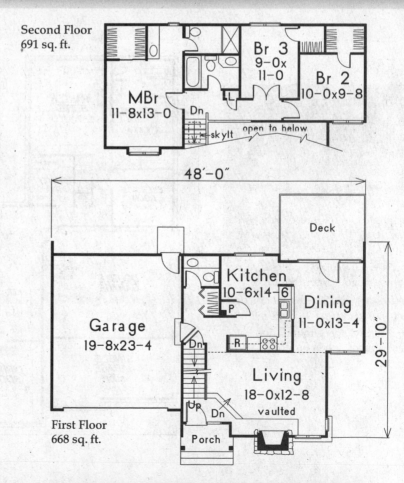

Second Floor
691 sq. ft.

Br 3
9-0x 11-0

Br 2
10-0x9-8

MBr
11-8x13-0

Dn

skylt

open to below

48'-0"

Deck

Kitchen
10-6x14-6

Dining
11-0x13-4

Garage
19-8x23-4

Dn

P

R

29'-10"

Living
18-0x12-8
vaulted

Up

Dn

First Floor
668 sq. ft.

Porch

TO ORDER BLUEPRINTS USE THE FORM ON PAGE 15 OR CALL TOLL-FREE 1-877-671-6036
View thousands more home plans online at www.familyhandyman.com/homeplans

93

The Family Handyman

Elegant European Styling

Plan #710-060D-0010

© Copyright MCMXCVIII — Ralph Jones

2,600 total square feet of living area

Price Code E

Special features

- Formal entry has large openings to dining and great rooms both with coffered ceilings

- Great room has corner fireplace and atrium doors leading to rear covered porch

- Morning room with rear view and an angled eating bar is sunny and bright

- Exercise room could easily serve as an office or computer room

- 4 bedrooms, 2 1/2 baths, 3-car side entry garage

- Slab or crawl space foundation, please specify when ordering

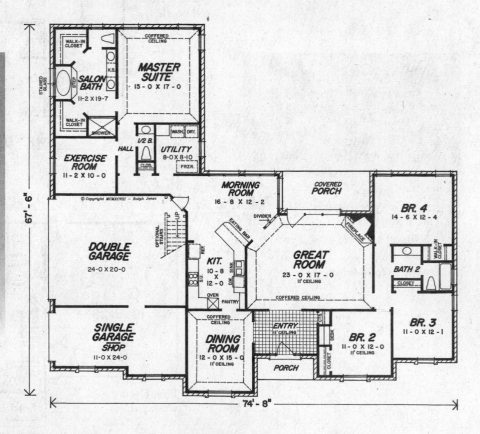

Country-Style With Large Porch   Plan #710-001D-0031

1,501 total square feet of living area   **Price Code B**

Special features

- Spacious kitchen with dining area is open to the outdoors
- Convenient utility room is adjacent to garage
- Master bedroom with private bath, dressing area and access to large covered porch
- Large family room creates openness
- 3 bedrooms, 2 baths, 2-car side entry garage
- Basement foundation, drawings also include crawl space and slab foundations

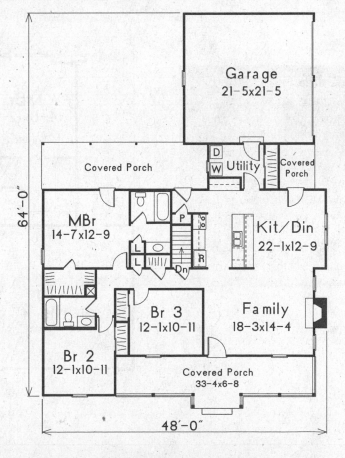

TO ORDER BLUEPRINTS USE THE FORM ON PAGE 15 OR CALL TOLL-FREE 1-877-671-6036
View thousands more home plans online at www.familyhandyman.com/homeplans

95

Window Adds Character

Plan #710-022D-0018

1,368 total square feet of living area

Price Code A

Special features

- Entry foyer steps down to open living area which combines great room and formal dining area
- Vaulted master bedroom includes box bay window, large vanity, separate tub and shower
- Cozy breakfast area features direct access to the patio and pass-through kitchen
- Handy linen closet located in hall
- 3 bedrooms, 2 baths, 2-car garage
- Basement foundation

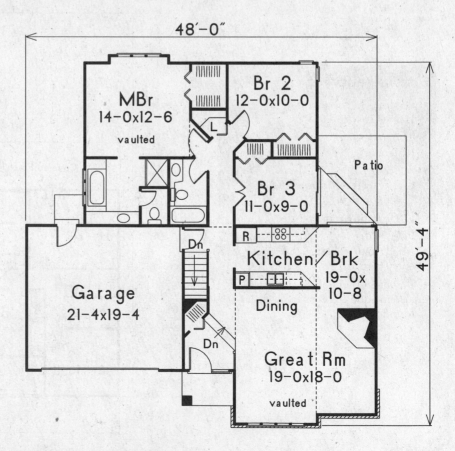

48'-0"

49'-4"

MBr
14-0x12-6
vaulted

Br 2
12-0x10-0

L

Br 3
11-0x9-0

Patio

R

Dn

Kitchen/Brk
19-0x 10-8

Dining

P

Garage
21-4x19-4

Dn

Great Rm
19-0x18-0
vaulted

TO ORDER BLUEPRINTS USE THE FORM ON PAGE 15 OR CALL TOLL-FREE 1-877-671-6036
View thousands more home plans online at www.familyhandyman.com/homeplans

Dining With A View

Plan #710-007D-0038

1,524 total square feet of living area

Price Code B

Special features

- Delightful balcony overlooks two-story entry illuminated by oval window
- Roomy first floor master bedroom offers quiet privacy
- All bedrooms feature one or more walk-in closets
- 3 bedrooms, 2 1/2 baths, 2-car garage
- Basement foundation, drawings also include crawl space and slab foundations

Second Floor
573 sq. ft.

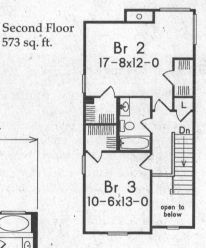

Br 2
17-8x12-0

Br 3
10-6x13-0

open to below

Dn

L

38'-0"

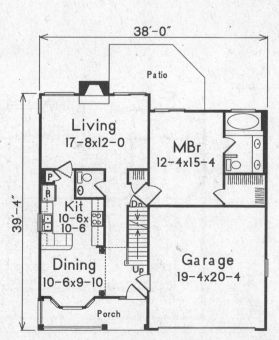

Patio

Living
17-8x12-0

MBr
12-4x15-4

39'-4"

P
R

Kit
10-6x
10-6

Dn

Dining
10-6x9-10

Up

Garage
19-4x20-4

Porch

First Floor
951 sq. ft.

TO ORDER BLUEPRINTS USE THE FORM ON PAGE 15 OR CALL TOLL-FREE 1-877-671-6036
View thousands more home plans online at www.familyhandyman.com/homeplans

97

Traditional Farmhouse Feeling   Plan #710-062D-0042

2,582 total square feet of living area   **Price Code D**

Special features

- Both the family and living rooms are warmed by hearths
- The master bedroom on the second floor has a bayed sitting room and a private bath with whirlpool tub
- Old-fashioned window seat in second floor landing is a charming touch
- 4 bedrooms, 3 baths, 2-car side entry garage
- Basement or crawl space foundation, please specify when ordering

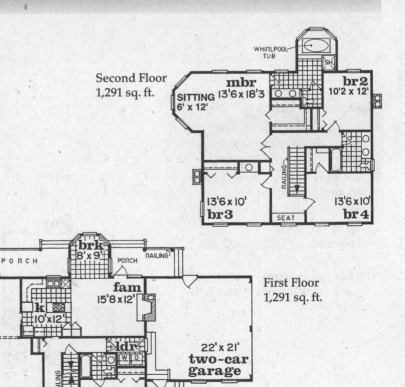

Second Floor 1,291 sq. ft.

WHIRLPOOL TUB

mbr 13'6 x 18'3
SITTING 6' x 12'
br2 10'2 x 12'
SH

13'6 x 10' br3
SEAT
13'6 x 10' br4
RAILING

First Floor 1,291 sq. ft.

RAILING   PORCH   brk 8' x 9'   PORCH   RAILING

din 15' x 12'
fam 15'8 x 12'
k 10'x 12'

ldr   W D
22' x 21' two~car garage

13'6 x 18'8 liv
RAILING
13'6 x 10' den

PORCH

RAILING   RAILING

Width: 64'-6"
Depth: 41'-0"

Luxurious Master Bedroom

Plan #710-065D-0036

2,587 total square feet of living area

Price Code D

Special features

- High windows above French doors in the great room create a spectacular view
- The spacious kitchen serves the breakfast and dining rooms with ease
- The second floor offers plenty of space with three bedrooms and a storage area
- 4 bedrooms, 3 1/2 baths, 2-car side entry garage
- Basement foundation

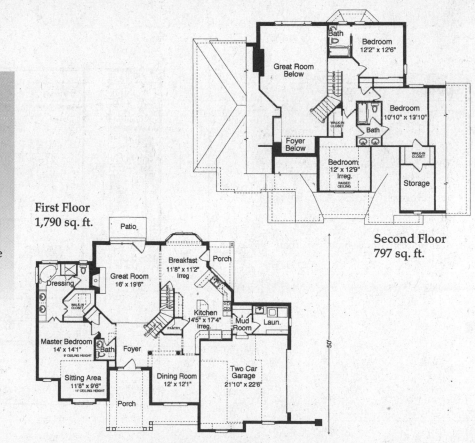

First Floor 1,790 sq. ft.

Second Floor 797 sq. ft.

TO ORDER BLUEPRINTS USE THE FORM ON PAGE 15 OR CALL TOLL-FREE 1-877-671-6036
View thousands more home plans online at www.familyhandyman.com/homeplans

99

Traditional Southern Style Home   Plan #710-028D-0004

1,785 total square feet of living area

Price Code B

Special features

- 9' ceilings throughout home
- Luxurious master bath includes whirlpool tub and separate shower
- Cozy breakfast area is convenient to kitchen
- 3 bedrooms, 3 baths, 2-car detached garage
- Basement, crawl space or slab foundation, please specify when ordering

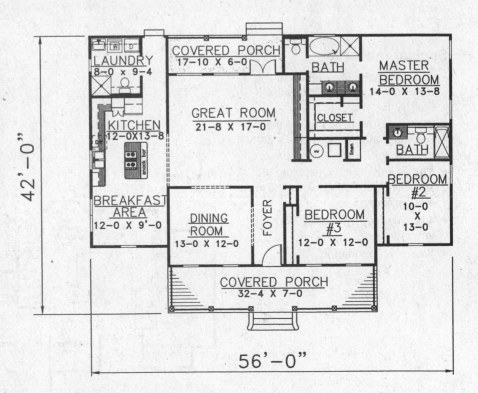

LAUNDRY 8-0 X 9-4

COVERED PORCH 17-10 X 6-0

BATH

MASTER BEDROOM 14-0 X 13-8

KITCHEN 12-0X13-8

GREAT ROOM 21-8 X 17-0

CLOSET

linen

BATH

BREAKFAST AREA 12-0 X 9-0

DINING ROOM 13-0 X 12-0

FOYER

BEDROOM #3 12-0 X 12-0

BEDROOM #2 10-0 X 13-0

COVERED PORCH 32-4 X 7-0

42'-0"

56'-0"

Spacious And Functional Home   Plan #710-004D-0001

2,505 total square feet of living area   **Price Code D**

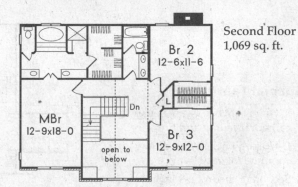

Second Floor
1,069 sq. ft.

Br 2
12–6x11–6

MBr
12–9x18–0

Dn

Br 3
12–9x12–0

open to below

Special features

- The garage features extra storage area and ample workspace
- Laundry room accessible from the garage and the outdoors
- Deluxe raised tub and immense walk-in closet grace master bath
- 3 bedrooms, 2 1/2 baths, 2-car side entry garage
- Basement foundation, drawings also include crawl space foundation

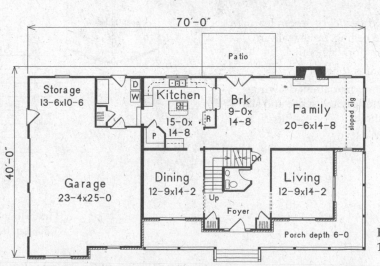

70'–0"

40'–0"

Patio

Storage
13–6x10–6

Kitchen
15–0x
14–8

Brk
9–0x
14–8

Family
20–6x14–8

sloped clg

Garage
23–4x25–0

Dining
12–9x14–2

Living
12–9x14–2

Foyer

Up

Porch depth 6–0

First Floor
1,436 sq. ft.

Spacious A-Frame

Plan #710-001D-0077

1,769 total square feet of living area

Price Code B

Special features

- Living room boasts an elegant cathedral ceiling and fireplace
- U-shaped kitchen and dining area combine for easy living
- Secondary bedrooms include double closets
- Secluded master bedroom features a sloped ceiling, large walk-in closet and private bath
- 3 bedrooms, 2 baths
- Basement foundation, drawings also include crawl space and slab foundations

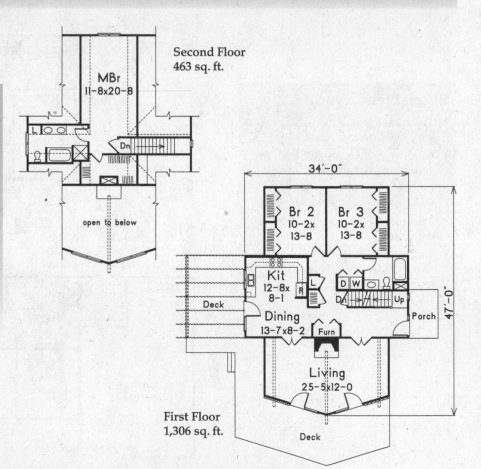

Second Floor
463 sq. ft.

MBr
11-8x20-8

Dn

open to below

34'-0"

47'-0"

Br 2
10-2x
13-8

Br 3
10-2x
13-8

Kit
12-8x
8-1

Deck

Dining
13-7x8-2

Furn

Porch

Up

Living
25-5x12-0

First Floor
1,306 sq. ft.

Deck

COUNTRY CHARMER

Plan #710-016D-0058

2,874 total square feet of living area

Price Code G

Special features

- Openness characterizes the casual areas
- The kitchen is separated from the bayed breakfast nook by an island workspace
- Stunning great room has dramatic vaulted ceiling and a corner fireplace
- Unfinished loft on the second floor has an additional 300 square feet of living area
- 4 bedrooms, 3 baths, 3-car side entry garage
- Basement, crawl space or slab foundation, please specify when ordering

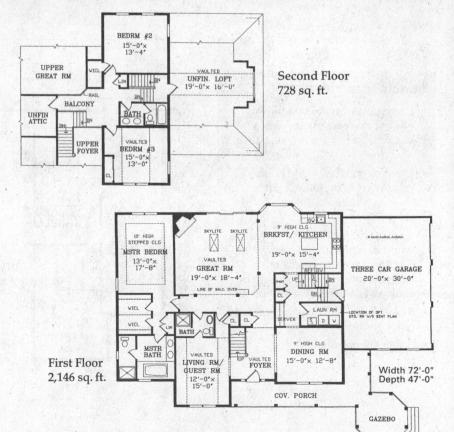

Second Floor
728 sq. ft.

First Floor
2,146 sq. ft.

Width 72'-0"
Depth 47'-0"

TO ORDER BLUEPRINTS USE THE FORM ON PAGE 15 OR CALL TOLL-FREE 1-877-671-6036
View thousands more home plans online at www.familyhandyman.com/homeplans

103

Prestige In A Classic Ranch

Plan #710-007D-0050

2,723 total square feet of living area

Price Code E

Special features

- Large porch invites you into an elegant foyer which accesses a vaulted study with private hall and coat closet

- Great room is second to none, comprised of fireplace, built-in shelves, vaulted ceiling and a 1 1/2 story window wall

- A spectacular hearth room with vaulted ceiling and masonry fireplace opens to an elaborate kitchen featuring two snack bars, cooking island and walk-in pantry

- 3 bedrooms, 2 1/2 baths, 3-car side entry garage

- Basement foundation

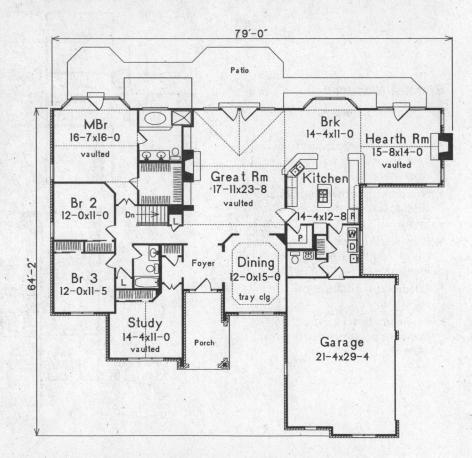

79'-0"

Patio

MBr
16-7x16-0
vaulted

Brk
14-4x11-0

Hearth Rm
15-8x14-0
vaulted

Br 2
12-0x11-0

Great Rm
17-11x23-8
vaulted

Kitchen
14-4x12-8

Dn

Foyer

Dining
12-0x15-0
tray clg

Br 3
12-0x11-5

64'-2"

Study
14-4x11-0
vaulted

Porch

Garage
21-4x29-4

TO ORDER BLUEPRINTS USE THE FORM ON PAGE 15 OR CALL TOLL-FREE 1-877-671-6036
View thousands more home plans online at www.familyhandyman.com/homeplans

Porch Adds Country Charm

Plan #710-029D-0002

1,619 total square feet of living area

Price Code B

Special features

- Private second floor bedroom and bath
- Kitchen features a snack bar and adjacent dining area
- Master bedroom has a private bath
- Centrally located washer and dryer
- 3 bedrooms, 3 baths
- Basement foundation, drawings also include crawl space and slab foundations

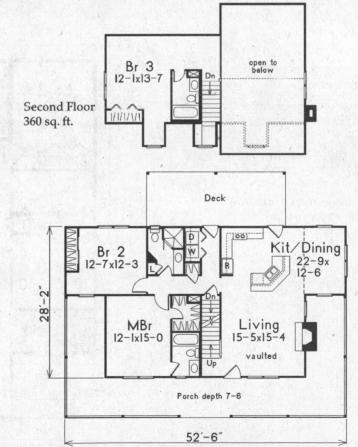

Second Floor
360 sq. ft.

Br 3
12-1x13-7

open to below

Dn

Deck

Br 2
12-7x12-3

Kit/Dining
22-9x 12-6

MBr
12-1x15-0

Living
15-5x15-4
vaulted

Dn

Up

28'-2"

Porch depth 7-6

52'-6"

First Floor
1,259 sq. ft.

TO ORDER BLUEPRINTS USE THE FORM ON PAGE 15 OR CALL TOLL-FREE 1-877-671-6036
View thousands more home plans online at www.familyhandyman.com/homeplans

105

Three Bedroom Luxury

Plan #710-007D-0107

1,161 total square feet of living area

Price Code AA

Special features

- Brickwork and feature window add elegance to home for a narrow lot
- Living room enjoys a vaulted ceiling, fireplace and opens to kitchen
- U-shaped kitchen offers a breakfast area with bay window, snack bar and built-in pantry
- 3 bedrooms, 2 baths
- Basement foundation

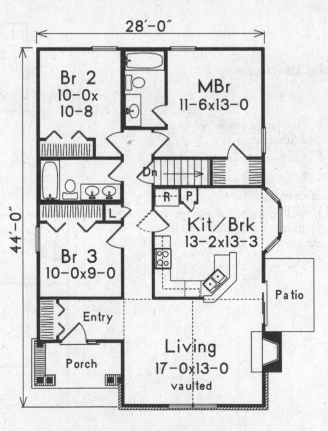

28'-0"

44'-0"

Br 2
10-0x
10-8

MBr
11-6x13-0

Dn

R   P

Br 3
10-0x9-0

Kit/Brk
13-2x13-3

Patio

Entry

Porch

Living
17-0x13-0
vaulted

106

TO ORDER BLUEPRINTS USE THE FORM ON PAGE 15 OR CALL TOLL-FREE 1-877-671-6036
View thousands more home plans online at www.familyhandyman.com/homeplans

Plenty Of Built-Ins

Plan #710-020D-0013

3,012 total square feet of living area

Price Code E

Special features

- Master bedroom has sitting area with entertainment center/library
- Utility room has a sink and includes lots of storage and counterspace
- Future space above garage has an additional 336 square feet of living area
- 4 bedrooms, 3 1/2 baths, 2-car side entry garage
- Crawl space, slab or basement foundation, please specify when ordering

Width: 62'-0"
Depth: 86'-0"

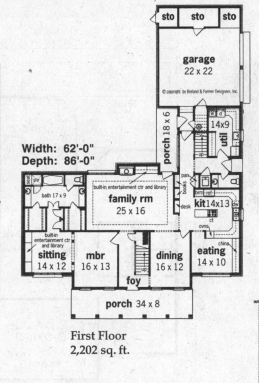

sto sto sto

garage
22 x 22

© copyright by Breland & Farmer Designers, Inc.

porch 18 x 6

w d
14x9
util

built-in entertainment ctr and library

family rm
25 x 16

pan
books
brm ref
desk
kit 14x13
ct
china

bath 17 x 9

built-in entertainment ctr and library

sitting
14 x 12

mbr
16 x 13

foy

dining
16 x 12

ovns

eating
14 x 10

porch 34 x 8

First Floor
2,202 sq. ft.

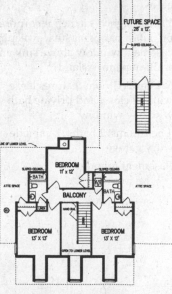

Second Floor
810 sq. ft.

FUTURE SPACE
28' x 12'
SLOPED CEILINGS

OUTLINE OF LOWER LEVEL

SLOPED CEILINGS   BEDROOM   SLOPED CEILINGS
11' x 12'
BATH   BATH
ATTIC SPACE   ATTIC SPACE
BALCONY
BEDROOM   HAND RAIL   BEDROOM
13' x 13'   13' x 12'
OPEN TO LOWER LEVEL

TO ORDER BLUEPRINTS USE THE FORM ON PAGE 15 OR CALL TOLL-FREE 1-877-671-6036
View thousands more home plans online at www.familyhandyman.com/homeplans

107

KITCHEN Is Center Of Activity   Plan #710-007D-0017

1,882 total square feet of living area

Price Code C

Special features

- Handsome brick facade
- Spacious great room and dining room combination brightened by unique corner windows and patio access
- Well-designed kitchen incorporates breakfast bar peninsula, sweeping casement window above sink and walk-in pantry island
- Master bedroom features large walk-in closet and private bath with bay window
- 4 bedrooms, 2 baths, 2-car side entry garage
- Basement foundation

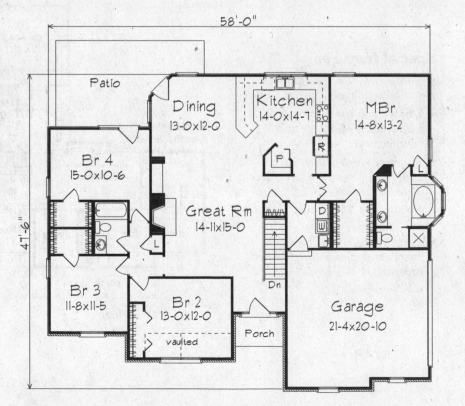

Country-Style Covered Porch

Plan #710-016D-0048

2,567 total square feet of living area

Price Code F

Special features

- Breakfast room has a 12' cathedral ceiling and a bayed area full of windows
- Great room has a stepped ceiling, built-in media center and a corner fireplace
- Bonus room on the second floor has an additional 300 square feet of living area
- 4 bedrooms, 3 baths, 2-car side entry garage
- Basement, crawl space or slab foundation, please specify when ordering

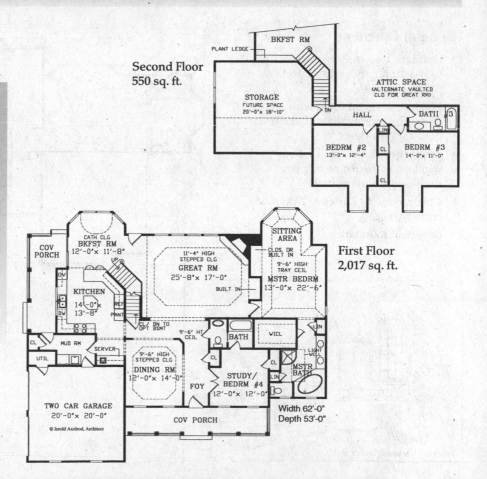

Second Floor
550 sq. ft.

First Floor
2,017 sq. ft.

Width 62'-0"
Depth 53'-0"

© Jerold Axelrod, Architect

TO ORDER BLUEPRINTS USE THE FORM ON PAGE 15 OR CALL TOLL-FREE 1-877-671-6036
View thousands more home plans online at www.familyhandyman.com/homeplans

109

The Family Handyman

Irresistible Grandeur

Plan #710-007D-0006

2,624 total square feet of living area

Price Code E

Special features

- Dramatic two-story entry opens to bayed dining room through classic colonnade
- Magnificent great room with 18' ceiling brightly lit with three palladian windows
- Master bedroom includes bay window, walk-in closets, plant shelves and sunken bath
- 4 bedrooms, 2 1/2 baths, 2-car side entry garage
- Basement foundation

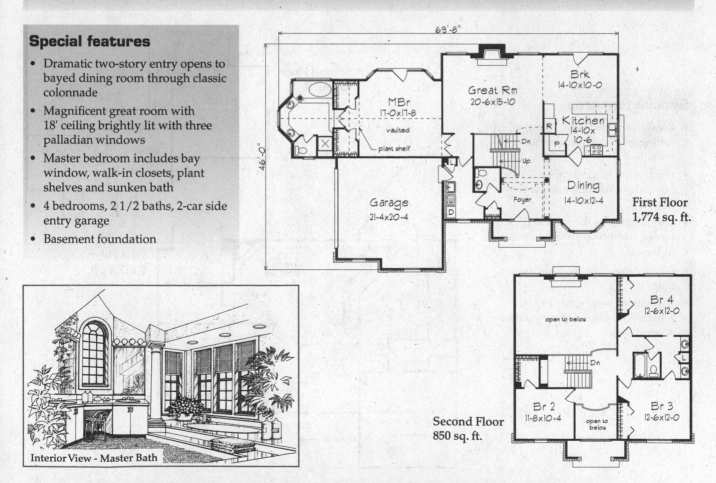

Interior View - Master Bath

69'-8"

46'-0"

MBr 17-0x17-8
vaulted
plant shelf

Great Rm 20-6x15-10

Brk 14-10x10-0

Kitchen 14-10x 10-6

Garage 21-4x20-4

Dn
Up

Foyer

Dining 14-10x12-4

First Floor 1,774 sq. ft.

Br 4 12-6x12-0

open to below

Dn

Br 2 11-8x10-4

Br 3 12-6x12-0

open to below

Second Floor 850 sq. ft.

TO ORDER BLUEPRINTS USE THE FORM ON PAGE 15 OR CALL TOLL-FREE 1-877-671-6036
View thousands more home plans online at www.familyhandyman.com/homeplans

Master Bedroom Opens To Porch   Plan #710-024D-0024

2,481 total square feet of living area   Price Code D

Special features

- All bedrooms separate from main living areas for privacy
- Enormous master bath with double walk-in closets
- Unique covered porch off living area and breakfast room
- Cozy fireplace with built-in bookshelves in living area
- 4 bedrooms, 2 1/2 baths, 2-car side entry garage
- Crawl space or slab foundation, please specify when ordering

Width: 56'-8"
Depth: 86'-0"

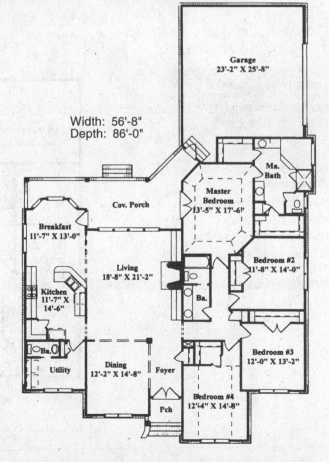

Garage 23'-2" X 25'-8"

Ma. Bath

Master Bedroom 13'-5" X 17'-6"

Cov. Porch

Breakfast 11'-7" X 13'-0"

Bedroom #2 11'-8" X 14'-0"

Living 18'-8" X 21'-2"

Kitchen 11'-7" X 14'-6"

Ba.

Bedroom #3 12'-0" X 13'-2"

Ba.

Utility

Dining 12'-2" X 14'-8"

Foyer

Bedroom #4 12'-4" X 14'-8"

Pch

TO ORDER BLUEPRINTS USE THE FORM ON PAGE 15 OR CALL TOLL-FREE 1-877-671-6036
View thousands more home plans online at www.familyhandyman.com/homeplans

111

Distinctive Style For A Small Lot — Plan #710-007D-0060

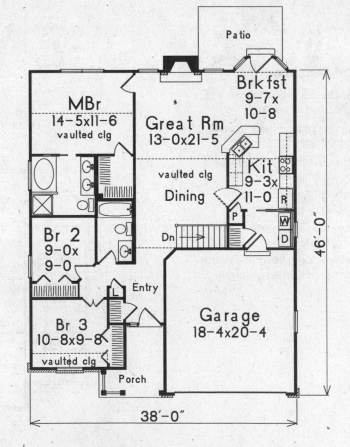

1,268 total square feet of living area

Price Code B

Special features

- Multiple gables, large porch and arched windows create classy exterior
- Innovative design provides openness in great room, kitchen and breakfast room
- Secondary bedrooms have private hall with bath
- 3 bedrooms, 2 baths, 2-car garage
- Basement foundation, drawings also include crawl space and slab foundations

Patio

MBr
14-5x11-6
vaulted clg

Brk fst
9-7x
10-8

Great Rm
13-0x21-5

vaulted clg

Kit
9-3x
11-0

Dining

Br 2
9-0x
9-0

Dn

P

W

D

R

Entry

L

Br 3
10-8x9-8

vaulted clg

Garage
18-4x20-4

Porch

46'-0"

38'-0"

The Family Handyman

Spacious Living Arrangement   Plan #710-021D-0001

2,396 total square feet of living area

Price Code D

Special features

- Generously wide entry welcomes guests
- Central living area with a 12' ceiling and large fireplace serves as a convenient traffic hub
- Kitchen is secluded, yet has easy access to the living, dining and breakfast areas
- Deluxe master bath has a walk-in closet, oversized tub, shower and other amenities
- Energy efficient home with 2" x 6" exterior walls
- 4 bedrooms, 2 baths, 2-car garage
- Slab foundation, drawings also include basement and crawl space foundations

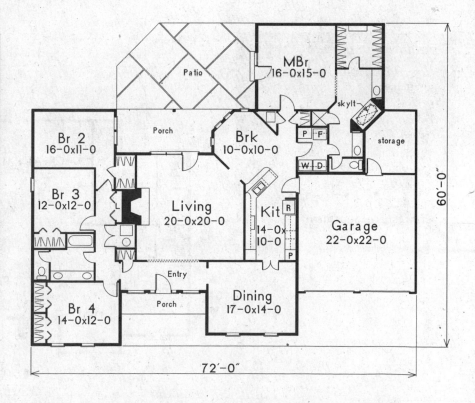

TO ORDER BLUEPRINTS USE THE FORM ON PAGE 15 OR CALL TOLL-FREE 1-877-671-6036
View thousands more home plans online at www.familyhandyman.com/homeplans

113

Great Views At Rear Of Home   Plan #710-011D-0010

2,197 total square feet of living area   **Price Code C**

Special features

- Centrally located great room opens to kitchen, breakfast nook and private backyard
- Den located off entry ideal for home office
- Vaulted master bath has spa tub, shower and double vanity
- 3 bedrooms, 2 1/2 baths, 3-car garage
- Crawl space foundation

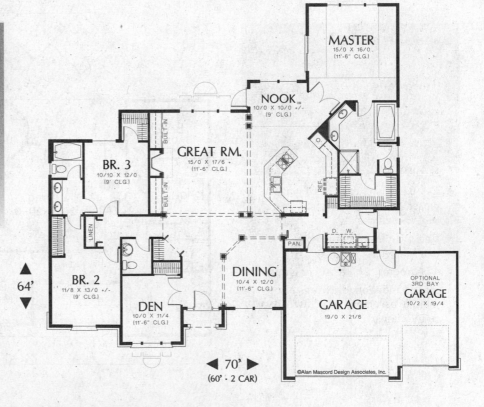

TO ORDER BLUEPRINTS USE THE FORM ON PAGE 15 OR CALL TOLL-FREE 1-877-671-6036
View thousands more home plans online at www.familyhandyman.com/homeplans

Impressive Foyer

Plan #710-035D-0032

1,856 total square feet of living area

Price Code C

Special features

- Beautiful covered porch creates a Southern accent
- Kitchen has an organized feel with lots of cabinetry
- Large foyer has a grand entrance and leads into family room through columns and an arched opening
- 3 bedrooms, 2 baths, 2-car side entry garage
- Walk-out basement, crawl space or slab foundation, please specify when ordering

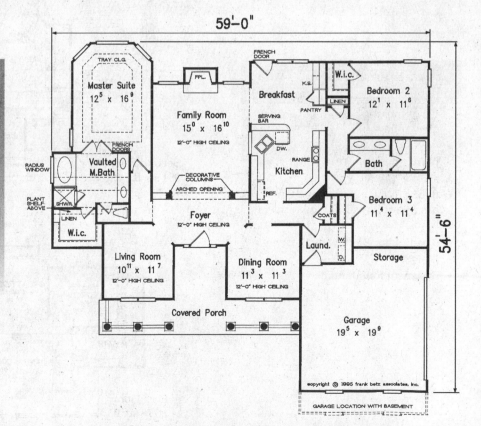

TO ORDER BLUEPRINTS USE THE FORM ON PAGE 15 OR CALL TOLL-FREE 1-877-671-6036
View thousands more home plans online at www.familyhandyman.com/homeplans

115

A Media Nook In The Great Room   Plan #710-072D-0005

2,729 total square feet of living area   **Price Code E**

Special features

- Formal dining room has lovely views into the beautiful two-story great room
- Second floor loft area makes a perfect home office or children's computer area
- Bonus room on the second floor has an additional 300 square feet of living area
- 3 bedrooms, 2 1/2 baths, 2-car garage
- Basement foundation

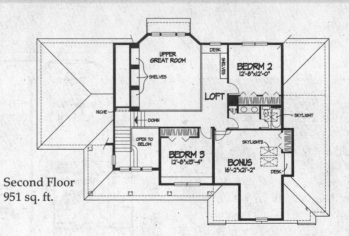

Second Floor
951 sq. ft.

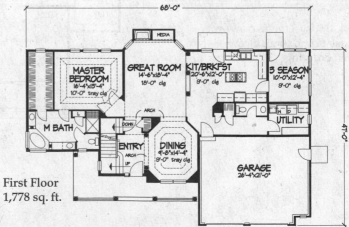

First Floor
1,778 sq. ft.

Porches Bring Outdoor Living In — Plan #710-024D-0027

2,500 total square feet of living area

Price Code D

Special features

- Master bedroom has its own separate wing with front porch, double walk-in closets, private bath and access to back porch and patio
- Large unfinished gameroom on the second floor has an additional 359 square feet of living area
- Living area is oversized and has a fireplace
- 3 bedrooms, 3 baths
- Basement, slab or crawl space foundation, please specify when ordering

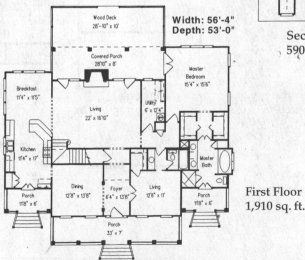

Width: 56'-4"
Depth: 53'-0"

Second Floor
590 sq. ft.

First Floor
1,910 sq. ft.

Affordable Upscale, Amenity Full — Plan #710-006D-0001

1,643 total square feet of living area

Price Code B

Special features

- Family room has vaulted ceiling, open staircase and arched windows allowing for plenty of light
- Kitchen captures full use of space, with pantry, storage, ample counterspace and work island
- Large closets and storage areas throughout
- Roomy master bath has a skylight for natural lighting plus separate tub and shower
- Rear of house provides ideal location for future screened-in porch
- 3 bedrooms, 2 baths, 2-car side entry garage
- Basement foundation, drawings also include slab and crawl space foundations

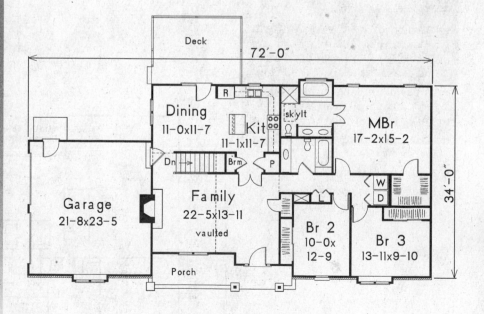

THE Family **Handyman**

Classic Exterior
Plan #710-007D-0049

1,791 total square feet of living area

Price Code C

Special features

- Vaulted great room and octagon-shaped dining area enjoy views of covered patio
- Kitchen features a pass-through to dining area, center island, large walk-in pantry and breakfast room with large bay window
- Master bedroom is vaulted with sitting area
- 4 bedrooms, 2 baths, 2-car garage with storage
- Basement foundation, drawings also include crawl space and slab foundations

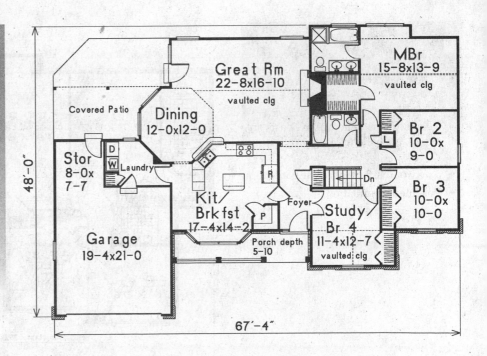

Covered Patio

Great Rm
22-8x16-10
vaulted clg

MBr
15-8x13-9
vaulted clg

Dining
12-0x12-0

Stor
8-0x
7-7

Laundry

Br 2
10-0x
9-0

Kit/
Brkfst
17-4x14-2

Foyer

Study
Br 4
11-4x12-7
vaulted clg

Br 3
10-0x
10-0

Porch depth
5-10

Garage
19-4x21-0

48'-0"

67'-4"

TO ORDER BLUEPRINTS USE THE FORM ON PAGE 15 OR CALL TOLL-FREE 1-877-671-6036
View thousands more home plans online at www.familyhandyman.com/homeplans

119

Country Flair In A Flexible Ranch — Plan #710-051D-0053

1,461 total square feet of living area

Price Code A

Special features

- Casual dining room
- Cathedral ceilings in great room and dining room give home a spacious feel
- Relaxing master bedroom boasts an expansive bath and large walk-in closet
- 3 bedrooms, 2 baths, 2-car garage
- Basement foundation

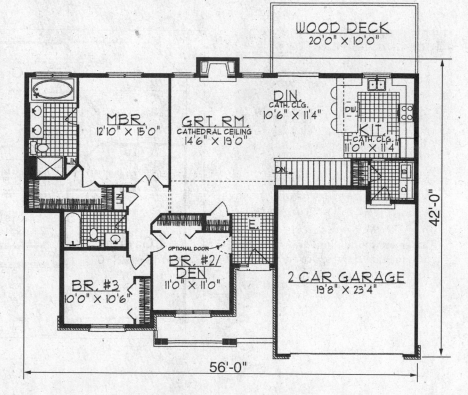

Covered Porch Highlights Home — Plan #710-040D-0032

1,808 total square feet of living area

Price Code C

Special features

- Master bedroom has a walk-in closet, double vanities and separate tub and shower
- Two second floor bedrooms share a study area and full bath
- Partially covered patio is complete with a skylight
- Side entrance opens to utility room with convenient counterspace and laundry sink
- 3 bedrooms, 2 1/2 baths, 2-car side entry garage
- Basement foundation

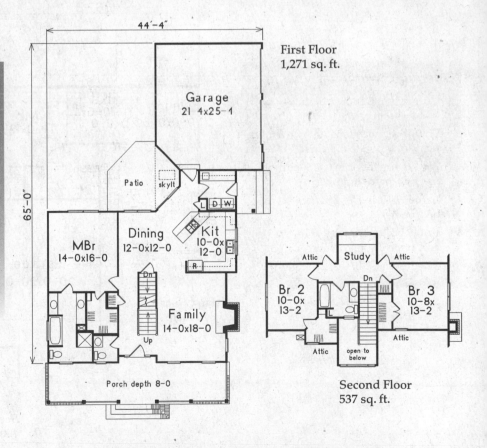

First Floor
1,271 sq. ft.

44'-4"

65'-0"

Garage
21-4x25-1

Patio   sky lt

L D W

Dining
12-0x12-0

Kit
10-0x
12-0

R

MBr
14-0x16-0

Dn

Family
14-0x18-0

Up

Porch depth 8-0

Study

Attic   Attic

Br 2
10-0x
13-2

Dn

Br 3
10-8x
13-2

Attic

Attic   open to
below

Second Floor
537 sq. ft.

TO ORDER BLUEPRINTS USE THE FORM ON PAGE 15 OR CALL TOLL-FREE 1-877-671-6036
View thousands more home plans online at www.familyhandyman.com/homeplans

121

Floor-To-Ceiling Window — Plan #710-022D-0002

1,246 total square feet of living area

Price Code A

Special features

- Corner living room window adds openness and light
- Out-of-the-way kitchen with dining area accesses the outdoors
- Private first floor master bedroom has a corner window
- Large walk-in closet is located in bedroom #3
- Easily built perimeter allows economical construction
- 3 bedrooms, 2 baths, 2-car garage
- Basement foundation

36'-8"

Deck

Dining
9-0x9-6

Kit
12-0x
9-0

MBr
14-0x12-8

Dn

Living
12-4x17-0

vaulted

Up

plant shelf

Garage
20-0x20-0

38'-8"

First Floor
846 sq. ft.

Br 2
11-6x10-0

open to below

Dn

Br 3
13-0x9-0

Second Floor
400 sq. ft.

Great Room Is Core Of Home Plan #710-027D-0006

2,076 total square feet of living area

Price Code C

Special features

- Vaulted great room has fireplace flanked by windows and skylights that welcome the sun
- Kitchen leads to vaulted breakfast room and rear deck
- Study located off foyer provides great location for home office
- Large bay windows grace master bedroom and bath
- 3 bedrooms, 2 baths, 2-car garage
- Basement foundation

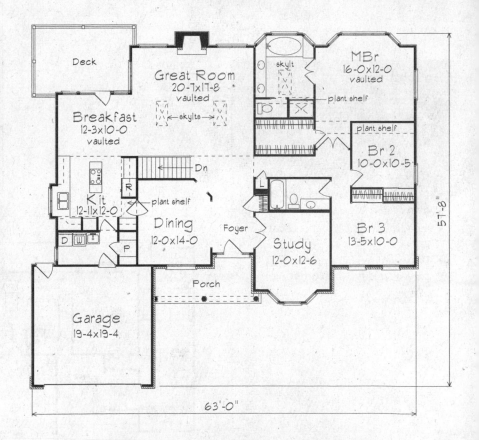

TO ORDER BLUEPRINTS USE THE FORM ON PAGE 15 OR CALL TOLL-FREE 1-877-671-6036
View thousands more home plans online at www.familyhandyman.com/homeplans

123

Windows Add Plenty Of Light
Plan #710-056D-0017

2,460 total square feet of living area

Price Code D

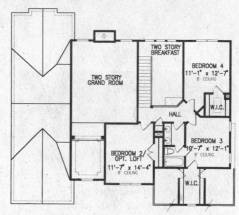

Second Floor
709 sq. ft.

First Floor
1,751 sq. ft.

Special features

- Convenient first floor master bedroom has double walk-in closets and an optional study/living room attached

- Two-story breakfast and grand rooms are open and airy

- Laundry room has a sink and overhead cabinets for convenience

- 4 bedrooms, 2 1/2 baths, 2-car garage

- Basement or slab foundation, please specify when ordering

124

TO ORDER BLUEPRINTS USE THE FORM ON PAGE 15 OR CALL TOLL-FREE 1-877-671-6036
View thousands more home plans online at www.familyhandyman.com/homeplans

Expansive Glass Wall   Plan #710-062D-0048

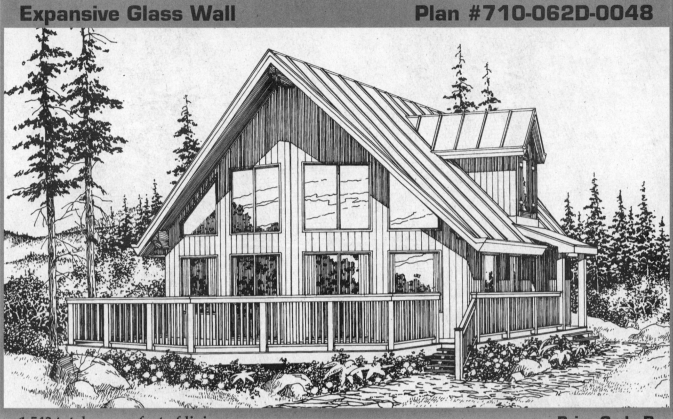

1,543 total square feet of living area   **Price Code B**

Special features

- Enormous sundeck makes this a popular vacation style
- A woodstove warms the vaulted living and dining rooms
- A vaulted kitchen has a prep island and breakfast bar
- Second floor vaulted master bedroom has private bath and walk-in closet
- 3 bedrooms, 2 baths
- Crawl space foundation

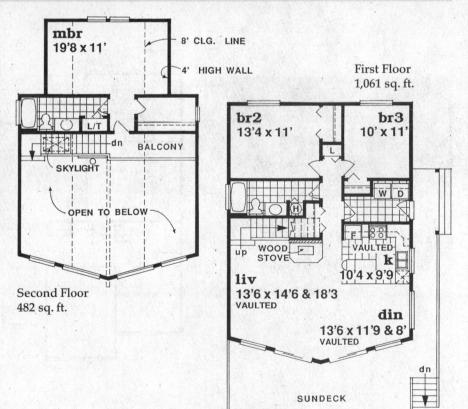

mbr 19'8 x 11'

8' CLG. LINE

4' HIGH WALL

L/T

dn   BALCONY

SKYLIGHT

OPEN TO BELOW

Second Floor 482 sq. ft.

First Floor 1,061 sq. ft.

br2 13'4 x 11'

br3 10' x 11'

L

W D

up   WOOD STOVE

VAULTED

F

liv 13'6 x 14'6 & 18'3 VAULTED

k 10'4 x 9'9

din 13'6 x 11'9 & 8' VAULTED

dn

SUNDECK

Width: 28'-0"
Depth: 39'-9"

Varied Ceiling Heights

Plan #710-055D-0032

2,439 total square feet of living area

Price Code D

Special features

- Enter columned gallery area just before reaching family room with see-through fireplace
- Master suite has a corner whirlpool tub
- Double-door entrance into study
- 4 bedrooms, 3 baths, 2-car garage
- Slab, crawl space, basement or walk-out basement foundation, please specify when ordering

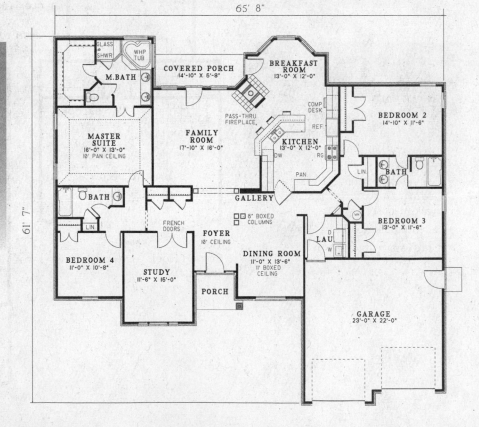

Charm Wrapped In A Veranda

Plan #710-037D-0009

2,059 total square feet of living area

Price Code C

Special features

- Octagon-shaped breakfast room offers plenty of windows and creates a view to the veranda
- First floor master bedroom has large walk-in closet and deluxe bath
- 9' ceilings throughout the home
- Secondary bedrooms and bath feature dormers and are adjacent to cozy sitting area
- 3 bedrooms, 2 1/2 baths, 2-car detached garage
- Slab foundation, drawings also include basement and crawl space foundations

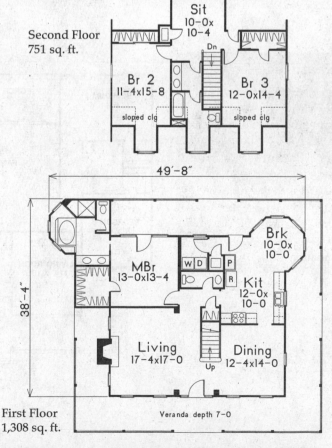

Second Floor
751 sq. ft.

Sit
10-0x
10-4

Dn

Br 2
11-4x15-8

Br 3
12-0x14-4

sloped clg   sloped clg

49'-8"

38'-4"

MBr
13-0x13-4

W D   P
R

Brk
10-0x
10-0

Kit
12-0x
10-0

Living
17-4x17-0

Up

Dining
12-4x14-0

First Floor
1,308 sq. ft.

Veranda depth 7-0

TO ORDER BLUEPRINTS USE THE FORM ON PAGE 15 OR CALL TOLL-FREE 1-877-671-6036
View thousands more home plans online at www.familyhandyman.com/homeplans

127

Unique Three-Way Fireplace   Plan #710-026D-0166

2,126 total square feet of living area

Price Code C

Special features

- Elegant bay windows in master bedroom welcome the sun
- Double vanities in master bath are separated by a large whirlpool tub
- Secondary bedrooms each include a walk-in closet
- Nook has access to the outdoors onto the rear porch
- 3 bedrooms, 2 baths, 2-car side entry garage
- Slab foundation

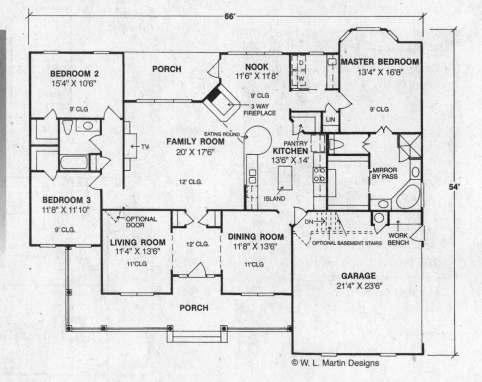

BEDROOM 2
15'4" X 10'6"
9' CLG

PORCH

NOOK
11'6" X 11'8"
9' CLG
3 WAY FIREPLACE

MASTER BEDROOM
13'4" X 16'8"
9' CLG

FAMILY ROOM
20' X 17'6"
12' CLG.

EATING ROUND

LIN

PANTRY

KITCHEN
13'6" X 14'

MIRROR BY PASS

ISLAND

BEDROOM 3
11'8" X 11'10"
9' CLG.

OPTIONAL DOOR

LIVING ROOM
11'4" X 13'6"
11'CLG

12' CLG.

DINING ROOM
11'8" X 13'6"
11'CLG

DN

OPTIONAL BASEMENT STAIRS

WORK BENCH

GARAGE
21'4" X 23'6"

PORCH

© W. L. Martin Designs

66'

54'

Drive Under Garage Design

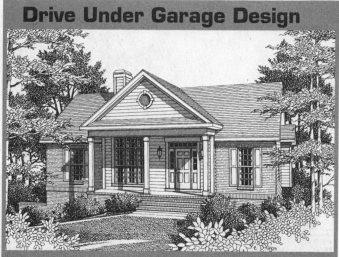

Plan #710-052D-0005

1,268 total square feet of living area

Price Code A

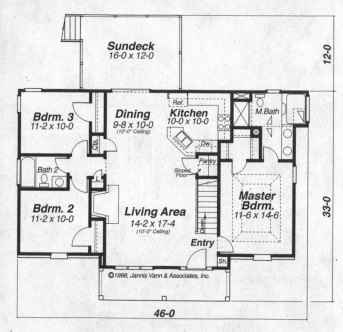

Special features

- Raised gable porch is a focal point creating a dramatic look
- 10' ceilings throughout living and dining areas
- Open kitchen is well-designed
- Master bedroom offers tray ceiling and private bath with both a garden tub and a 4' shower
- 3 bedrooms, 2 baths, 2-car drive under garage
- Basement foundation

Cottage-Style Adds Charm

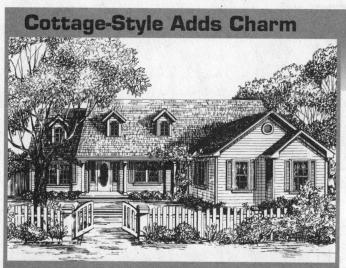

Plan #710-043D-0008

1,496 total square feet of living area

Price Code A

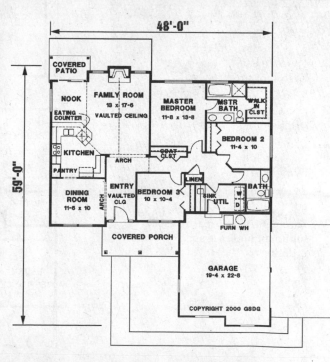

Special features

- Large utility room with sink and extra counterspace
- Covered patio off breakfast nook extends dining to the outdoors
- Eating counter in kitchen overlooks vaulted family room
- 3 bedrooms, 2 baths, 2-car side entry garage
- Crawl space foundation

The Family Handyman

A Great Plan With Cozy Charm — Plan #710-016D-0021

1,892 total square feet of living area

Price Code D

Special features

- Victorian home includes folk charm
- This split bedroom plan places a lovely master bedroom on the opposite end of the other two bedrooms for privacy
- Central living and dining areas combine creating a great place for entertaining
- Bonus room on the second floor has an additional 285 square feet of living area
- 3 bedrooms, 2 1/2 baths, 2-car side entry garage
- Basement, crawl space or slab foundation, please specify when ordering

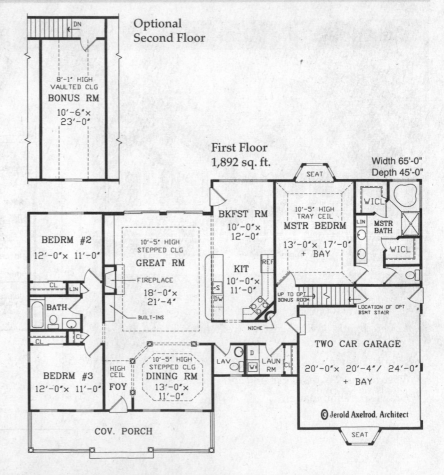

Optional Second Floor

8'-1" HIGH VAULTED CLG
BONUS RM
10'-6" x 23'-0"

First Floor
1,892 sq. ft.

Width 65'-0"
Depth 45'-0"

SEAT

BEDRM #2
12'-0" x 11'-0"

10'-5" HIGH STEPPED CLG
GREAT RM
FIREPLACE
18'-0" x 21'-4"
BUILT-INS

BKFST RM
10'-0" x 12'-0"

10'-5" HIGH TRAY CEIL
MSTR BEDRM
13'-0" x 17'-0" + BAY

WICL
LIN
MSTR BATH
WICL

KIT
10'-0" x 11'-0"
REF

CL LIN
BATH

UP TO OPT BONUS ROOM

LOCATION OF OPT BSMT STAIR

NICHE

BEDRM #3
12'-0" x 11'-0"

HIGH CEIL
FOY

10'-5" HIGH STEPPED CLG
DINING RM
13'-0" x 11'-0"

LAV
D
W
LAUN RM

TWO CAR GARAGE
20'-0" x 20'-4" / 24'-0" + BAY

© Jerold Axelrod, Architect

COV. PORCH

SEAT

Convenient Pool Bath

Plan #710-047D-0046

2,597 total square feet of living area

Price Code D

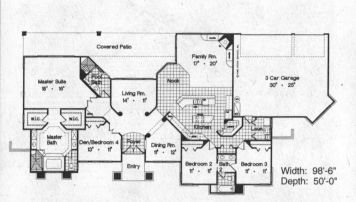

Width: 98'-6"
Depth: 50'-0"

Special features

- Angled design creates unlimited views and spaces that appear larger
- Den/bedroom #4 makes a perfect home office or guest suite
- Island kitchen with view to nook and family room includes a walk-in pantry
- Pool bath is shared by outdoor and indoor areas
- 4 bedrooms, 3 baths, 3-car rear entry garage
- Slab foundation

Great Recreation Room

Plan #710-068D-0016

2,750 total square feet of living area

Price Code E

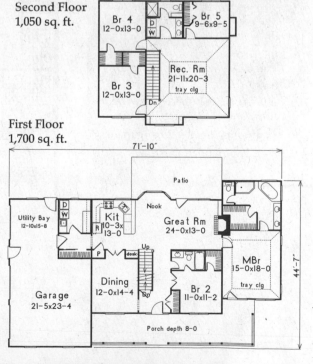

Second Floor
1,050 sq. ft.

First Floor
1,700 sq. ft.

Special features

- Oversized rooms throughout
- 9' ceilings on first floor
- Unique utility bay workshop off garage
- Spacious master bedroom with luxurious bath
- Optional sixth bedroom plan also included
- 5 bedrooms, 3 1/2 baths, 2-car side entry garage
- Basement foundation, drawings also include crawl space and slab foundations

TO ORDER BLUEPRINTS USE THE FORM ON PAGE 15 OR CALL TOLL-FREE 1-877-671-6036
View thousands more home plans online at www.familyhandyman.com/homeplans

131

TERRIFIC RANCH

Plan #710-051D-0027

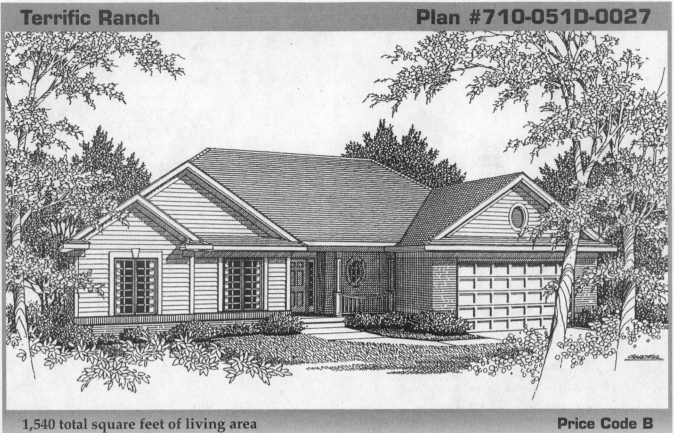

1,540 total square feet of living area

Price Code B

Special features

- Spacious master bedroom has a large walk-in closet and sweeping windows overlooking yard
- First floor laundry conveniently located between the garage and kitchen
- Living room features a cathedral ceiling and corner fireplace
- 3 bedrooms, 2 baths, 2-car garage
- Basement foundation

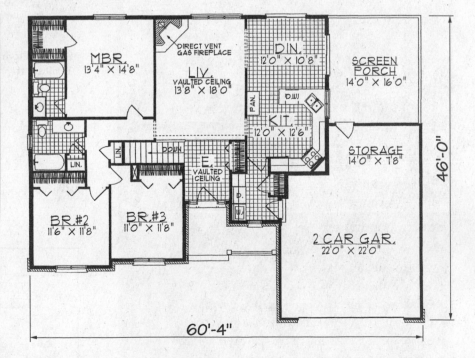

Cozy Home For Family Living

Plan #710-025D-0006

1,612 total square feet of living area

Price Code B

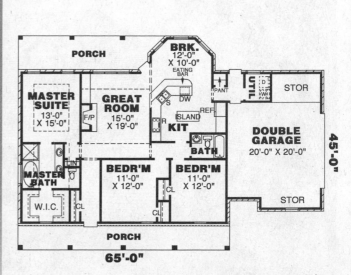

Special features

- Covered porch in rear of home creates an outdoor living area
- Master suite is separated from other bedrooms for privacy
- Eating bar in kitchen extends into breakfast area for additional seating
- 3 bedrooms, 2 baths, 2-car side entry garage
- Slab foundation

Seating At Breakfast Bar

Plan #710-068D-0012

2,544 total square feet of living area

Price Code D

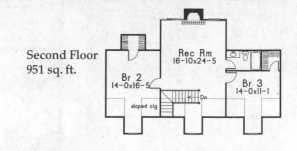

Second Floor
951 sq. ft.

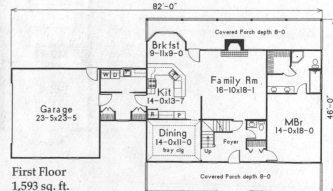

First Floor
1,593 sq. ft.

Special features

- Central family room becomes gathering place
- Second floor recreation room is a great game room for children
- First floor master bedroom is secluded from main living areas
- 3 bedrooms, 2 1/2 baths, 2-car side entry garage
- Basement foundation, drawings also include crawl space and slab foundations

TO ORDER BLUEPRINTS USE THE FORM ON PAGE 15 OR CALL TOLL-FREE 1-877-671-6036
View thousands more home plans online at www.familyhandyman.com/homeplans

133

Grand Entry Foyer   **Plan #710-015D-0044**

2,148 total square feet of living area   **Price Code C**

Special features

- 9' ceilings throughout this home
- 11' ceilings in great room, kitchen, nook and foyer
- Eating bar in kitchen extends the dining space for extra guests or casual seating
- 3 bedrooms, 2 baths, 2-car side entry garage
- Basement foundation

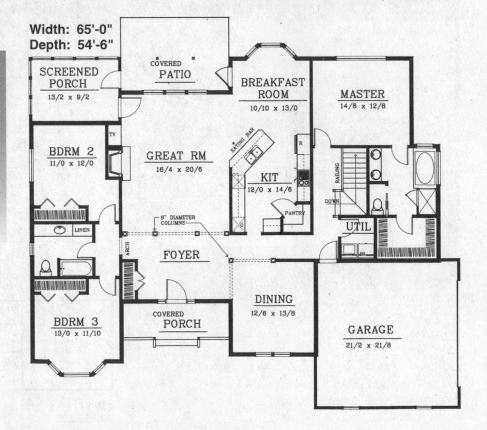

Width: 65'-0"
Depth: 54'-6"

SCREENED PORCH 13/2 x 9/2

COVERED PATIO

BREAKFAST ROOM 10/10 x 13/0

MASTER 14/8 x 12/8

BDRM 2 11/0 x 12/0

GREAT RM 16/4 x 20/6

EATING BAR

KIT 12/0 x 14/6

RAILING

DOWN

UTIL

LINEN

8" DIAMETER COLUMNS

PANTRY

FOYER

ARCH

BDRM 3 13/0 x 11/10

COVERED PORCH

DINING 12/6 x 13/8

GARAGE 21/2 x 21/8

Modern Rustic Design

Plan #710-049D-0007

1,118 total square feet of living area

Price Code AA

Special features

- Convenient kitchen has direct access into garage and looks out onto front covered porch
- The covered patio is enjoyed by both the living room and master suite
- Octagon-shaped dining room adds interest to the front exterior while the interior is sunny and bright
- 2 bedrooms, 2 baths, 2-car garage
- Slab foundation

Gabled And Arched Brick Entry

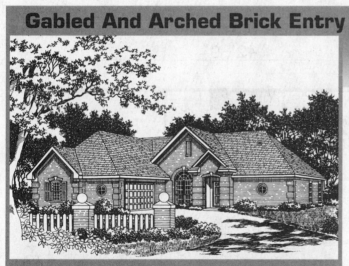

Plan #710-018D-0008

2,109 total square feet of living area

Price Code C

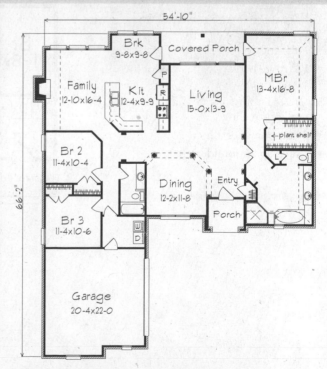

Special features

- 12' ceilings in living and dining rooms
- Nearby kitchen is an integral part of the breakfast room
- Secluded and generous-sized master bedroom includes a plant shelf, walk-in closet and private bath
- Stately columns and circle-top window frame dining room
- 3 bedrooms, 2 baths, 2-car side entry garage
- Slab foundation, drawings also include crawl space foundation

Rustic Plan With Modern Features   Plan #710-058D-0029

1,000 total square feet of living area   **Price Code AA**

Special features

- Large mud room with separate covered porch entrance
- Full-length covered front porch
- Bedrooms on opposite sides of the home for privacy
- Vaulted ceiling creates an open and spacious feeling
- 2 bedrooms, 1 bath
- Crawl space foundation

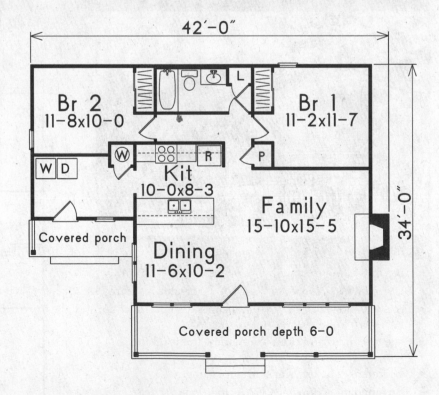

Br 2
11-8x10-0

Br 1
11-2x11-7

W D

W   R

P

Kit
10-0x8-3

Family
15-10x15-5

Covered porch

Dining
11-6x10-2

Covered porch depth 6-0

42'-0"

34'-0"

Oversized Front Porch

Plan #710-038D-0048

1,146 total square feet of living area

Price Code AA

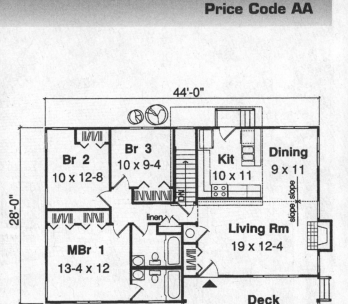

Special features

- Master bedroom has private bath
- Well-organized kitchen is loaded with cabinetry
- A sloped ceiling in the living and dining rooms creates a comfortable atmosphere
- 3 bedrooms, 2 baths
- Basement, slab or crawl space foundation, please specify when ordering

Appealing Facade

Plan #710-034D-0010

2,178 total square feet of living area

Price Code C

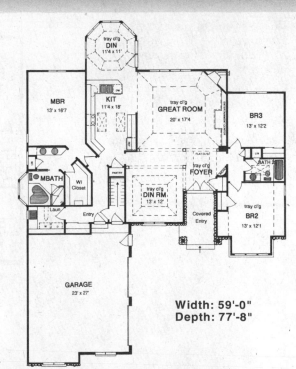

Special features

- Large foyer leads to a sunny great room with corner fireplace and expansive entertainment center
- Kitchen and dining area are efficiently designed
- Master bedroom has private bath with step-up tub and a bay window
- 3 bedrooms, 2 baths, 2-car side entry garage
- Basement foundation

TO ORDER BLUEPRINTS USE THE FORM ON PAGE 15 OR CALL TOLL-FREE 1-877-671-6036
View thousands more home plans online at www.familyhandyman.com/homeplans

137

Handyman THE Family

Comfortable Ranch   Plan #710-051D-0040

1,495 total square feet of living area   **Price Code A**

Special features

- Dining room has vaulted ceiling creating a large formal gathering area with access to a screened porch
- Cathedral ceiling in great room adds spaciousness
- Nice-sized entry with coat closet
- 3 bedrooms, 2 baths, 2-car garage
- Basement foundation

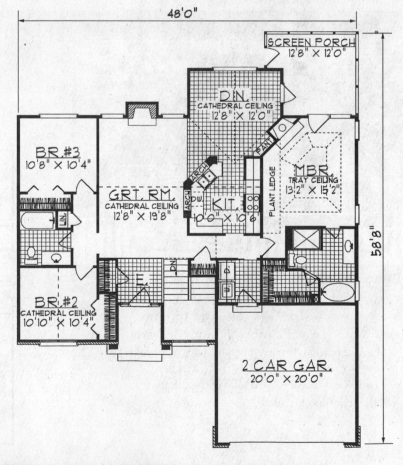

Formal Facade

Plan #710-019D-0010

1,890 total square feet of living area

Price Code C

WIDTH 65-10

DEPTH 53-5

MASTER BATH

PORCH

BRKFST RM 10-8 X 11-8 10 FT CLG

UTIL 8-0 x 5-8

STORAGE

STORAGE

MASTER BEDRM 14-4 X 15-6 10 FT CLG

FP

LIVING ROOM 17-4 X 15-8 10 FT CLG

KITCHEN 10-8 X 13-6 10 FT CLG

GARAGE

COPYRIGHT LARRY E. BELK

BATH 2

LIN

PAN

FOYER 10 FT CLG

DINING ROOM 11-0 X 13-0, 10 FT COFFERED CLG

BEDROOM 2 12-6 X 11-6

BEDROOM 3 12-0 X 13-4 10 FT CLG

PORCH

Special features

- 10' ceilings give this home a spacious feel
- Efficient kitchen has breakfast bar which overlooks living room
- Master bedroom has a private bath with walk-in closet
- 3 bedrooms, 2 baths, 2-car side entry garage
- Crawl space or slab foundation, please specify when ordering

Country-Style With Large Rooms

Plan #710-001D-0045

1,197 total square feet of living area

Price Code AA

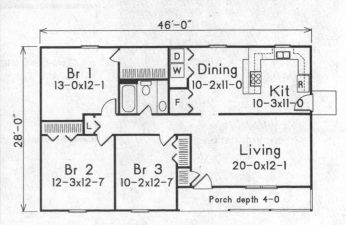

46'-0"

28'-0"

Br 1 13-0x12-1

D
W
F

Dining 10-2x11-0

Kit 10-3x11-0

R

L

Br 2 12-3x12-7

Br 3 10-2x12-7

Living 20-0x12-1

Porch depth 4-0

Special features

- U-shaped kitchen includes ample workspace, breakfast bar, laundry area and direct access to the outdoors
- Large living room with convenient coat closet
- Bedroom #1 features large walk-in closet
- 3 bedrooms, 1 bath
- Crawl space foundation, drawings also include basement and slab foundations

Spacious Feel To This Home — Plan #710-065D-0028

1,611 total square feet of living area — Price Code B

Special features

- Sliding doors lead to a delightful screened porch creating a wonderful summer retreat
- Master bedroom has a lavishly appointed dressing room and large walk-in closet
- The kitchen offers an abundance of cabinets and counterspace with convenient access to the laundry room and garage
- 3 bedrooms, 2 baths, 2-car side entry garage
- Basement foundation

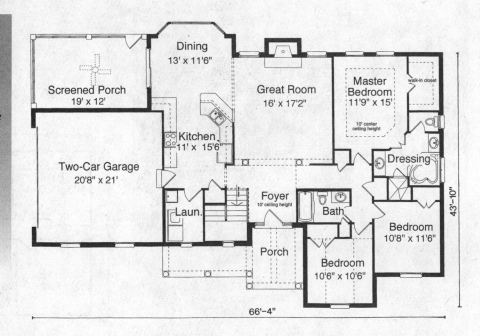

Expansive Counterspace

Plan #710-020D-0009

2,123 total square feet of living area

Price Code E

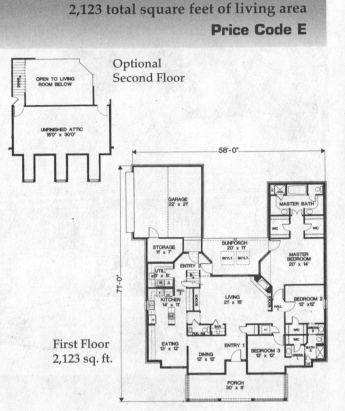

Optional
Second Floor

OPEN TO LIVING ROOM BELOW

UNFINISHED ATTIC
15'0" x 30'0"

58'-0"

71'-0"

GARAGE
22' x 2T

STORAGE
11' x 7'

SUNPORCH
20' x 11'
SKYLT. SKYLT.

MASTER BATH

WIC WIC

UTIL.
8' x 8'

ENTRY 2

MASTER BEDROOM
20' x 14'

KITCHEN
14' x 11'

HALL

LIVING
21' x 15'

HALL

BEDROOM 2
12' x 12'

WIC

EATING
13' x 12'

DINING
12' x 12'

ENTRY 1

BEDROOM 3
12' x 12'

WIC
BATH 3

PORCH
30' x 8'

First Floor
2,123 sq. ft.

Special features

- Energy efficient home with 2" x 6" exterior walls
- Living room has wood burning fireplace, built-in bookshelves and a wet bar
- Skylights make the sunporch bright and comfortable
- Unfinished attic has an additional 450 square feet of living area
- 3 bedrooms, 2 1/2 baths, 2-car side entry garage
- Crawl space, slab or basement foundation, please specify when ordering

Layout Creates Open Living Area

Plan #710-001D-0067

1,285 total square feet of living area

Price Code B

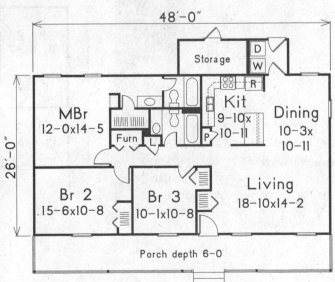

48'-0"

26'-0"

Storage

D
W

MBr
12'-0x14'-5

Furn
L

Kit
9-10x
10-11

Dining
10-3x
10-11

P

R

Br 2
.15-6x10-8

Br 3
10-1x10-8

Living
18-10x14-2

Porch depth 6-0

Special features

- Accommodating home with ranch-style porch
- Large storage area on back of home
- Master bedroom includes dressing area, private bath and built-in bookcase
- Kitchen features pantry, breakfast bar and complete view to dining room
- 3 bedrooms, 2 baths
- Crawl space foundation, drawings also include basement and slab foundations

TO ORDER BLUEPRINTS USE THE FORM ON PAGE 15 OR CALL TOLL-FREE 1-877-671-6036
View thousands more home plans online at www.familyhandyman.com/homeplans

141

Classic Ranch Has Grand Appeal   Plan #710-005D-0001

1,400 total square feet of living area   **Price Code B**

Special features

- Master bedroom is secluded for privacy
- Large utility room has additional cabinet space
- Covered porch provides an outdoor seating area
- Roof dormers add great curb appeal
- Living room and master bedroom feature vaulted ceilings
- Oversized two-car garage has storage space
- 3 bedrooms, 2 baths, 2-car garage
- Basement foundation, drawings also include crawl space foundation

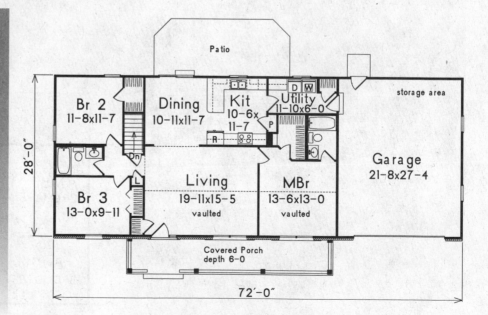

Patio

Br 2
11-8x11-7

Dining
10-11x11-7

Kit
10-6x
11-7

Utility
11-10x6-0

storage area

28'-0"

Br 3
13-0x9-11

Living
19-11x15-5
vaulted

MBr
13-6x13-0
vaulted

Garage
21-8x27-4

Covered Porch
depth 6-0

72'-0"

Private Bedrooms

Plan #710-068D-0010

1,849 total square feet of living area

Price Code C

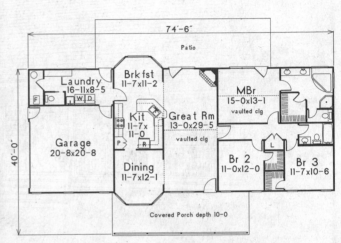

Special features

- Enormous laundry/mud room has many extras
- Lavish master bath has corner jacuzzi tub, double sinks, separate shower and walk-in closet
- Secondary bedrooms include walk-in closets
- Kitchen has wrap-around eating counter and is positioned between dining area and breakfast room for convenience
- 3 bedrooms, 2 1/2 baths, 2-car side entry garage
- Slab foundation, drawings also include crawl space foundation

Luxurious Master Bath

Plan #710-034D-0002

1,456 total square feet of living area

Price Code A

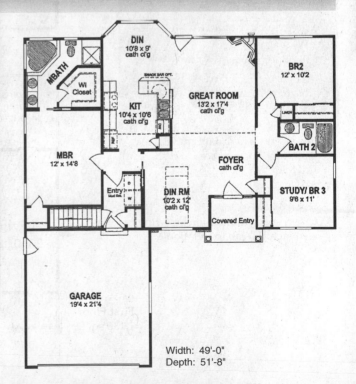

Special features

- Open floor plan adds spaciousness to this design
- Bayed dining area creates a cheerful setting
- Corner fireplace in great room is a terrific focal point
- 3 bedrooms, 2 baths, 2-car garage
- Basement foundation

TO ORDER BLUEPRINTS USE THE FORM ON PAGE 15 OR CALL TOLL-FREE 1-877-671-6036
View thousands more home plans online at www.familyhandyman.com/homeplans

143

Inviting Screened-In Rear Porch   Plan #710-021D-0016

1,600 total square feet of living area

Price Code B

Special features

- Energy efficient home with 2" x 6" exterior walls
- First floor master bedroom is accessible from two points of entry
- Master bath dressing area includes separate vanities and a mirrored make-up counter
- Second floor bedrooms have generous storage space and share a full bath
- 3 bedrooms, 2 baths, 2-car side entry garage
- Crawl space foundation, drawings also include slab foundation

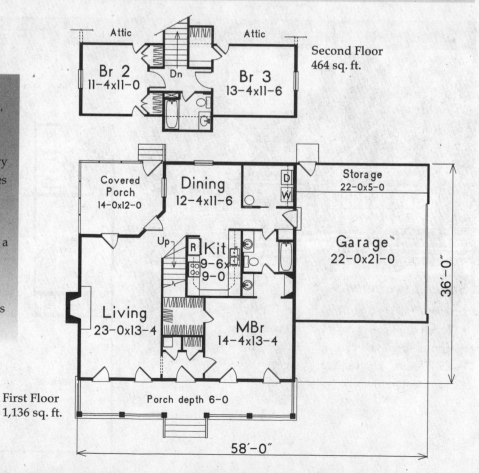

Attic

Br 2
11-4x11-0

Dn

Attic

Br 3
13-4x11-6

Second Floor
464 sq. ft.

Covered Porch
14-0x12-0

Dining
12-4x11-6

Storage
22-0x5-0

Up

Kit
9-6x 9-0

Garage
22-0x21-0

Living
23-0x13-4

MBr
14-4x13-4

36'-0"

First Floor
1,136 sq. ft.

Porch depth 6-0

58'-0"

Lovely, Spacious Floor Plan

Plan #710-058D-0016

1,558 total square feet of living area

Price Code B

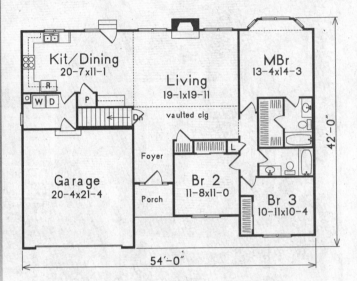

Special features

- Spacious utility room located conveniently between garage and kitchen/dining area
- Bedrooms separated off main living area by hallway
- Enormous living area with fireplace and vaulted ceiling opens to kitchen and dining area
- Master bedroom is enhanced with large bay window, walk-in closet and private bath
- 3 bedrooms, 2 baths, 2-car garage
- Basement foundation

Private Master Bedroom

Plan #710-034D-0020

2,018 total square feet of living area

Price Code C

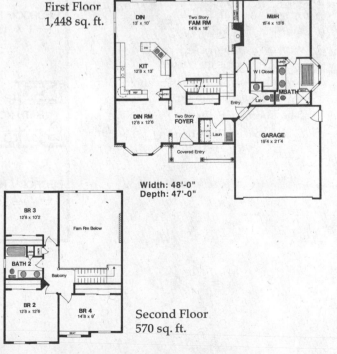

First Floor
1,448 sq. ft.

Width: 48'-0"
Depth: 47'-0"

Second Floor
570 sq. ft.

Special features

- Family room is situated near dining area and kitchen creating a convenient layout
- First floor master bedroom features private bath with step-up tub and bay window
- Laundry area located on the first floor
- 4 bedrooms, 2 1/2 baths, 2-car garage
- Basement foundation

TO ORDER BLUEPRINTS USE THE FORM ON PAGE 15 OR CALL TOLL-FREE 1-877-671-6036
View thousands more home plans online at www.familyhandyman.com/homeplans

145

Perfect Home For Family Living   Plan #710-028D-0006

1,700 total square feet of living area

Price Code B

Special features

- Oversized laundry room has large pantry and storage area as well as access to the outdoors
- Master bedroom is separated from other bedrooms for privacy
- Raised snack bar in kitchen allows extra seating for dining
- 3 bedrooms, 2 baths
- Crawl space foundation

50—0 WIDE X 42—0 DEEP
(INCLUDING COVERED PORCH)

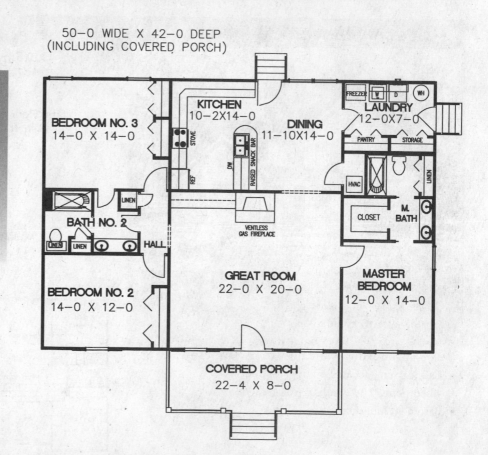

TO ORDER BLUEPRINTS USE THE FORM ON PAGE 15 OR CALL TOLL-FREE 1-877-671-6036
View thousands more home plans online at www.familyhandyman.com/homeplans

Large Porch Is Welcoming

Special features

- U-shaped kitchen opens into living area by a 42" high counter
- Oversized bay window and French door accent dining room
- Gathering space is created by the large living room
- Convenient utility room and linen closet
- 1 bedroom, 1 bath
- Slab foundation

Plan #710-037D-0017

829 total square feet of living area

Price Code AAA

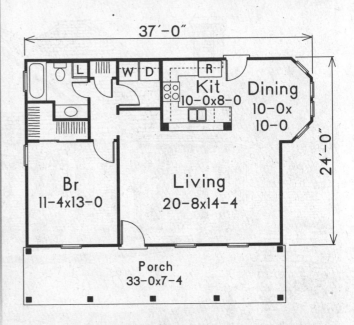

Bright And Beautiful

Special features

- Open and airy with two-story foyer and family room
- Den is secluded from the rest of the home
- Second floor bedrooms have walk-in closets and share a bath
- Optional bonus room has an additional 276 square feet of living area
- 4 bedrooms, 3 baths, 2-car garage
- Walk-out basement, slab or crawl space foundation, please specify when ordering

Plan #710-035D-0029

2,349 total square feet of living area

Price Code D

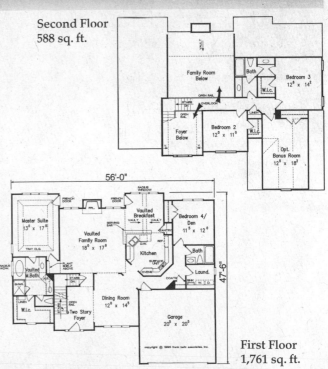

TO ORDER BLUEPRINTS USE THE FORM ON PAGE 15 OR CALL TOLL-FREE 1-877-671-6036
View thousands more home plans online at www.familyhandyman.com/homeplans

147

Great Home For A Narrow Lot — Plan #710-036D-0056

1,604 total square feet of living area

Price Code B

Special features

- Ideal design for a narrow lot
- Living and dining areas combine for a spacious feel
- Secluded study has double-doors for privacy
- Master bedroom has a spacious private bath
- 3 bedrooms, 2 baths, 2-car garage
- Slab foundation

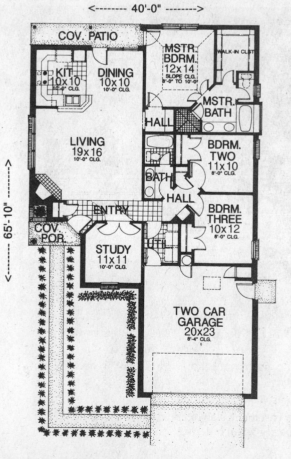

Ranch With A Tudor Influence

Plan #710-069D-0019

2,162 total square feet of living area

Price Code C

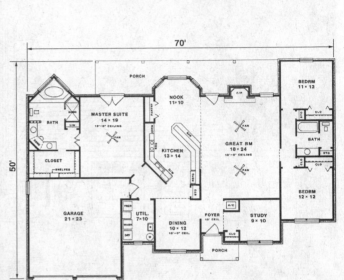

Special features

- 10' ceilings in great room, dining room, master suite and foyer
- Enormous great room overlooks kitchen with oversized snack bar
- Luxurious master bath boasts a triangular whirlpool tub drenched in light from large windows
- 3 bedrooms, 2 baths, 2-car garage
- Crawl space or slab foundation, please specify when ordering

Peaceful Shaded Front Porch

Plan #710-001D-0072

1,288 total square feet of living area

Price Code A

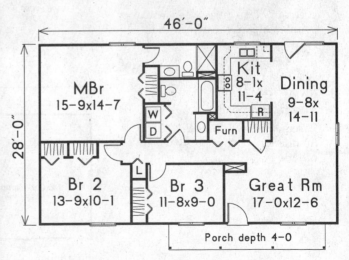

Special features

- Kitchen, dining area and great room join to create an open living space
- Master bedroom includes private bath
- Secondary bedrooms include ample closet space
- Hall bath features convenient laundry closet
- Dining room accesses the outdoors
- 3 bedrooms, 2 baths
- Crawl space foundation, drawings also include basement and slab foundations

Screened Area Perfect For Relaxing   Plan #710-038D-0037

1,434 total square feet of living area

Price Code A

Special features

- Private second floor master bedroom features a private bath and a roomy walk-in closet
- A country kitchen with peninsula counter adjoins the living room creating the feeling of a larger living area
- The living room has a warm fireplace and a tall ceiling
- 3 bedrooms, 2 baths, 2-car garage
- Basement, crawl space or slab foundation, please specify when ordering

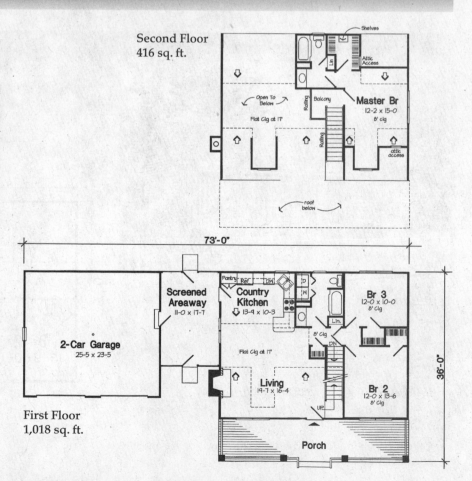

Second Floor
416 sq. ft.

First Floor
1,018 sq. ft.

TO ORDER BLUEPRINTS USE THE FORM ON PAGE 15 OR CALL TOLL-FREE 1-877-671-6036
View thousands more home plans online at www.familyhandyman.com/homeplans

Stonework Entry Adds Character

Plan #710-010D-0005

1,358 total square feet of living area

Price Code A

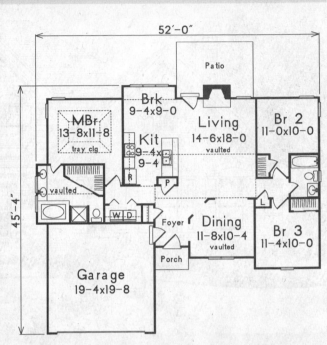

Special features

- Vaulted master bath has walk-in closet, double-bowl vanity, large tub, shower and toilet area
- Galley kitchen opens to both the living room and the breakfast area
- Vaulted ceiling joins dining and living rooms
- Breakfast room with full wall of windows
- 3 bedrooms, 2 baths, 2-car garage
- Slab foundation

Grand Covered Entry

Plan #710-025D-0051

3,369 total square feet of living area

Price Code F

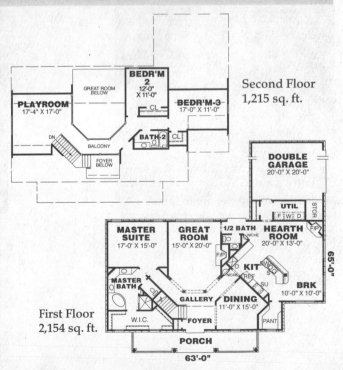

Special features

- Large playroom overlooks to great room below and makes a great casual family area
- Extra storage is located in garage
- Well-planned hearth room and kitchen are open and airy
- Foyer flows into unique diagonal gallery area creating a dramatic entrance into the great room
- 3 bedrooms, 2 1/2 baths, 2-car side entry garage
- Walk-out basement foundation

TO ORDER BLUEPRINTS USE THE FORM ON PAGE 15 OR CALL TOLL-FREE 1-877-871-6036
View thousands more home plans online at www.familyhandyman.com/homeplans

151

Outstanding For Entertaining

Plan #710-007D-0001

2,597 total square feet of living area

Price Code E

Special features

- Large U-shaped kitchen features island cooktop and breakfast bar
- Entry and great room enhanced by sweeping balcony
- Bedrooms #2 and #3 share a bath, while the fourth bedroom has a private bath
- Vaulted great room with transomed arch windows
- 4 bedrooms, 3 1/2 baths, 2-car side entry garage
- Walk-out basement foundation, drawings also include crawl space and slab foundations

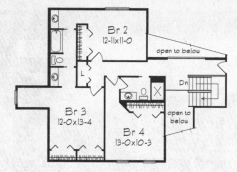

Second Floor
855 sq. ft.

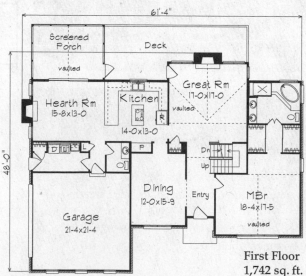

First Floor
1,742 sq. ft.

All The Amenities

Plan #710-026D-0137

1,758 total square feet of living area

Price Code B

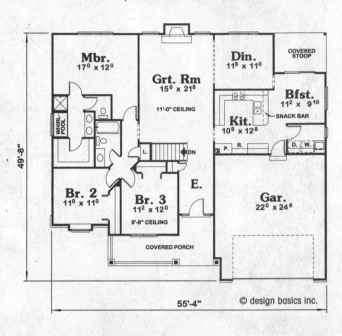

Special features

- Secluded covered porch off breakfast area is a charming touch
- Great room and dining area combine for terrific entertaining possibilities
- Master bedroom with all the amenities
- Spacious foyer area opens into large great room with 11' ceiling
- 3 bedrooms, 2 baths, 2-car garage
- Basement foundation

Covered Porch Surrounds Home

Plan #710-068D-0006

1,399 total square feet of living area

Price Code A

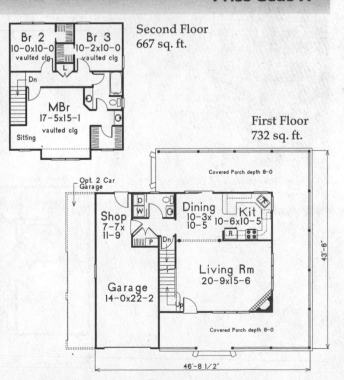

Special features

- Living room overlooks dining area through arched columns
- Laundry room contains handy half bath
- Spacious master bedroom includes sitting area, walk-in closet and plenty of sunlight
- 3 bedrooms, 1 1/2 baths, 1-car garage
- Basement foundation, drawings also include crawl space and slab foundations

TO ORDER BLUEPRINTS USE THE FORM ON PAGE 15 OR CALL TOLL-FREE 1-877-671-6036
View thousands more home plans online at www.familyhandyman.com/homeplans

153

Dining Room Has Butler's Pantry   Plan #710-043D-0011

2,422 total square feet of living area

Price Code D

Special features

- Covered porches invite guests into home
- Convenient and private first floor master suite
- Family room has vaulted ceiling
- 10' ceiling in dining room has a formal feel
- Kitchen has walk-in pantry and eating bar
- 3 bedrooms, 2 1/2 baths, 3-car side entry garage
- Crawl space foundation

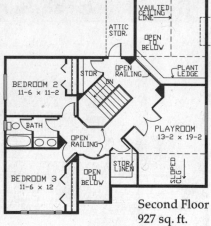

Second Floor
927 sq. ft.

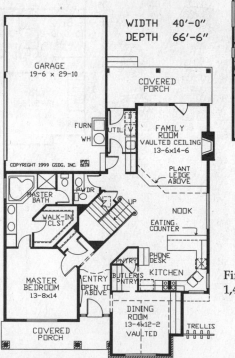

WIDTH 40'-0"
DEPTH 66'-6"

First Floor
1,495 sq. ft.

TO ORDER BLUEPRINTS USE THE FORM ON PAGE 15 OR CALL TOLL-FREE 1-877-671-6036
View thousands more home plans online at www.familyhandyman.com/homeplans

Elaborate Dining Room

Plan #710-035D-0028

1,779 total square feet of living area

Price Code B

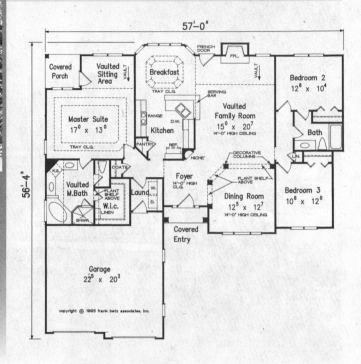

Special features

- Well-designed floor plan has vaulted family room with fireplace and access to the outdoors
- Decorative columns separate dining area from foyer
- A vaulted ceiling adds spaciousness in master bath with walk-in closet
- 3 bedrooms, 2 baths, 2-car garage
- Walk-out basement, slab or crawl space foundation, please specify when ordering

Warm And Inviting

Plan #710-019D-0011

1,955 total square feet of living area

Price Code C

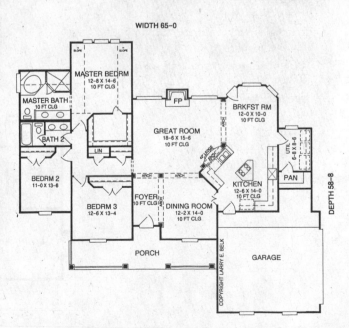

Special features

- Porch adds outdoor area to this design
- Dining and great rooms visible from foyer through a series of elegant archways
- Kitchen overlooks great room and breakfast room
- 3 bedrooms, 2 baths, 2-car side entry garage
- Crawl space or slab foundation, please specify when ordering

Ideal For Entertaining

Plan #710-052D-0048

1,870 total square feet of living area

Price Code C

Special features

- Kitchen is open to the living and dining areas
- Breakfast area has cathedral ceiling creating a sunroom effect
- Master bedroom is spacious with all the amenities
- Second floor bedrooms share hall bath
- 3 bedrooms, 2 1/2 baths, 2-car drive under garage
- Basement foundation

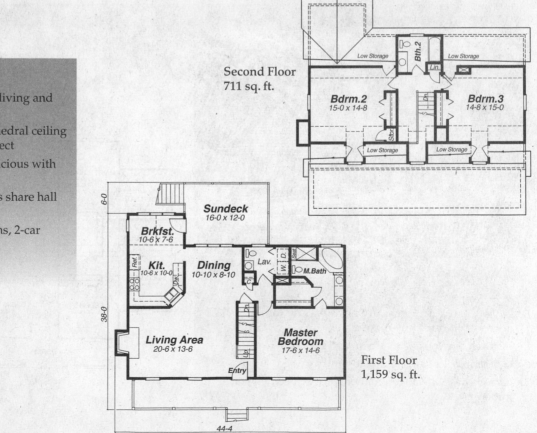

Second Floor
711 sq. ft.

Low Storage   Bth.2   Low Storage

Lin.

Bdrm.2
15-0 x 14-8

Bdrm.3
14-8 x 15-0

Stor.

Low Storage   Low Storage

First Floor
1,159 sq. ft.

Sundeck
16-0 x 12-0

Brkfst.
10-6 x 7-6

Kit.
10-6 x 10-0

Dining
10-10 x 8-10

Lav.

W. D.

M.Bath

Living Area
20-6 x 13-6

Master
Bedroom
17-6 x 14-6

Entry

6-0

38-0

44-4

Carport With Storage

Special features

- Country charm with covered front porch
- Dining area looks into family room with fireplace
- Master suite has walk-in closet and private bath
- 3 bedrooms, 2 baths, 2-car attached carport
- Slab or crawl space foundation, please specify when ordering

Plan #710-039D-0002

1,333 total square feet of living area

Price Code A

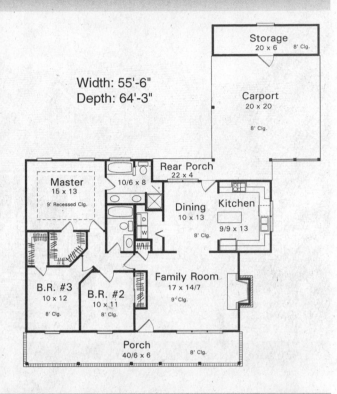

Width: 55'-6"
Depth: 64'-3"

Attractive Styling

Special features

- Dining area has 10' high sloped ceiling
- Kitchen opens to large living room with fireplace and has access to a covered porch
- Master suite features private bath, double walk-in closets and whirlpool tub
- 3 bedrooms, 2 baths, 2-car garage
- Slab or crawl space foundation, please specify when ordering

Plan #710-030D-0004

1,791 total square feet of living area

Price Code B

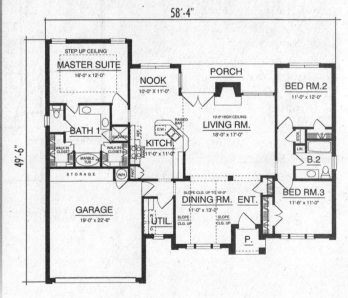

TO ORDER BLUEPRINTS USE THE FORM ON PAGE 15 OR CALL TOLL-FREE 1-877-671-6036
View thousands more home plans online at www.familyhandyman.com/homeplans

157

1,926 total square feet of living area

Price Code C

Special features

- Large covered rear porch is spacious enough for entertaining
- L-shaped kitchen is compact yet efficient and includes a snack bar for extra dining space
- Oversized utility room has counterspace, extra shelves and space for a second refrigerator
- Secluded master suite has a private bath and a large walk-in closet
- 3 bedrooms, 2 baths, 2-car side entry garage
- Slab or crawl space foundation, please specify when ordering

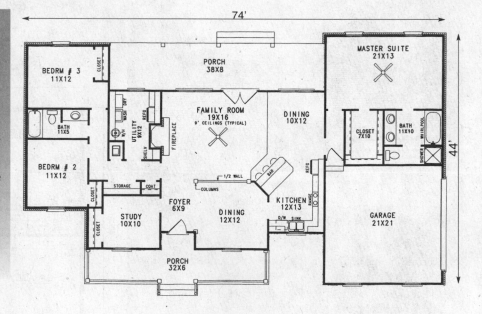

Gabled, Covered Front Porch

Plan #710-001D-0036
1,320 total square feet of living area

Price Code A

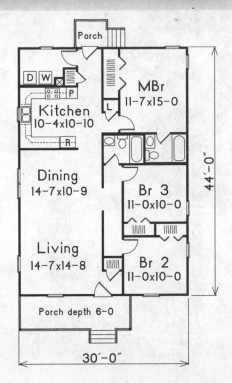

Special features

- Functional U-shaped kitchen features pantry
- Large living and dining areas join to create an open atmosphere
- Secluded master bedroom includes private full bath
- Covered front porch opens into large living area with convenient coat closet
- Utility/laundry room located near the kitchen
- 3 bedrooms, 2 baths
- Crawl space foundation

Raised Plantation Styling

Plan #710-060D-0028
2,287 total square feet of living area

Price Code D

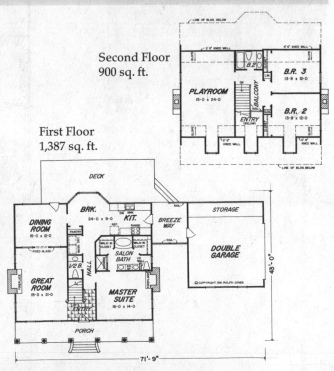

Second Floor
900 sq. ft.

First Floor
1,387 sq. ft.

Special features

- Two-story foyer has balcony
- Great room includes a fireplace and decorative fixed glass between dining room
- Large kitchen and breakfast room with great view to rear
- Second floor has two bedrooms, balcony and large playroom
- 3 bedrooms, 2 1/2 baths, 2-car side entry garage
- Slab or crawl space foundation, please specify when ordering

TO ORDER BLUEPRINTS USE THE FORM ON PAGE 15 OR CALL TOLL-FREE 1-877-671-6036
View thousands more home plans online at www.familyhandyman.com/homeplans

159

Fountain Graces Entry

Plan #710-048D-0004

2,397 total square feet of living area

Price Code E

Special features

- Covered entrance with fountain leads to double-door entry and foyer
- Kitchen features two pantries and opens into breakfast and family rooms
- Master bath features huge walk-in closet, electric clothes carousel, double-bowl vanity and corner tub
- 3 bedrooms, 2 1/2 baths, 2-car garage
- Slab foundation

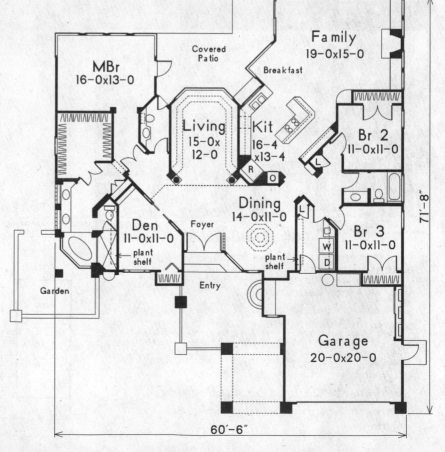

TO ORDER BLUEPRINTS USE THE FORM ON PAGE 15 OR CALL TOLL-FREE 1-877-671-6036
View thousands more home plans online at www.familyhandyman.com/homeplans

THE FAMILY Handyman

Secluded Living Room

Plan #710-035D-0021

1,978 total square feet of living area

Price Code C

Special features

- Elegant arched openings throughout interior
- Vaulted living room off foyer
- Master suite with cheerful sitting room and a private bath
- 3 bedrooms, 2 1/2 baths, 2-car garage
- Walk-out basement, slab or crawl space foundation, please specify when ordering

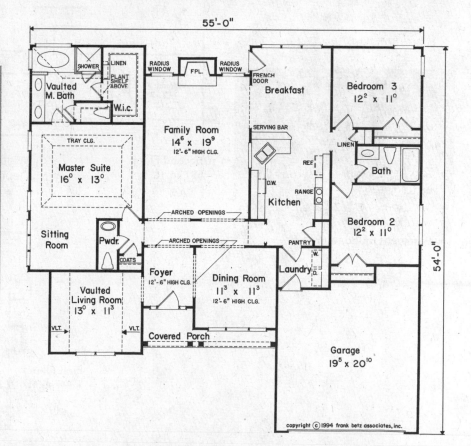

TO ORDER BLUEPRINTS USE THE FORM ON PAGE 15 OR CALL TOLL-FREE 1-877-671-6036
View thousands more home plans online at www.familyhandyman.com/homeplans

161

The Family Handyman

COVERED FRONT PORCH

Plan #710-039D-0017

1,966 total square feet of living area

Price Code C

Special features

- Private dining room remains focal point when entering the home
- Kitchen and breakfast room join to create a functional area
- Lots of closet space in second floor bedrooms
- 3 bedrooms, 2 1/2 baths, 2-car side entry garage
- Basement foundation

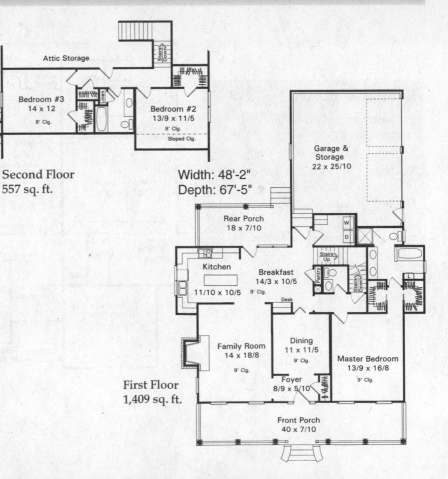

Second Floor
557 sq. ft.

Attic Storage

Bedroom #3
14 x 12
8' Clg.

Bedroom #2
13/9 x 11/5
8' Clg.
Sloped Clg.

Width: 48'-2"
Depth: 67'-5"

Garage & Storage
22 x 25/10

Rear Porch
18 x 7/10

Kitchen
11/10 x 10/5

Breakfast
14/3 x 10/5
9' Clg.

Family Room
14 x 18/8
9' Clg.

Dining
11 x 11/5
9' Clg.

Master Bedroom
13/9 x 16/8
9' Clg.

Foyer
8/9 x 5/10

First Floor
1,409 sq. ft.

Front Porch
40 x 7/10

TO ORDER BLUEPRINTS USE THE FORM ON PAGE 15 OR CALL TOLL-FREE 1-877-671-6036
View thousands more home plans online at www.familyhandyman.com/homeplans

162

The Family Handyman

Open Breakfast/Family Room

Plan #710-02?

2,135 total square feet of living area

Price Code D

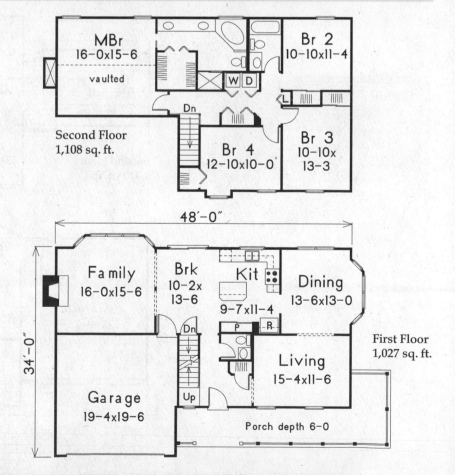

Special features

- Family room features extra space, impressive fireplace and full wall of windows that joins breakfast room creating spacious entertainment area
- Washer and dryer conveniently located on the second floor
- Kitchen features island counter and pantry
- 4 bedrooms, 2 1/2 baths, 2-car garage
- Basement foundation

Second Floor 1,108 sq. ft.

MBr 16-0x15-6 vaulted

Br 2 10-10x11-4

Br 3 10-10x 13-3

Br 4 12-10x10-0

First Floor 1,027 sq. ft.

Family 16-0x15-6

Brk 10-2x 13-6

Kit 9-7x11-4

Dining 13-6x13-0

Living 15-4x11-6

Garage 19-4x19-6

48'-0"

34'-0"

Porch depth 6-0

TO ORDER BLUEPRINTS USE THE FORM ON PAGE 15 OR CALL TOLL-FREE 1-877-671-6036
View thousands more home plans online at www.familyhandyman.com/homeplans

163

Handsome Traditional

Plan #710-053D-0017

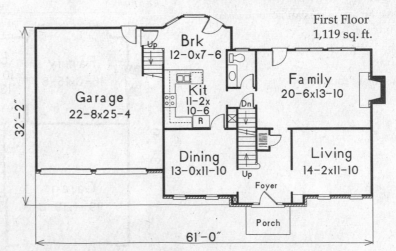

2,529 total square feet of living area

Price Code E

Special features

- Distinguished appearance enhances this home's classic interior arrangement
- Bonus room over the garage, which is included in the square footage, has direct access from the attic and the second floor hall
- Garden tub, walk-in closet and coffered ceiling enhance the master bedroom suite
- 4 bedrooms, 2 1/2 baths, 2-car garage
- Basement foundation

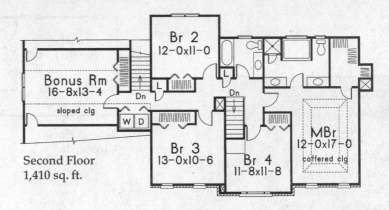

Bonus Rm
16-8x13-4
sloped clg

Br 2
12-0x11-0

Br 3
13-0x10-6

Br 4
11-8x11-8

MBr
12-0x17-0
coffered clg

Second Floor
1,410 sq. ft.

First Floor
1,119 sq. ft.

Garage
22-8x25-4

Brk
12-0x7-6

Kit
11-2x
10-6

Family
20-6x13-10

Dining
13-0x11-10

Living
14-2x11-10

Foyer

Porch

32'-2"

61'-0"

Step Into Elegant Foyer

Plan #710-019D-0021

2,838 total square feet of living area

Price Code E

Special features

- Elegant foyer is enormous and spotlights a grand staircase to the second floor
- Cozy study tucked away for privacy
- Sunny kitchen and breakfast area have cathedral ceilings
- 4 bedrooms, 3 baths, 2-car garage
- Basement, crawl space or slab foundation, please specify when ordering

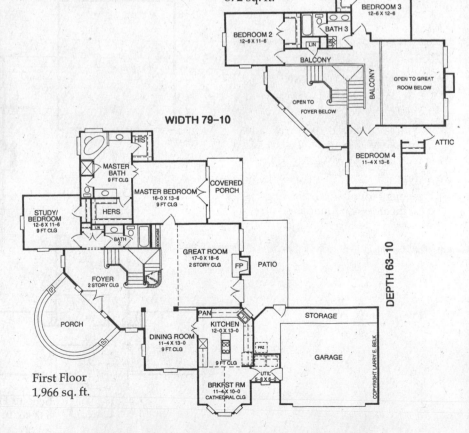

Second Floor 872 sq. ft.

BEDROOM 3 12-6 X 12-6

BEDROOM 2 12-6 X 11-6

BATH 3

LIN

BALCONY

OPEN TO GREAT ROOM BELOW

BALCONY

OPEN TO FOYER BELOW

ATTIC

BEDROOM 4 11-4 X 13-6

WIDTH 79-10

DEPTH 63-10

HIS

MASTER BATH 9 FT CLG

MASTER BEDROOM 16-0 X 13-6 9 FT CLG

COVERED PORCH

STUDY/ BEDROOM 12-6 X 11-6 9 FT CLG

HERS

LIN

BATH 2

BOOKCASE

GREAT ROOM 17-0 X 18-6 2 STORY CLG

FP

PATIO

FOYER 2 STORY CLG

PORCH

PAN

STORAGE

KITCHEN 12-0 X 13-0

FRZ

GARAGE

DINING ROOM 11-4 X 13-0 9 FT CLG

9 FT CLG

UTIL 5-8 X 6-0

COPYRIGHT LARRY E. BELK

First Floor 1,966 sq. ft.

BRKFST RM 11-4 X 10-0 CATHEDRAL CLG

TO ORDER BLUEPRINTS USE THE FORM ON PAGE 15 OR CALL TOLL-FREE 1-877-671-6036
View thousands more home plans online at www.familyhandyman.com/homeplans

165

Breezeway Joins Living Space   Plan #710-040D-0024

1,874 total square feet of living area   **Price Code C**

Special features

- 9' ceilings throughout first floor
- Two-story foyer opens into large family room with fireplace
- First floor master bedroom includes private bath with tub and shower
- 4 bedrooms, 2 1/2 baths, 2-car garage
- Basement foundation, drawings also include slab foundation

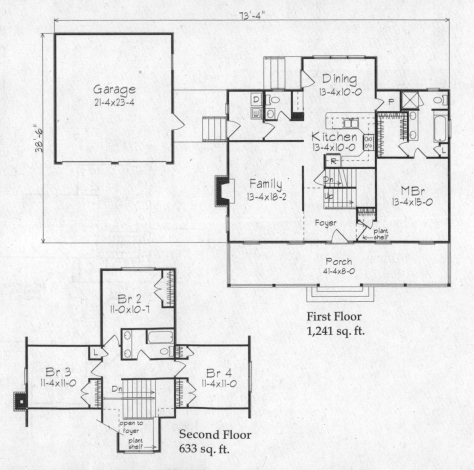

First Floor
1,241 sq. ft.

Second Floor
633 sq. ft.

TO ORDER BLUEPRINTS USE THE FORM ON PAGE 15 OR CALL TOLL-FREE 1-877-671-6036
View thousands more home plans online at www.familyhandyman.com/HOMEPLANS

Elegant Family Room

Plan #710-023D-0010

2,558 total square feet of living area

Price Code D

Special features

- 9' ceilings throughout home
- Angled counter in kitchen serves breakfast and family rooms
- Entry foyer flanked by formal living and dining rooms
- Garage includes storage space
- 4 bedrooms, 3 baths, 2-car side entry garage
- Slab foundation, drawings also include crawl space foundation

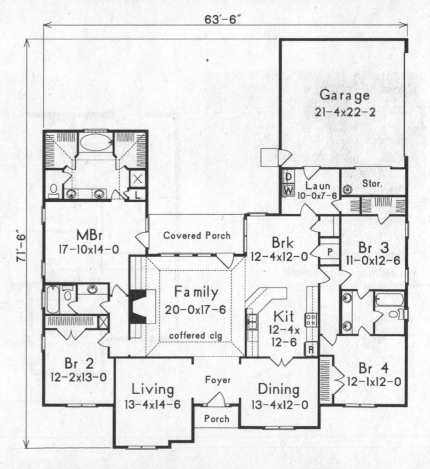

TO ORDER BLUEPRINTS USE THE FORM ON PAGE 15 OR CALL TOLL-FREE 1-877-671-6036
View thousands more home plans online at www.familyhandyman.com/homeplans

167

Spacious Foyer Welcomes Guests   Plan #710-065D-0022

1,593 total square feet of living area   **Price Code B**

Special features

- The rear porch is a pleasant surprise and perfect for enjoying the outdoors
- Great room is filled with extras like a corner fireplace, sloping ceiling and view to the outdoors
- Separating the kitchen from the dining area is a large island with seating
- 3 bedrooms, 2 baths, 2-car garage
- Basement foundation

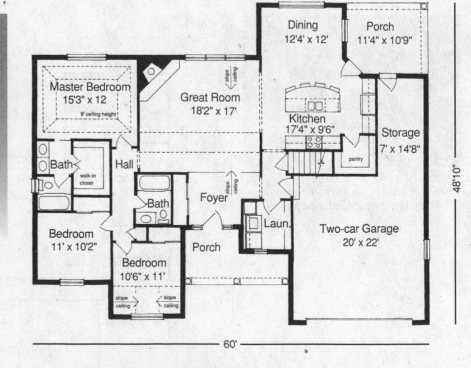

TO ORDER BLUEPRINTS USE THE FORM ON PAGE 15 OR CALL TOLL-FREE 1-877-671-6036
View thousands more home plans online at www.familyhandyman.com/homeplans

Open Living

Plan #710-041D-0001

2,003 total square feet of living area

Price Code D

Special features

- Octagon-shaped dining room with tray ceiling and deck overlook
- L-shaped island kitchen serves living and dining rooms
- Master bedroom boasts luxury bath and walk-in closet
- Living room features columns, elegant fireplace and 10' ceiling
- 3 bedrooms, 2 baths, 2-car garage
- Basement foundation

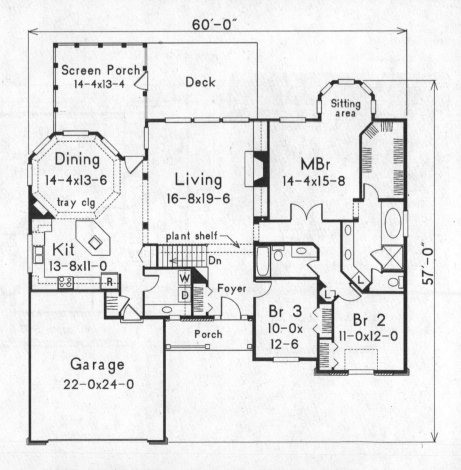

TO ORDER BLUEPRINTS USE THE FORM ON PAGE 15 OR CALL TOLL-FREE 1-877-671-6036
View thousands more home plans online at www.familyhandyman.com/homeplans

169

Ranch Offers Country Elegance

Plan #710-007D-0085

1,787 total square feet of living area

Price Code B

Special features

- Large great room with fireplace and vaulted ceiling features three large skylights and windows galore
- Cooking is sure to be a pleasure in this L-shaped well-appointed kitchen which includes bayed breakfast area with access to rear deck
- Every bedroom offers a spacious walk-in closet with a convenient laundry room just steps away
- 415 square feet of optional living area available on the lower level
- 3 bedrooms, 2 baths, 2-car drive under garage
- Walk-out basement foundation

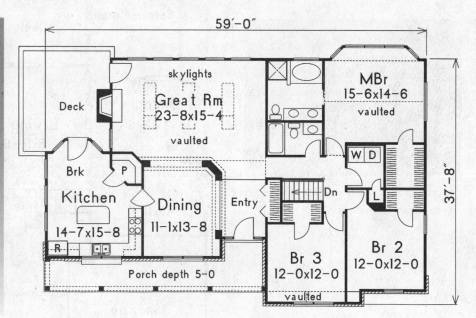

A Ranch With Many Luxuries
Plan #710-035D-0041

2,403 total square feet of living area

Price Code D

Special features

- Cozy family room with high coffered ceiling and a fireplace flanked by bookcases
- Vaulted breakfast room with wall of windows
- Master suite has private bath with double walk-in closets and access to a vaulted living room with wet bar
- 3 bedrooms, 2 1/2 baths, 2-car side entry garage
- Slab, crawl space, or walk-out basement foundation, please specify when ordering

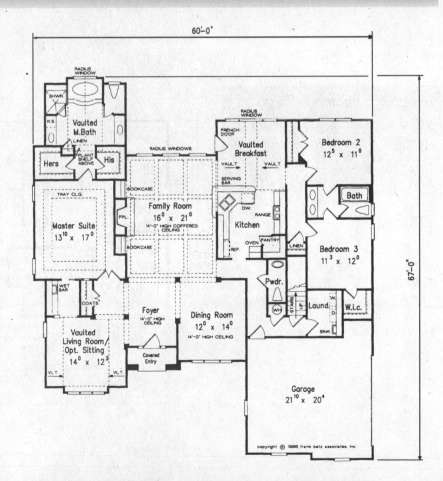

TO ORDER BLUEPRINTS USE THE FORM ON PAGE 15 OR CALL TOLL-FREE 1-877-671-6036
View thousands more home plans online at www.familyhandyman.com/homeplans

171

Central Fireplace In Living Area
Plan #710-001D-0029

1,260 total square feet of living area

Price Code A

Special features

- Spacious kitchen and dining area feature a large pantry, storage area, easy access to garage and laundry room
- Pleasant covered front porch adds a practical touch
- Master bedroom with a private bath adjoins two other bedrooms, all with plenty of closet space
- 3 bedrooms, 2 baths, 2-car garage
- Basement foundation, drawings also include crawl space and slab foundations

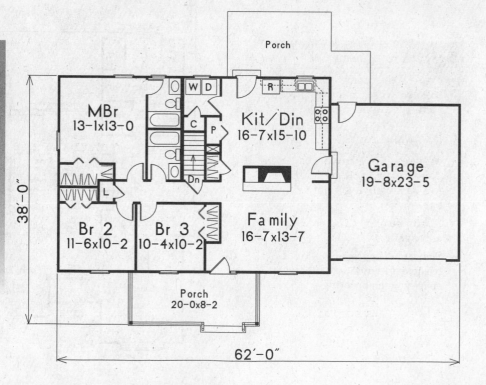

TO ORDER BLUEPRINTS USE THE FORM ON PAGE 15 OR CALL TOLL-FREE 1-877-671-6036
View thousands more home plans online at www.familyhandyman.com/homeplans

The Family Handyman

TERRIFIC CURB APPEAL

Plan #710-013D-0022

1,992 total square feet of living area

Price Code C

Special features

- Interesting angled walls add drama to many of the living areas including family room, master bedroom and breakfast area
- Covered porch includes spa and an outdoor kitchen with sink, refrigerator and cooktop
- Enter majestic master bath to find a dramatic corner oversized tub
- 4 bedrooms, 3 baths, 2-car side entry garage
- Basement, crawl space or slab foundation, please specify when ordering

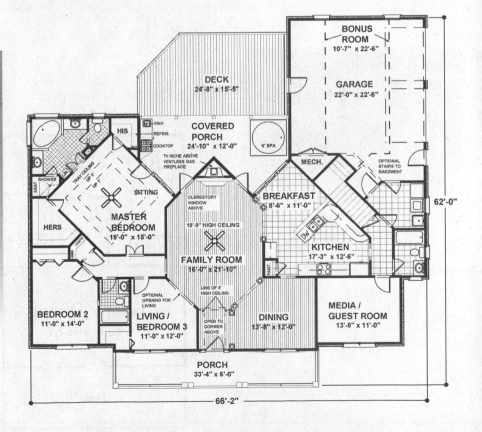

TO ORDER BLUEPRINTS USE THE FORM ON PAGE 15 OR CALL TOLL-FREE 1-877-671-6036
View thousands more home plans online at www.familyhandyman.com/homeplans

173

1,154 total square feet of living area

Price Code AA

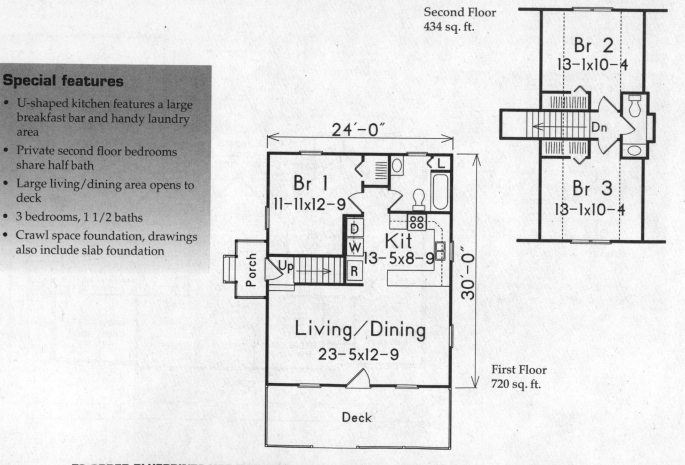

Special features

- U-shaped kitchen features a large breakfast bar and handy laundry area
- Private second floor bedrooms share half bath
- Large living/dining area opens to deck
- 3 bedrooms, 1 1/2 baths
- Crawl space foundation, drawings also include slab foundation

Second Floor
434 sq. ft.

Br 2
13-1x10-4

Dn

Br 3
13-1x10-4

24'-0"

Br 1
11-11x12-9

Kit
13-5x8-9

D
W
R

Up

Porch

30'-0"

Living/Dining
23-5x12-9

First Floor
720 sq. ft.

Deck

174

TO ORDER BLUEPRINTS USE THE FORM ON PAGE 15 OR CALL TOLL-FREE 1-877-671-6036
View thousands more home plans online at www.familyhandyman.com/homeplans

Massive Ranch Has Class — Plan #710-001D-0007

2,874 total square feet of living area

Price Code E

Special features

- Large family room with sloped ceiling and wood beams adjoins the kitchen and breakfast area with windows on two walls
- Large foyer opens to family room with massive stone fireplace and open stairs to the basement
- Private master bedroom with raised tub under the bay window, dramatic dressing area and a huge walk-in closet
- 4 bedrooms, 2 1/2 baths, 2-car side entry garage
- Basement foundation

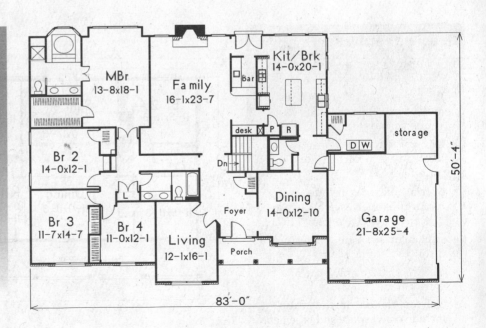

TO ORDER BLUEPRINTS USE THE FORM ON PAGE 15 OR CALL TOLL-FREE 1-877-671-6036
View thousands more home plans online at www.familyhandyman.com/homeplans

175

Charming Country Style

Plan #710-021D-0006

1,600 total square feet of living area

Price Code C

Special features

- Energy efficient home with 2" x 6" exterior walls
- Impressive sunken living room has massive stone fireplace and a 16' vaulted ceiling
- Dining room is conveniently located next to kitchen and divided for privacy
- Special amenities include sewing room, glass shelves in kitchen and master bath and a large utility area
- Sunken master bedroom features a distinctive sitting room
- 3 bedrooms, 2 baths, 2-car side entry garage
- Slab foundation, drawings also include crawl space and basement foundations

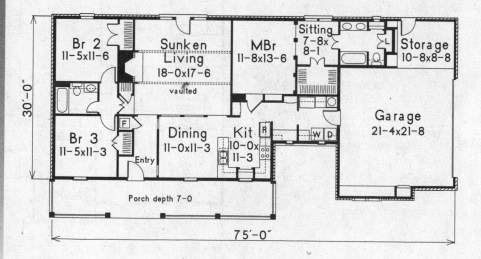

Br 2
11-5x11-6

Sunken Living
18-0x17-6
vaulted

MBr
11-8x13-6

Sitting
7-8x
8-1

Storage
10-8x8-8

Br 3
11-5x11-3

Dining
11-0x11-3

Kit
10-0x
11-3

Garage
21-4x21-8

Entry

30'-0"

Porch depth 7-0

75'-0"

Sophisticated Ranch

Plan #710-007D-0057

2,808 total square feet of living area

Price Code F

Special features

- An impressive front exterior showcases three porches for quiet times
- Large living and dining rooms flank an elegant entry
- Bedroom #3 shares a porch with the living room and a spacious bath with bedroom #2
- Vaulted master bedroom enjoys a secluded screened porch and sumptuous bath with corner tub, double vanities and huge walk-in closet
- Living room can easily convert to an optional fourth bedroom
- 3 bedrooms, 2 1/2 baths, 3-car side entry garage
- Basement foundation

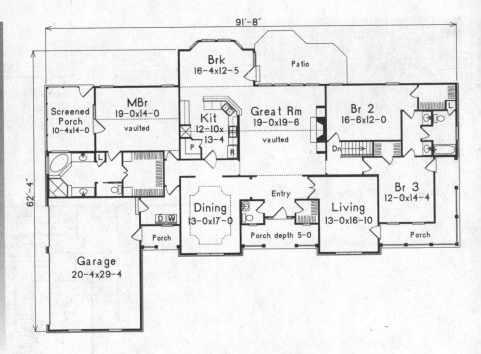

TO ORDER BLUEPRINTS USE THE FORM ON PAGE 15 OR CALL TOLL-FREE 1-877-671-6036
View thousands more home plans online at www.familyhandyman.com/homeplans

177

Efficient Floor Plan

Plan #710-024D-0007

1,609 total square feet of living area

Price Code B

Special features

- Sunny bay window in breakfast room
- U-shaped kitchen with pantry
- Spacious utility room
- Bedrooms on second floor feature dormers
- Family room includes plenty of space for entertaining
- 3 bedrooms, 2 1/2 baths, 2-car garage
- Slab foundation

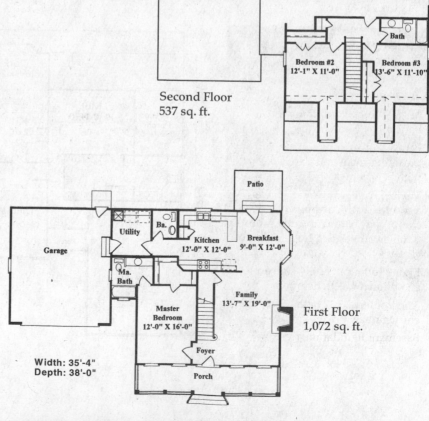

Second Floor
537 sq. ft.

Bath

Bedroom #2
12'-1" X 11'-0"

Bedroom #3
13'-6" X 11'-10"

First Floor
1,072 sq. ft.

Patio

Utility

Ba.

Kitchen
12'-0" X 12'-0"

Breakfast
9'-0" X 12'-0"

Garage

Ma. Bath

Family
13'-7" X 19'-0"

Master Bedroom
12'-0" X 16'-0"

Foyer

Porch

Width: 35'-4"
Depth: 38'-0"

TO ORDER BLUEPRINTS USE THE FORM ON PAGE 15 OR CALL TOLL-FREE 1-877-671-6036
View thousands more home plans online at www.familyhandyman.com/homeplans

Economical Ranch For Easy Living   Plan #710-014D-0005

1,314 total square feet of living area

Price Code A

Special features

- Energy efficient home with 2" x 6" exterior walls
- Covered porch adds immediate appeal and welcoming charm
- Open floor plan combined with vaulted ceiling offers spacious living
- Functional kitchen complete with pantry and eating bar
- Cozy fireplace in the living room
- Private master bedroom features a large walk-in closet and bath
- 3 bedrooms, 2 baths, 2-car garage
- Basement foundation

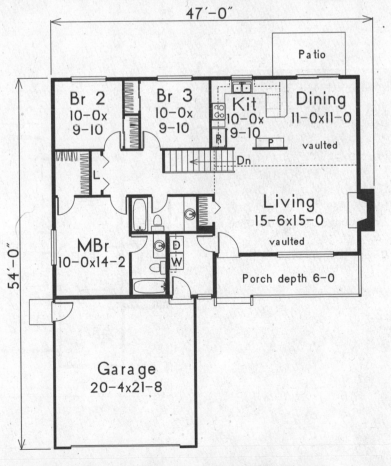

TO ORDER BLUEPRINTS USE THE FORM ON PAGE 15 OR CALL TOLL-FREE 1-877-671-6036
View thousands more home plans online at www.familyhandyman.com/homeplans

179

Distinctive Ranch

Plan #710-051D-0039

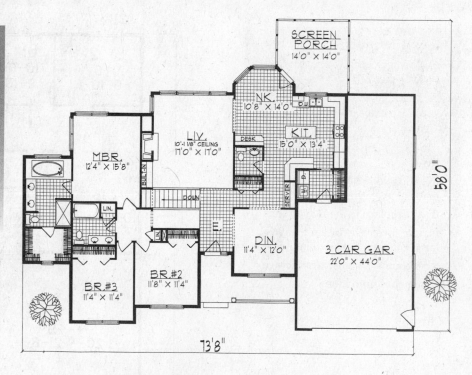

FREILING

1,962 total square feet of living area

Price Code C

Special features

- Formal dining room has a butler's pantry for entertaining
- Open living room offers a fireplace, built-in cabinetry and exceptional views to the outdoors
- Kitchen has work island and planning desk
- 3 bedrooms, 2 1/2 baths, 3-car garage
- Basement foundation

Impressive Corner Fireplace

Plan #710-053D-0042

1,458 total square feet of living area

Price Code A

Special features

- Convenient snack bar joins kitchen with breakfast room
- Large living room has fireplace, plenty of windows, vaulted ceiling and nearby plant shelf
- Master bedroom offers a private bath with vaulted ceiling, walk-in closet, plant shelf and coffered ceiling
- Corner windows provide abundant light in breakfast room
- 3 bedrooms, 2 baths, 2-car garage
- Crawl space foundation, drawings also include slab foundation

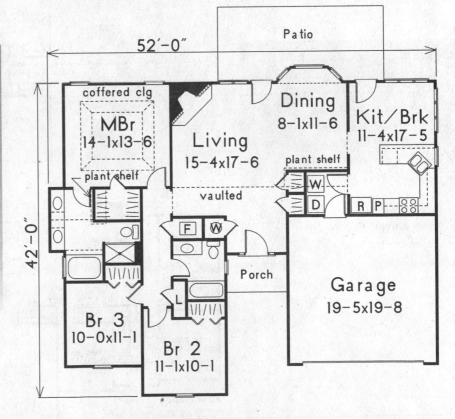

TO ORDER BLUEPRINTS USE THE FORM ON PAGE 15 OR CALL TOLL-FREE 1-877-671-6036
View thousands more home plans online at www.familyhandyman.com/homeplans

181

Brick Traditional

Plan #710-056D-0019

2,737 total square feet of living area

Price Code E

Special features

- T-stairs make any room easily accessible
- Two-story foyer and grand room create spacious feeling
- Master bedroom has gorgeous bay window and a sitting area
- Bedroom #4 has its own private bath
- 5 bedrooms, 4 baths, 2-car side entry garage
- Basement foundation

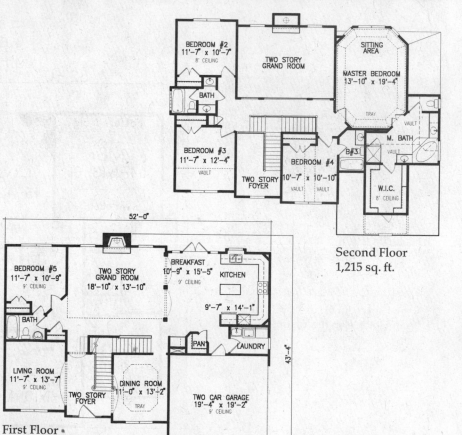

Second Floor
1,215 sq. ft.

First Floor
1,522 sq. ft.

Dramatic U-Shaped Stairs   Plan #710-011D-0025

2,287 total square feet of living area   Price Code E

Special features

- Wrap-around porch creates an inviting feeling
- First floor windows have transom windows above
- Den has see-through fireplace into the family area
- 3 bedrooms, 2 1/2 baths, 2-car side entry garage
- Crawl space foundation

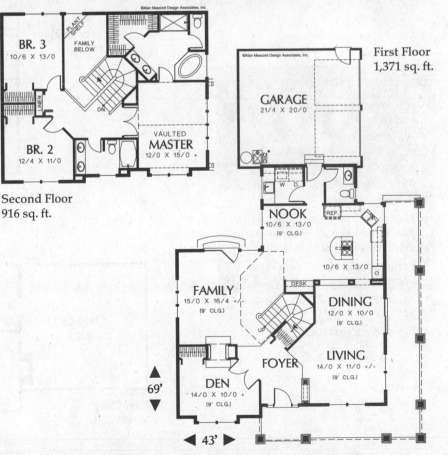

©Alan Mascord Design Associates, Inc.

BR. 3
10/6 X 13/0

FAMILY BELOW

PLANT SHELF

LINEN

DN.

BR. 2
12/4 X 11/0

VAULTED MASTER
12/0 X 15/0 +

Second Floor
916 sq. ft.

©Alan Mascord Design Associates, Inc.

First Floor
1,371 sq. ft.

GARAGE
21/4 X 20/0

W   D.

REF.

NOOK
10/6 X 13/0
(9' CLG.)

10/6 X 13/0

FAMILY
15/0 X 16/4 +/-
(9' CLG.)

DESK

DINING
12/0 X 10/0
(9' CLG.)

UP

FOYER

LIVING
14/0 X 11/0 +/-
(9' CLG.)

DEN
14/0 X 10/0 +
(9' CLG.)

69'

43'

TO ORDER BLUEPRINTS USE THE FORM ON PAGE 15 OR CALL TOLL-FREE 1-877-671-6036
View thousands more home plans online at www.familyhandyman.com/homeplans

183

COUNTRY CLASSIC

Plan #710-014D-0014

1,921 total square feet of living area

Price Code D

Special features

- Energy efficient home with 2" x 6" exterior walls
- Sunken family room includes a built-in entertainment center and coffered ceiling
- Sunken formal living room features a coffered ceiling
- Master bedroom dressing area has double sinks, spa tub, shower and French door to private deck
- Large front porch adds to home's appeal
- 3 bedrooms, 2 1/2 baths, 2-car garage
- Basement foundation

Second Floor
863 sq. ft.

Deck

MBr
13-2x14-2

open to below

Dn

Br 2
12-2x
11-6

Br 3
10-8x11-6

62'-0"

Patio

Nook
10-4x11-4

Kit
10-0x
11-4

Dining
10-4x11-4

Garage
23-8x23-4

Sunken
Family
13-2x15-6

coffered clg

Dn

Up

Sunken
Living
13-2x15-6

coffered clg

28'-0"

First Floor
1,058 sq. ft.

Porch depth 6-0

Bounty Of Bay Windows

Plan #710-035D-0035

2,322 total square feet of living area

Price Code D

Special features

- Vaulted family room has fireplace and access to kitchen
- Decorative columns and arched openings surround dining area
- Master suite has a sitting room and grand scale bath
- Kitchen includes island with serving bar
- 3 bedrooms, 2 1/2 baths, 2-car side entry garage
- Walk-out basement, crawl space or slab foundation, please specify when ordering

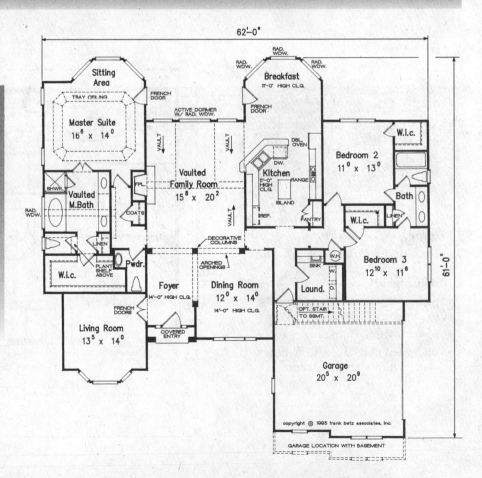

TO ORDER BLUEPRINTS USE THE FORM ON PAGE 15 OR CALL TOLL-FREE 1-877-671-6036
View thousands more home plans online at www.familyhandyman.com/homeplans

185

Rustic Stone Exterior

Plan #710-017D-0008

1,466 total square feet of living area

Price Code B

Special features

- Energy efficient home with 2" x 6" exterior walls
- Foyer separates the living room from the dining room and contains a generous coat closet
- Large living room with corner fireplace, bay window and pass-through to the kitchen
- Informal breakfast area opens to a large terrace through sliding glass doors which brightens area
- Master bedroom has a large walk-in closet and private bath
- 3 bedrooms, 2 baths, 2-car garage
- Basement foundation, drawings also include slab foundation

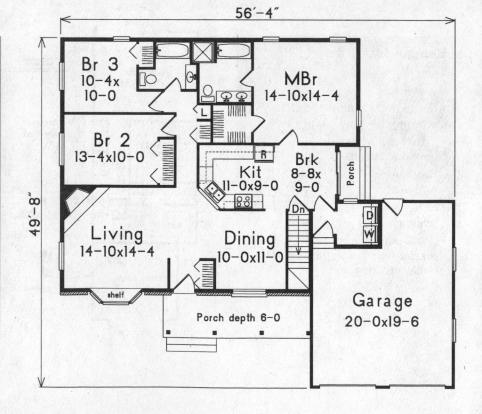

56'-4"

49'-8"

Br 3
10-4x
10-0

MBr
14-10x14-4

Br 2
13-4x10-0

Kit
11-0x9-0

Brk
8-8x
9-0

Porch

Living
14-10x14-4

Dn

Dining
10-0x11-0

D
W

shelf

Garage
20-0x19-6

Porch depth 6-0

Dramatic Atrium Ambiance — Plan #710-007D-0010

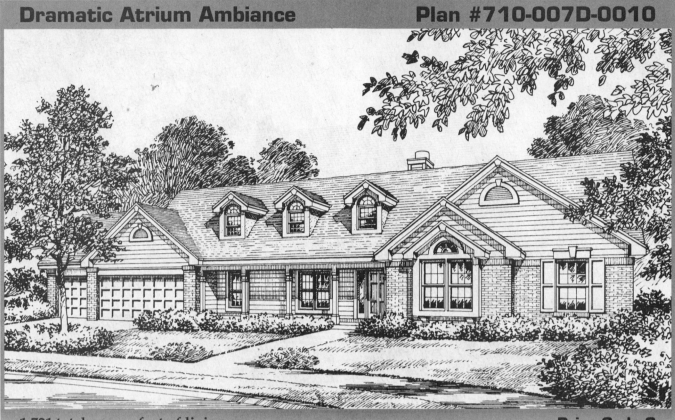

1,721 total square feet of living area

Price Code C

Special features

- Roof dormers add great curb appeal
- Vaulted dining and great rooms immersed in light from atrium window wall
- Breakfast room opens onto covered porch
- Functionally designed kitchen
- 3 bedrooms, 2 baths, 3-car garage
- Walk-out basement foundation, drawings also include crawl space and slab foundations

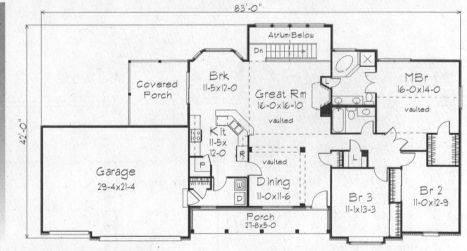

Rear View

TO ORDER BLUEPRINTS USE THE FORM ON PAGE 15 OR CALL TOLL-FREE 1-877-671-6036
View thousands more home plans online at www.familyhandyman.com/homeplans

187

Southern Elegance

Plan #710-028D-0017

2,669 total square feet of living area

Price Code E

Special features

- Nice-sized corner pantry in kitchen
- Guest bedroom, located off the great room, has a full bath and would make an excellent office
- Master bath has double walk-in closets, whirlpool tub and a large shower
- 3 bedrooms, 3 1/2 baths, 2-car side entry garage
- Basement or slab foundation, please specify when ordering

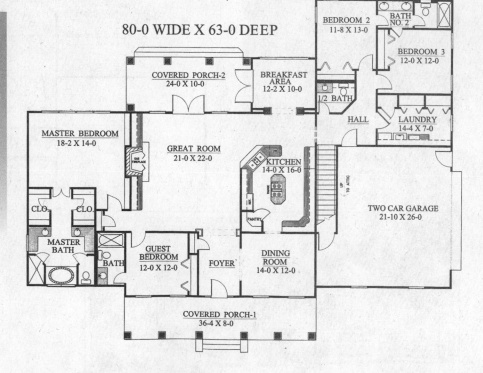

80-0 WIDE X 63-0 DEEP

TO ORDER BLUEPRINTS USE THE FORM ON PAGE 15 OR CALL TOLL-FREE 1-877-671-6036
View thousands more home plans online at www.familyhandyman.com/homeplans

188

The Family Handyman

Private First Floor Master Bedroom   Plan #710-036D-0055

3,017 total square feet of living area

Price Code E

Special features

- Impressive two-story entry has curved staircase
- Family room has unique elliptical vault above window
- Master bedroom includes a private covered patio and bath with walk-in closet
- Breakfast area overlooks great room
- Bonus room on the second floor has an additional 234 square feet of living area
- 4 bedrooms, 3 1/2 baths, 3-car side entry garage
- Slab foundation

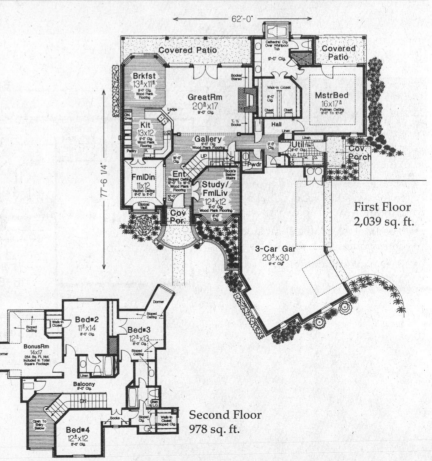

First Floor
2,039 sq. ft.

Second Floor
978 sq. ft.

TO ORDER BLUEPRINTS USE THE FORM ON PAGE 15 OR CALL TOLL-FREE 1-877-671-6036
View thousands more home plans online at www.familyhandyman.com/homeplans

189

Graciously Designed Traditional   Plan #710-058D-0021

1,477 total square feet of living area   **Price Code A**

Special features

- Oversized porch provides protection from the elements
- Innovative kitchen employs step-saving design
- Kitchen has snack bar which opens to the breakfast room with bay window
- 3 bedrooms, 2 baths, 2-car side entry garage with storage area
- Basement foundation

66'-8"

31'-8"

Storage 14-0x6-8

Lndry 7-9x6-4

Brkfst 11-2x12-0

MBr 11-8x15-3

Kit 11-4x11-4

Garage 22-0x19-4

Family 18-8x15-5

Br 2 11-0x12-0

Br 3 11-0x12-0

Covered Porch 22-0x7-4

Circular Stairway Adds To Entry   Plan #710-021D-0020

2,360 total square feet of living area

Price Code D

Special features

- Master bedroom includes sitting area and large bath
- Sloped family room ceiling provides view from second floor balcony
- Kitchen features island bar and walk-in butler's pantry
- 3 bedrooms, 2 1/2 baths, 2-car side entry garage
- Crawl space foundation, drawings also include slab and basement foundations

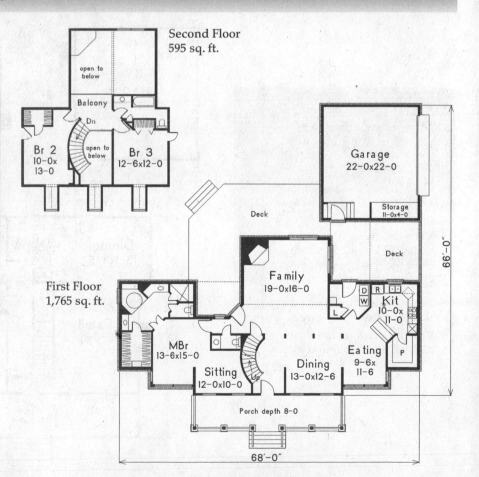

Second Floor
595 sq. ft.

open to below

Balcony

Dn

Br 2
10-0x
13-0

open to below

Br 3
12-6x12-0

Garage
22-0x22-0

Storage
11-0x4-0

Deck

Deck

Family
19-0x16-0

First Floor
1,765 sq. ft.

Kit
10-0x
11-0

MBr
13-6x15-0

Sitting
12-0x10-0

Dining
13-0x12-6

Eating
9-6x
11-6

Porch depth 8-0

66'-0"

68'-0"

TO ORDER BLUEPRINTS USE THE FORM ON PAGE 15 OR CALL TOLL-FREE 1-877-671-6036
View thousands more home plans online at www.familyhandyman.com/homeplans

191

Two-Story Foyer Is Spacious   Plan #710-040D-0001

1,814 total square feet of living area   **Price Code D**

Special features

- Large master bedroom includes a spacious bath with garden tub, separate shower and large walk-in closet
- Spacious kitchen and dining area brightened by large windows and patio access
- Detached two-car garage with walkway leading to house adds charm to this country home
- Large front porch
- 3 bedrooms, 2 1/2 baths, 2-car detached side entry garage
- Crawl space foundation, drawings also include slab foundation

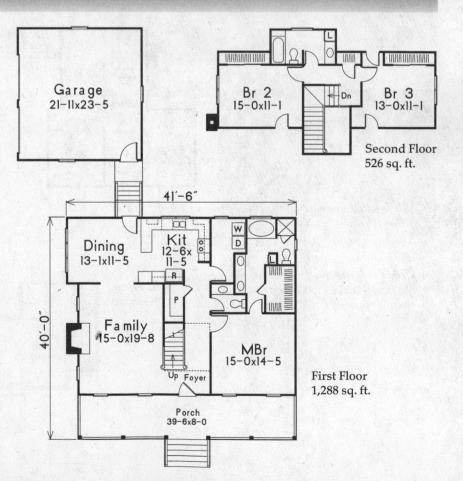

Garage
21-11x23-5

Br 2
15-0x11-1

Dn

Br 3
13-0x11-1

Second Floor
526 sq. ft.

41'-6"

Dining
13-1x11-5

Kit
12-6x
11-5

W
D

40'-0"

Family
15-0x19-8

MBr
15-0x14-5

Up   Foyer

First Floor
1,288 sq. ft.

Porch
39-6x8-0

TO ORDER BLUEPRINTS USE THE FORM ON PAGE 15 OR CALL TOLL-FREE 1-877-671-6036
View thousands more home plans online at www.familyhandyman.com/homeplans

Classic Elegance

Plan #710-007D-0062

2,483 total square feet of living area

Price Code D

Special features

- A large entry porch with open brick arches and palladian door welcomes guests
- The vaulted great room features an entertainment center alcove and the ideal layout for furniture placement
- The dining room is extra large with a stylish tray ceiling
- Study can easily be converted to a fourth bedroom
- 3 bedrooms, 2 baths, 2-car side entry garage
- Basement foundation

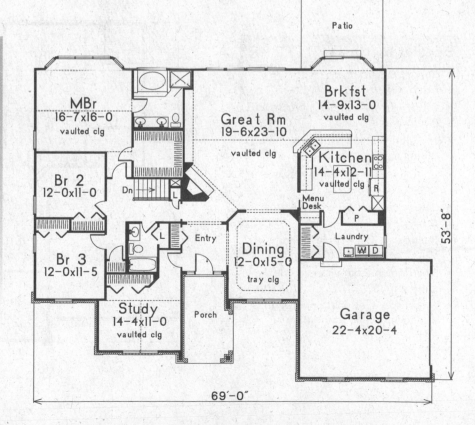

Patio

MBr
16-7x16-0
vaulted clg

Great Rm
19-6x23-10
vaulted clg

Brkfst
14-9x13-0
vaulted clg

Kitchen
14-4x12-11
vaulted clg

Br 2
12-0x11-0

Dn

Menu Desk

Entry

Laundry

Br 3
12-0x11-5

Dining
12-0x15-0
tray clg

Study
14-4x11-0
vaulted clg

Porch

Garage
22-4x20-4

53'-8"

69'-0"

TO ORDER BLUEPRINTS USE THE FORM ON PAGE 15 OR CALL TOLL-FREE 1-877-671-6036
View thousands more home plans online at www.familyhandyman.com/homeplans

193

Impressive Transom Windows Plan #710-021D-0011

1,800 total square feet of living area

Price Code D

Special features

- Energy efficient home with 2" x 6" exterior walls
- Covered front and rear porches add outdoor living area
- 12' ceilings in kitchen, eating area, dining and living rooms
- Private master bedroom features an expansive bath
- Side entry garage has two storage areas
- Pillared styling with brick and stucco exterior finish
- 3 bedrooms, 2 baths, 2-car side entry garage
- Crawl space foundation, drawings also include slab foundation

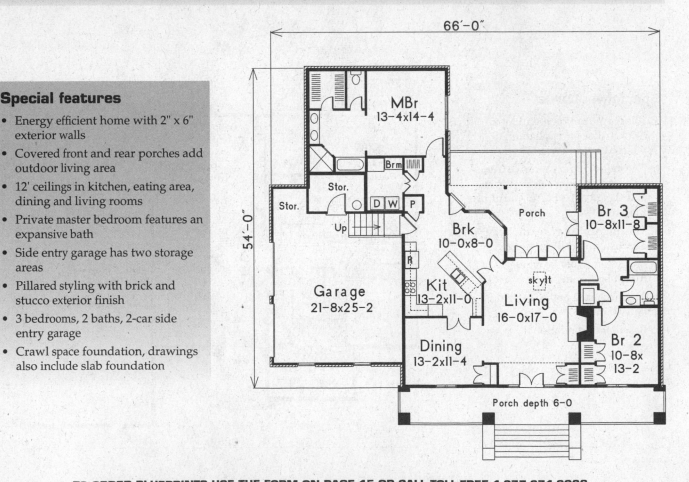

A Special Home For Views

Plan #710-007D-0075

1,684 total square feet of living area

Price Code B

Special features

- Delightful wrap-around porch anchored by full masonry fireplace
- The vaulted great room includes a large bay window, fireplace, dining balcony and atrium window wall
- Double walk in closets, large luxury bath and sliding doors to exterior balcony are a few fantastic features of the master bedroom
- Atrium opens to 611 square feet of optional living area on the lower level
- 3 bedrooms, 2 baths, 2-car drive under garage
- Walk-out basement foundation

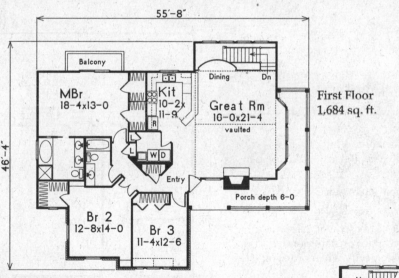

55'-8"

46'-4"

Balcony

MBr
18-4x13-0

Kit
10-2x
11-9

Dining

Dn

Great Rm
10-0x21-4
vaulted

First Floor
1,684 sq. ft.

W D

L

L

R

Entry

Br 2
12-8x14-0

Br 3
11-4x12-6

Porch depth 6-0

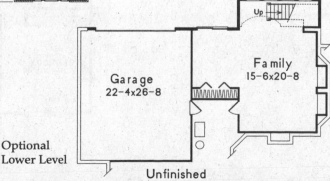

Up

Garage
22-4x26-8

Family
15-6x20-8

Optional
Lower Level

Unfinished

The Family
Handyman
Rear View

Master Suite Has Access Outdoors   Plan #710-055D-0024

1,680 total square feet of living area

Price Code B

Special features

- Enormous and luxurious master suite
- Kitchen and dining room have vaulted ceilings creating an open feeling
- Double sinks grace second bath
- 3 bedrooms, 2 baths, 2-car garage
- Walk-out basement, basement, crawl space or slab foundation, please specify when ordering

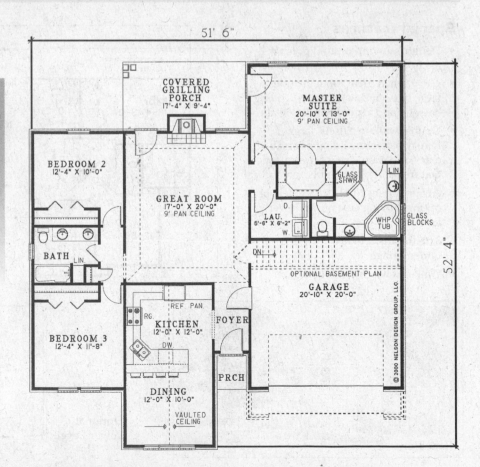

Ranch For A Country Setting

Plan #710-007D-0048

2,758 total square feet of living area

Price Code E

Special features

- Vaulted great room excels with fireplace, wet bar, plant shelves and skylights
- Fabulous master bedroom enjoys a fireplace, large bath, walk-in closet and vaulted ceiling
- Trendsetting kitchen and breakfast rooms adjoin spacious screened porch
- Convenient office near kitchen is perfect for computer room, hobby enthusiast or fifth bedroom
- 4 bedrooms, 2 1/2 baths, 3-car side entry garage
- Basement foundation

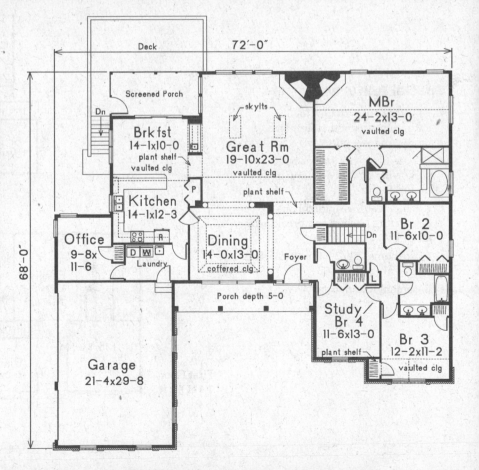

Deck

72'-0"

68'-0"

Screened Porch

Dn

Brkfst
14-1x10-0
plant shelf
vaulted clg

skylts

Great Rm
19-10x23-0
vaulted clg

MBr
24-2x13-0
vaulted clg

plant shelf

Kitchen
14-1x12-3

P

Office
9-8x
11-6

Dining
14-0x13-0
coffered clg

Foyer

Br 2
11-6x10-0

Dn

D W
Laundry
R

Study/
Br 4
11-6x13-0

Porch depth 5-0

plant shelf

Br 3
12-2x11-2

vaulted clg

Garage
21-4x29-8

TO ORDER BLUEPRINTS USE THE FORM ON PAGE 15 OR CALL TOLL-FREE 1-877-671-6036
View thousands more home plans online at www.familyhandyman.com/homeplans

197

Vaulted Ceilings Enhance Home   Plan #710-040D-0007

2,073 total square feet of living area   **Price Code D**

Special features

- Family room provides ideal gathering area with a fireplace, large windows and vaulted ceiling
- Private first floor master bedroom suite with a vaulted ceiling and luxury bath
- Kitchen features angled bar connecting kitchen and breakfast area
- 4 bedrooms, 2 1/2 baths, 2-car side entry garage
- Basement foundation

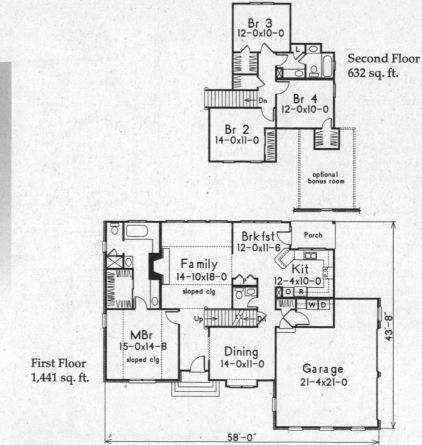

Second Floor
632 sq. ft.

Br 3
12-0x10-0

Br 4
12-0x10-0

Br 2
14-0x11-0

optional
bonus room

First Floor
1,441 sq. ft.

Brk fst
12-0x11-6

Porch

Family
14-10x18-0
sloped clg

Kit
12-4x10-0

MBr
15-0x14-8
sloped clg

Dining
14-0x11-0

Garage
21-4x21-0

43'-8"

58'-0"

Splendid Master Bedroom

Plan #710-065D-0013

2,041 total square feet of living area

Price Code C

Special features

- Great room accesses directly onto covered rear deck with ceiling fan above
- Private master bedroom has a beautiful octagon-shaped sitting area that opens and brightens the space
- Two secondary bedrooms share a full bath
- 3 bedrooms, 2 baths, 2-car side entry garage
- Basement or walk-out basement foundation, please specify when ordering

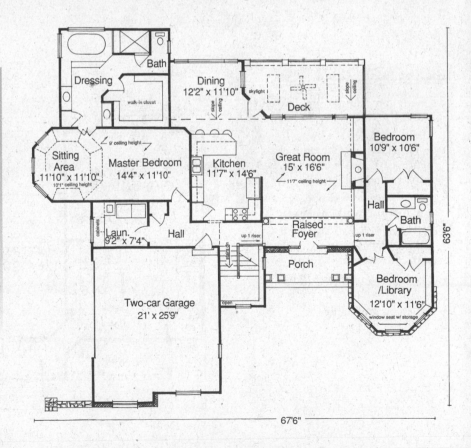

TO ORDER BLUEPRINTS USE THE FORM ON PAGE 15 OR CALL TOLL-FREE 1-877-671-6036
View thousands more home plans online at www.familyhandyman.com/homeplans

199

Appealing For A Narrow Lot

Plan #710-007D-0032

1,294 total square feet of living area

Price Code A

Special features

- Great room features fireplace and large bay with windows and patio doors
- Enjoy a laundry room immersed in light with large windows, arched transom and attractive planter box
- Vaulted master bedroom with bay window and walk-in closets
- Bedroom #2 boasts a vaulted ceiling, plant shelf and half bath, perfect for a studio
- 2 bedrooms, 1 full bath, 2 half baths, 1-car rear entry garage
- Basement foundation

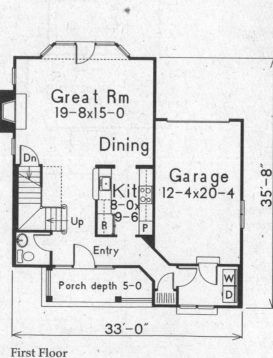

First Floor
718 sq. ft.

Second Floor
576 sq. ft.

TO ORDER BLUEPRINTS USE THE FORM ON PAGE 15 OR CALL TOLL-FREE 1-877-671-6036
View thousands more home plans online at www.familyhandyman.com/homeplans

Stylish Living

Plan #710-007D-0054

1,575 total square feet of living area

Price Code B

Special features

- Inviting porch leads to spacious living and dining rooms
- Kitchen with corner windows features an island snack bar, attractive breakfast room bay, convenient laundry and built-in pantry
- A luxury bath and walk-in closet adorn master bedroom suite
- 3 bedrooms, 2 1/2 baths, 2-car garage
- Basement foundation, drawings also include crawl space and slab foundations

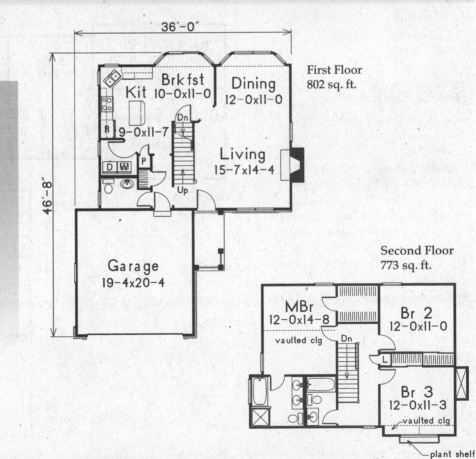

36'-0"

46'-8"

Kit 9-0x11-7

Brk fst 10-0x11-0

Dining 12-0x11-0

Living 15-7x14-4

Garage 19-4x20-4

First Floor 802 sq. ft.

Second Floor 773 sq. ft.

MBr 12-0x14-8
vaulted clg

Br 2 12-0x11-0

Br 3 12-0x11-3
vaulted clg

plant shelf

TO ORDER BLUEPRINTS USE THE FORM ON PAGE 15 OR CALL TOLL-FREE 1-877-671-6036
View thousands more home plans online at www.familyhandyman.com/homeplans

201

Home Offers Stylish Exterior — Plan #710-007D-0041

1,700 total square feet of living area

Price Code B

Special features

- Two-story entry with T-stair is illuminated with decorative oval window
- Skillfully designed U-shaped kitchen has a built-in pantry
- All bedrooms have generous closet storage and are common to spacious hall with walk-in cedar closet
- 4 bedrooms, 2 1/2 baths, 2-car side entry garage
- Basement foundation

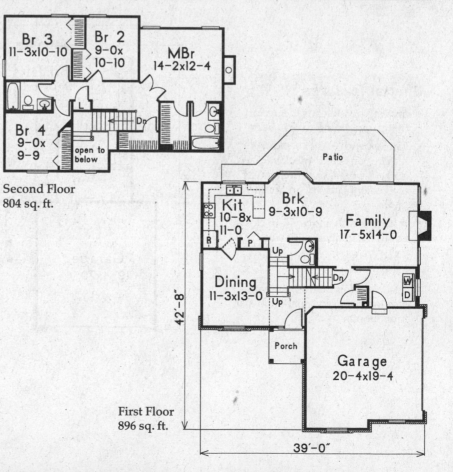

Br 3
11-3x10-10

Br 2
9-0x 10-10

MBr
14-2x12-4

Br 4
9-0x 9-9

open to below

Second Floor
804 sq. ft.

Patio

Kit
10-8x 11-0

Brk
9-3x10-9

Family
17-5x14-0

Dining
11-3x13-0

Porch

Garage
20-4x19-4

42'-8"

39'-0"

First Floor
896 sq. ft.

202

TO ORDER BLUEPRINTS USE THE FORM ON PAGE 15 OR CALL TOLL-FREE 1-877-671-6036
View thousands more home plans online at www.familyhandyman.com/homeplans

Impressive Victorian

Plan #710-001D-0003

2,286 total square feet of living area

Price Code E

Special features

- Fine architectural detail makes this home a showplace with its large windows, intricate brickwork and fine woodwork and trim
- Stunning two-story entry with attractive wood railing and balustrades in foyer
- Convenient wrap-around kitchen with window view, planning center and pantry
- Oversized master bedroom with walk-in closet and master bath
- 4 bedrooms, 2 1/2 baths, 2-car garage
- Basement foundation, drawings also include crawl space and slab foundations

Br 4
10-2x
10-8

Br 3
11-7x10-8

MBr
12-8x15-11
vaulted

open to below

Br 2
12-4x10-8

Second Floor
1,003 sq. ft.

64'-0"

Family
18-6x14-0

Bar

Brk
10-0x11-10

Kit
11-10x
10-6

34'-0"

Living
12-8x16-0

Entry

Up

Dining
11-0x13-0

Garage
19-4x23-4

W D

First Floor
1,283 sq. ft.

Porch depth 4-0

TO ORDER BLUEPRINTS USE THE FORM ON PAGE 15 OR CALL TOLL-FREE 1-877-671-6036
View thousands more home plans online at www.familyhandyman.com/homeplans

203

The Family Handyman

A GREAT MANOR HOUSE

Plan #710-001D-0012

3,368 total square feet of living area

Price Code F

Special features

- Sunken great room with cathedral ceiling, wooden beams, skylights and a masonry fireplace
- Octagon-shaped breakfast room has domed ceiling with beams, large windows and door to patio
- Private master bedroom has a deluxe bath and dressing area
- Oversized walk-in closets and storage areas in each bedroom
- 4 bedrooms, 3 full baths, 2 half baths, 2-car side entry garage
- Basement foundation

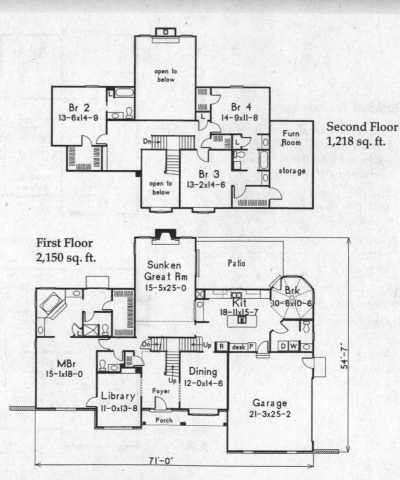

Second Floor
1,218 sq. ft.

First Floor
2,150 sq. ft.

TO ORDER BLUEPRINTS USE THE FORM ON PAGE 15 OR CALL TOLL-FREE 1-877-671-6036
View thousands more home plans online at www.familyhandyman.com/homeplans

Lake, Mountain Or Seaside Home   Plan #710-007D-0028

1,711 total square feet of living area

Price Code B

Special features

- Colossal entry leads to a vaulted great room with exposed beams, two-story window wall, brick fireplace, wet bar and balcony
- Bayed breakfast room shares the fireplace and joins a sun-drenched kitchen and deck
- Vaulted first floor master bedroom has double entry doors, closets and bookshelves
- Spiral stair and balcony dramatizes a loft that doubles as a spacious second bedroom
- 2 bedrooms, 2 1/2 baths
- Basement foundation

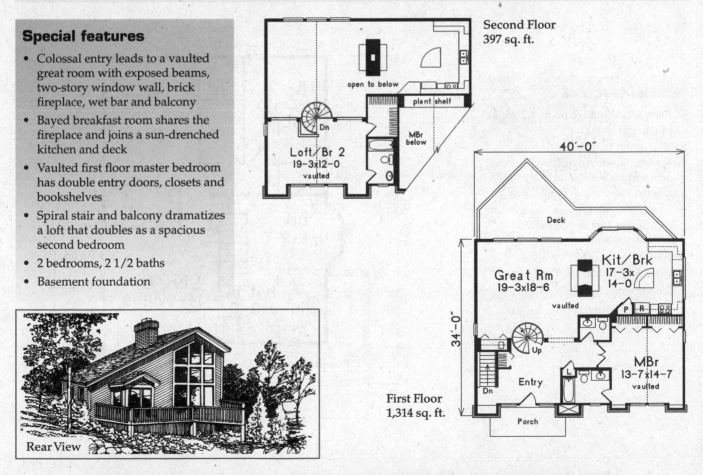

Second Floor
397 sq. ft.

open to below

plant shelf

MBr below

Loft/Br 2
19-3x12-0
vaulted

Dn

Rear View

40'-0"

Deck

Great Rm
19-3x18-6
vaulted

Kit/Brk
17-3x
14-0

34'-0"

Up

Entry

Dn

MBr
13-7x14-7
vaulted

Porch

First Floor
1,314 sq. ft.

Stylish Retreat For A Narrow Lot   Plan #710-007D-0105

1,084 total square feet of living area

Price Code AA

Special features

- Delightful country porch for quiet evenings
- The living room offers a front feature window which invites the sun and includes a fireplace and dining area with private patio
- The U-shaped kitchen features lots of cabinets and bayed breakfast room with built-in pantry
- Both bedrooms have walk-in closets and access to their own bath
- 2 bedrooms, 2 baths
- Basement foundation

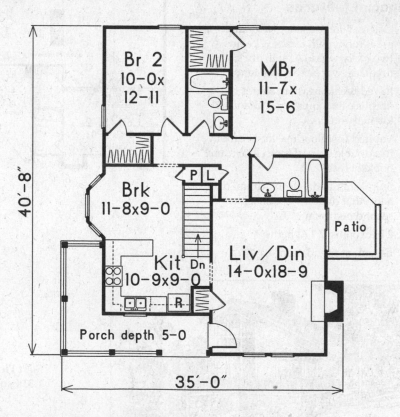

3,222 total square feet of living area   **Price Code F**

Special features

- Two-story foyer features central staircase and views to second floor, dining and living rooms
- Built-in breakfast booth surrounded by windows
- Gourmet kitchen with view to the great room
- Two-story great room features large fireplace and arched openings to the second floor
- Elegant master bedroom has separate reading room with bookshelves and fireplace
- 4 bedrooms, 3 1/2 baths, 2-car side entry garage
- Basement foundation, drawings also include crawl space and slab foundations

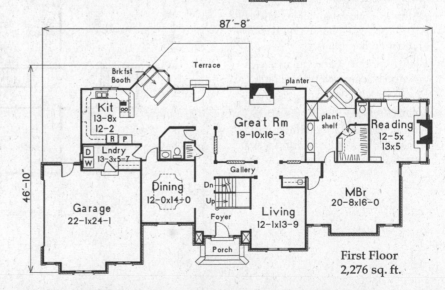

Second Floor
946 sq. ft.

Br 2
12-11x12-7

open to below

Br 3
12-0x13-3

Dn

open to below

Br 4
12-1x12-4

87'-8"

46'-10"

Brkfst Booth

Terrace

planter

Kit
13-8x
12-2

Great Rm
19-10x16-3

plant shelf

Reading
12-5x
13x5

Lndry
13-3x5-7

Gallery

Dining
12-0x14-0

Dn

Up

Living
12-1x13-9

MBr
20-8x16-0

Garage
22-1x24-1

Foyer

Porch

First Floor
2,276 sq. ft.

TO ORDER BLUEPRINTS USE THE FORM ON PAGE 15 OR CALL TOLL-FREE 1-877-671-6036
View thousands more home plans online at www.familyhandyman.com/homeplans

207

Distinctive Country Porch

Plan #710-007D-0011

2,182 total square feet of living area

Price Code D

Special features

- Meandering porch creates an inviting look
- Generous great room has four double-hung windows and gliding doors to exterior
- Highly functional kitchen features island/breakfast bar, menu desk and convenient pantry
- Each secondary bedroom includes generous closet and private bath
- 3 bedrooms, 3 1/2 baths, 2-car side entry garage
- Basement foundation, drawings also include crawl space and slab foundations

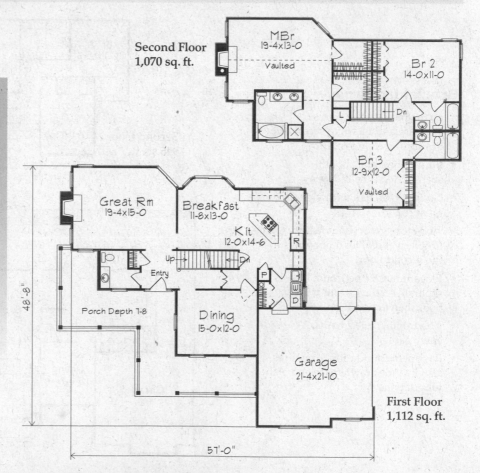

Second Floor
1,070 sq. ft.

MBr
19-4x13-0
Vaulted

Br 2
14-0x11-0

Br 3
12-9x12-0
Vaulted

Great Rm
19-4x15-0

Breakfast
11-8x13-0

Kit
12-0x14-6

Entry

Porch Depth 7-8

Dining
15-0x12-0

Garage
21-4x21-10

First Floor
1,112 sq. ft.

48'-8"

57'-0"

Comfortable Family Living   Plan #710-037D-0020

1,994 total square feet of living area   **Price Code D**

Special features

- Convenient entrance from the garage into the main living area through the utility room
- Standard 9' ceilings, bedroom #2 features a 12' vaulted ceiling and a 10' ceiling in the dining room
- Master bedroom offers a full bath with oversized tub, separate shower and walk-in closet
- Entry leads to formal dining room and attractive living room with double French doors and fireplace
- 3 bedrooms, 2 baths, 2-car garage
- Slab foundation

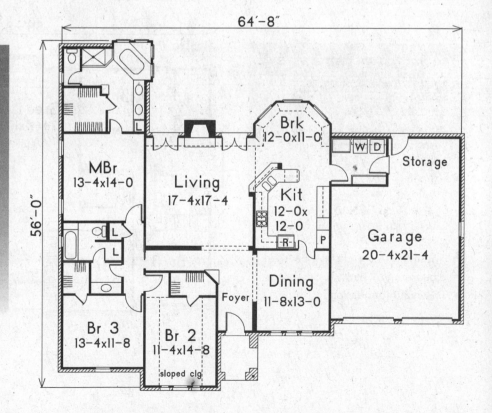

TO ORDER BLUEPRINTS USE THE FORM ON PAGE 15 OR CALL TOLL-FREE 1-877-671-6036
View thousands more home plans online at www.familyhandyman.com/homeplans

209

Handsome Accents

Plan #710-001D-0013

1,882 total square feet of living area

Price Code D

Special features

- Wide, handsome entrance opens to the vaulted great room with fireplace
- Living and dining areas are conveniently joined but still allow privacy
- Private covered porch extends breakfast area
- Practical passageway runs through laundry and mud room from garage to kitchen
- Vaulted ceiling in master bedroom
- 3 bedrooms, 2 baths, 2-car garage
- Basement foundation

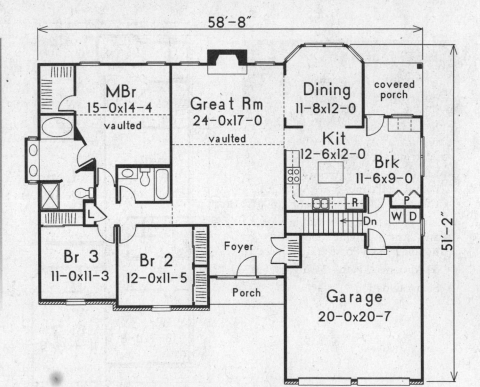

58'-8"

51'-2"

MBr 15-0x14-4 vaulted

Great Rm 24-0x17-0 vaulted

Dining 11-8x12-0

covered porch

Kit 12-6x12-0

Brk 11-6x9-0

Br 3 11-0x11-3

Br 2 12-0x11-5

Foyer

Porch

Garage 20-0x20-7

Bayed Dining Room

Plan #710-055D-0026

1,538 total square feet of living area

Price Code B

Special features

- Dining and great rooms highlighted in this design
- Master suite has many amenities
- Kitchen and laundry are accessible from any room in the house
- 3 bedrooms, 2 baths, 2-car garage
- Walk-out basement, basement, crawl space or slab foundation, please specify when ordering

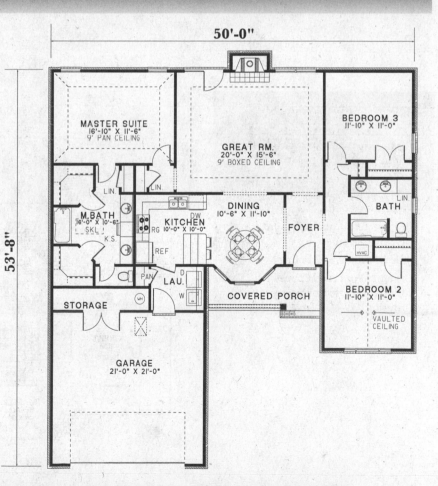

TO ORDER BLUEPRINTS USE THE FORM ON PAGE 15 OR CALL TOLL-FREE 1-877-671-6036
View thousands more home plans online at www.familyhandyman.com/homeplans

211

Porch Adds Warmth To Home   Plan #710-049D-0011

1,974 total square feet of living area   **Price Code C**

Special features

- Sunny bayed nook invites casual dining and shares its natural light with a snack counter and kitchen
- Spacious master bedroom occupies a bay window and offers a sumptuous bath
- Both second floor bedrooms have private balconies
- 3 bedrooms, 2 1/2 baths
- Basement or crawl space foundation, please specify when ordering

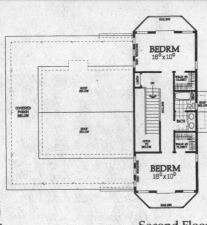

Second Floor
600 sq. ft.

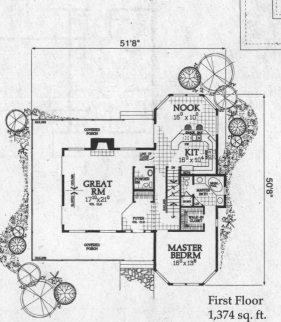

First Floor
1,374 sq. ft.

TO ORDER BLUEPRINTS USE THE FORM ON PAGE 15 OR CALL TOLL-FREE 1-877-671-6036
View thousands more home plans online at www.familyhandyman.com/homeplans

COURTYARD LENDS DISTINCTION

Plan #710-037D-0003

1,996 total square feet of living area

Price Code D

Special features

- Garden courtyard comes with large porch and direct access to master bedroom suite, breakfast room and garage
- Sculptured entrance has artful plant shelves and special niche in foyer
- Master bedroom boasts French doors, garden tub, desk with bookshelves and generous storage
- Plant shelves and high ceilings grace hallway
- 3 bedrooms, 2 baths, 2-car side entry garage
- Slab foundation, drawings also include crawl space foundation

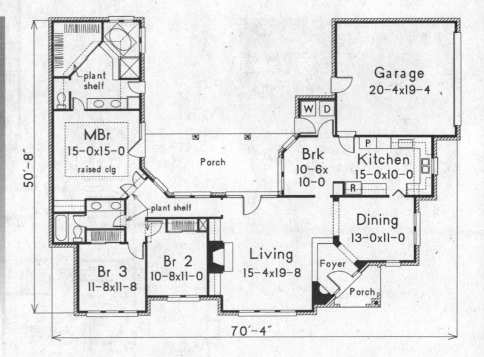

TO ORDER BLUEPRINTS USE THE FORM ON PAGE 15 OR CALL TOLL-FREE 1-877-671-6036
View thousands more home plans online at www.familyhandyman.com/homeplans

213

CHARMING COUNTRY FARMHOUSE

Plan #710-015D-0041

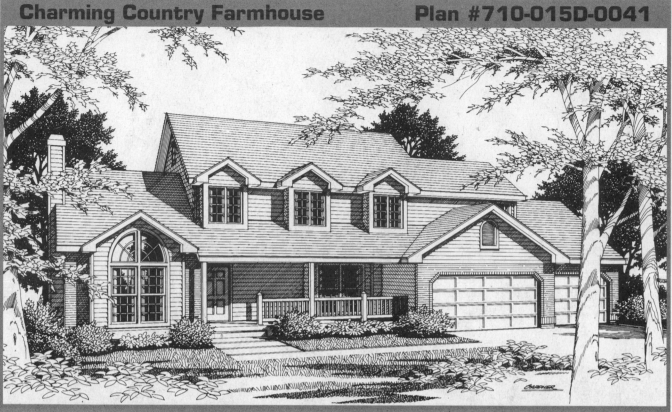

2,646 total square feet of living area

Price Code E

Special features

- Casual living areas of home located in the rear including a kitchen with eating bar overlooking an angled nook
- Private second floor master suite has a large walk-in closet, double sinks, spa tub and separate shower
- Two additional generous-sized bedrooms with dormered window seats and a large bonus room share a hall bath
- Bonus room on the second floor is included in the square footage
- 3 bedrooms, 2 1/2 baths, 3-car garage
- Basement foundation

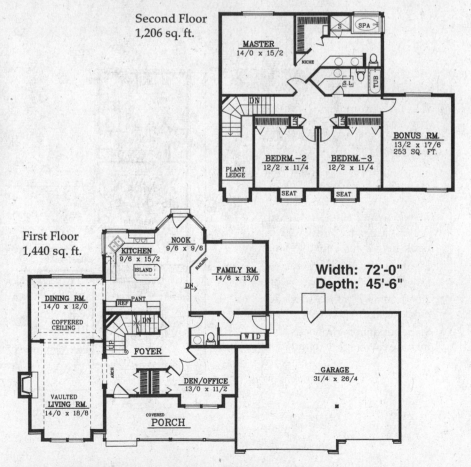

Second Floor
1,206 sq. ft.

MASTER
14/0 x 15/2

NICHE

SPA

TUB

S.L.

PLANT LEDGE

DN

BONUS RM.
13/2 x 17/6
253 SQ. FT.

BEDRM.-2
12/2 x 11/4

BEDRM.-3
12/2 x 11/4

SEAT

SEAT

First Floor
1,440 sq. ft.

KITCHEN
9/6 x 15/2

ISLAND

NOOK
9/6 x 9/6

RAILING

FAMILY RM.
14/6 x 13/0

DN

Width: 72'-0"
Depth: 45'-6"

DINING RM.
14/0 x 12/0

COFFERED CEILING

REF PANT

DN

W D

FOYER

UP

GARAGE
31/4 x 26/4

ARCH

DEN/OFFICE
13/0 x 11/2

VAULTED LIVING RM.
14/0 x 18/8

COVERED PORCH

TO ORDER BLUEPRINTS USE THE FORM ON PAGE 15 OR CALL TOLL-FREE 1-877-671-6036
View thousands more home plans online at www.familyhandyman.com/homeplans

Two-Story With Victorian Feel   Plan #710-038D-0044

1,982 total square feet of living area   Price Code C

Special features

- Spacious master bedroom has bath with corner whirlpool tub and sunny skylight above
- Breakfast area overlooks into great room
- Screened porch with skylight above extends the home outdoors and allows for another entertainment area
- 4 bedrooms, 2 1/2 baths
- Crawl space or slab foundation, please specify when ordering

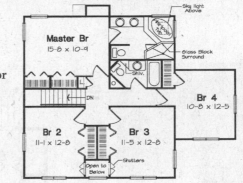

Second Floor
983 sq. ft.

Master Br
15-8 x 10-9

Br 4
10-8 x 12-5

Br 2
11-1 x 12-8

Br 3
11-5 x 12-8

Open to Below

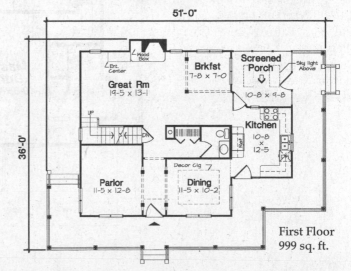

51'-0"

36'-0"

Great Rm
19-5 x 13-1

Brkfst
7-8 x 7-0

Screened Porch
10-8 x 9-8

Kitchen
10-8 x 12-5

Parlor
11-5 x 12-8

Dining
11-5 x 10-2

First Floor
999 sq. ft.

TO ORDER BLUEPRINTS USE THE FORM ON PAGE 15 OR CALL TOLL-FREE 1-877-671-6036
View thousands more home plans online at www.familyhandyman.com/HOMEPLANS

215

The Family Handyman

Formal Country Charm

Plan #710-052D-0011

1,325 total square feet of living area

Price Code A

Special features

- Sloped ceiling and a fireplace in living area creates a cozy feeling
- Formal dining and breakfast areas have an efficiently designed kitchen between them
- Master bedroom has a walk-in closet with luxurious private bath
- 3 bedrooms, 2 baths, 2-car drive under garage
- Basement or crawl space foundation, please specify when ordering

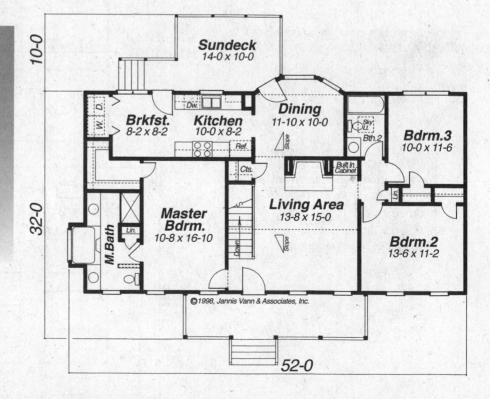

© 1998, Jannis Vann & Associates, Inc.

See-Through Fireplace

Plan #710-045D-0009

1,684 total square feet of living area

Price Code B

Special features

- Convenient double-doors in dining area provide access to a large deck
- Family room features several large windows for brightness
- Bedrooms separate from living areas for privacy
- Master bedroom offers a bath with walk-in closet, double-bowl vanity and both a shower and a whirlpool tub
- 3 bedrooms, 2 1/2 baths, 2-car garage
- Basement foundation

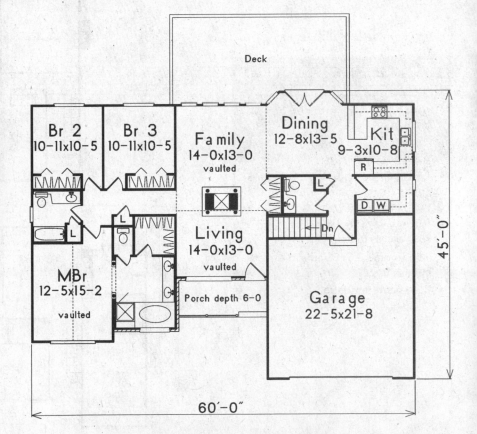

TO ORDER BLUEPRINTS USE THE FORM ON PAGE 15 OR CALL TOLL-FREE 1-877-671-6036
View thousands more home plans online at www.familyhandyman.com/homeplans

217

Balcony Offers Sweeping Views

Plan #710-027D-0007

2,444 total square feet of living area

Price Code D

Special features

- Laundry room with workspace, pantry and coat closet adjacent to kitchen
- Two bedrooms, study, full bath and plenty of closets on second floor
- Large walk-in closet and private bath make this master bedroom one you're sure to enjoy
- Kitchen with cooktop island and easy access to living area
- 3 bedrooms, 2 1/2 baths, 2-car side entry garage
- Basement foundation

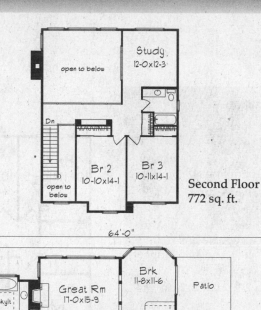

Second Floor
772 sq. ft.

First Floor
1,672 sq. ft.

OPEN RANCH DESIGN   Plan #710-022D-0011

1,630 total square feet of living area   **Price Code B**

Special features

- Crisp facade and full windows front and back offer open viewing
- Wrap-around rear deck is accessible from breakfast room, dining room and master bedroom
- Vaulted ceilings in living room and master bedroom
- Sitting area and large walk-in closet complement master bedroom
- 3 bedrooms, 2 baths, 2-car garage
- Basement foundation

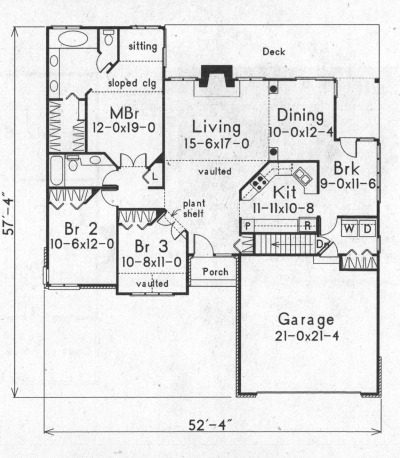

TO ORDER BLUEPRINTS USE THE FORM ON PAGE 15 OR CALL TOLL-FREE 1-877-671-6036
View thousands more home plans online at www.familyhandyman.com/homeplans

219

Flexible Layout For Various Uses   Plan #710-058D-0012

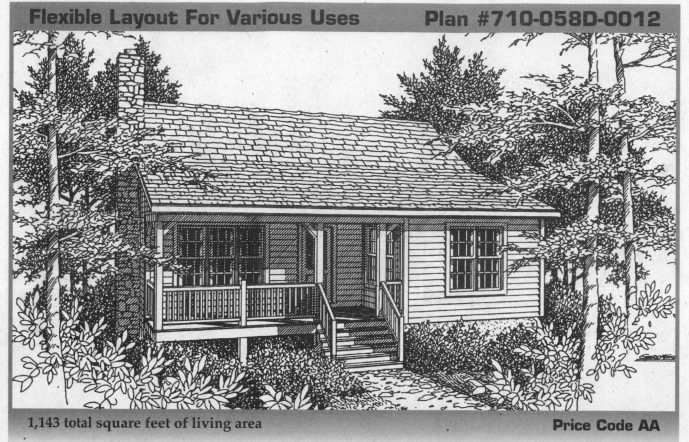

1,143 total square feet of living area   **Price Code AA**

Special features

- Enormous stone fireplace in family room adds warmth and character
- Spacious kitchen with breakfast bar overlooks family room
- Separate dining area great for entertaining
- Vaulted family room and kitchen create an open atmosphere
- 2 bedrooms, 1 bath
- Crawl space foundation

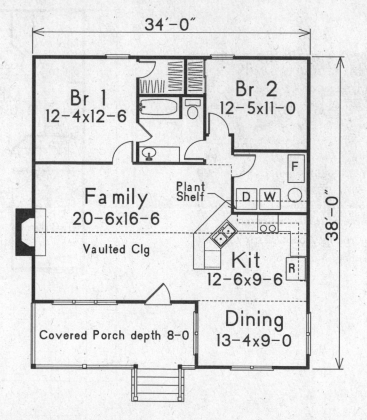

34'-0"

38'-0"

Br 1
12-4x12-6

Br 2
12-5x11-0

Family
20-6x16-6

Plant Shelf

F

D W

Vaulted Clg

Kit
12-6x9-6

R

Covered Porch depth 8-0

Dining
13-4x9-0

1,945 total square feet of living area

Price Code D

Special features

- Great room has a stepped ceiling and a fireplace
- Bayed dining area with stepped ceiling and French door leading to a covered porch
- Master bedroom has a tray ceiling, a bay window and a large walk-in closet
- 3 bedrooms, 2 1/2 baths, 2-car side entry garage
- Basement, crawl space or slab foundation, please specify when ordering

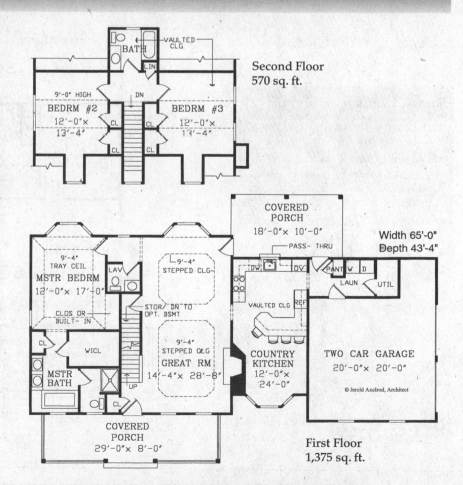

Second Floor
570 sq. ft.

BATH
VAULTED CLG
LIN
9'-0" HIGH
DN
BEDRM #2
12'-0" x
13'-4"
CL CL
BEDRM #3
12'-0" x
13'-4"
CL CL

Width 65'-0"
Depth 43'-4"

COVERED PORCH
18'-0" x 10'-0"
PASS-THRU

9'-4" TRAY CEIL
MSTR BEDRM
12'-0" x 17'-0"
LAV
9'-4" STEPPED CLG
DW
PANT W D
LAUN UTIL
CLOS OR BUILT-IN
STOR/ DN TO OPT. BSMT
VAULTED CLG
REF
CL
WICL
9'-4" STEPPED CLG
GREAT RM
14'-4" x 28'-8"
UP
COUNTRY KITCHEN
12'-0" x 24'-0"
TWO CAR GARAGE
20'-0" x 20'-0"
© Jerold Axelrod, Architect
MSTR BATH
CL

COVERED PORCH
29'-0" x 8'-0"

First Floor
1,375 sq. ft.

TO ORDER BLUEPRINTS USE THE FORM ON PAGE 15 OR CALL TOLL-FREE 1-877-671-6036
View thousands more home plans online at www.familyhandyman.com/homeplans

221

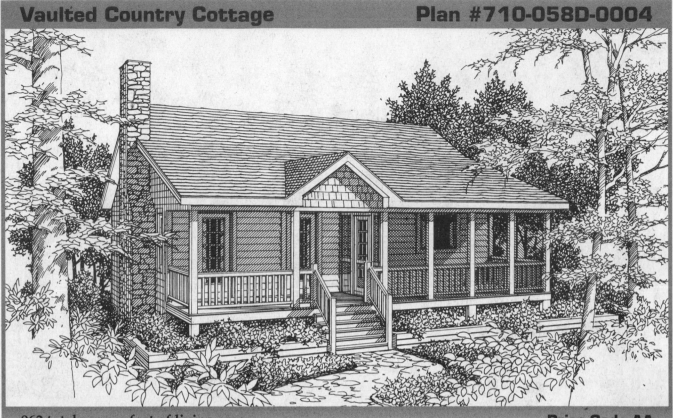

Vaulted Country Cottage

Plan #710-058D-0004

962 total square feet of living area

Price Code AA

Special features

- Both the kitchen and family room share warmth from the fireplace
- Charming facade features covered porch on one side, screened porch on the other and attractive planter boxes
- L-shaped kitchen boasts convenient pantry
- 2 bedrooms, 1 bath
- Crawl space foundation

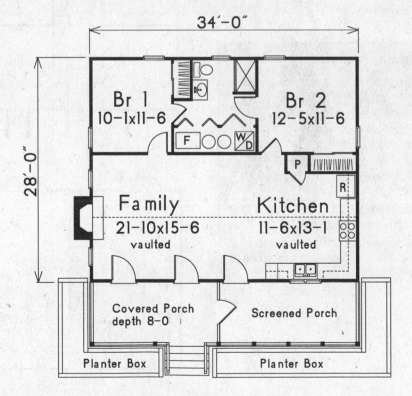

34'-0"

28'-0"

Br 1 10-1x11-6

Br 2 12-5x11-6

F

W/D

P

R

Family 21-10x15-6 vaulted

Kitchen 11-6x13-1 vaulted

Covered Porch depth 8-0

Screened Porch

Planter Box

Planter Box

MAGNIFICENT FACADE

Plan #710-048D-0010

J.N. HANSEN PT.L.

2,887 total square feet of living area

Price Code F

Special features

- Columned foyer opens into living room which has sunken wet bar that extends into pool area
- Stunning master bedroom accesses patio and offers view of pool through curved window wall
- Dining room boasts window walls
- Second floor includes two bedrooms, bath and shared balcony deck overlooking pool area
- 4 bedrooms, 2 1/2 baths, 2-car garage
- Slab foundation

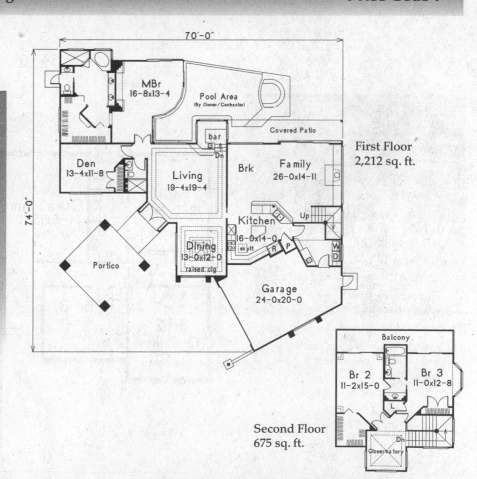

First Floor
2,212 sq. ft.

Second Floor
675 sq. ft.

TO ORDER BLUEPRINTS USE THE FORM ON PAGE 15 OR CALL TOLL-FREE 1-877-671-6036
View thousands more home plans online at www.familyhandyman.com/homeplans

223

High-Style Vaulted Ranch   Plan #710-014D-0007

1,453 total square feet of living area

Price Code A

Special features

- Decorative vents, window trim, shutters and brick blend to create dramatic curb appeal
- Energy efficient home with 2" x 6" exterior walls
- Kitchen opens to living area and includes salad sink in the island, pantry and handy laundry room
- Exquisite master bedroom is highlighted by a vaulted ceiling
- Dressing area with walk-in closet, private bath and spa tub/shower
- 3 bedrooms, 2 baths, 2-car garage
- Basement foundation, drawings also include crawl space foundation

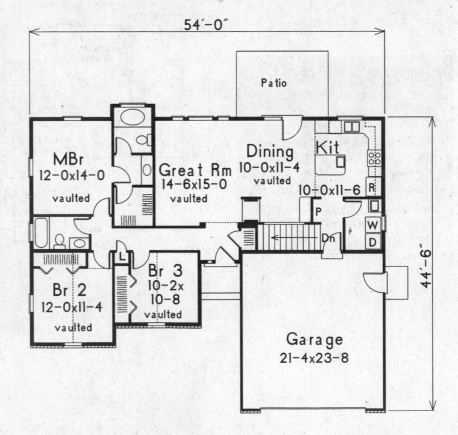

Formal And Informal Living

Plan #710-036D-0049

2,591 total square feet of living area

Price Code D

Special features

- Formal living area has a nice view extending past the covered patio
- Family room is adjacent to breakfast area and has a vaulted ceiling and fireplace creating a cozy atmosphere
- Master bedroom has a private sitting area and large private bath
- Gallery adds interest to entry
- 4 bedrooms, 3 baths, 3-car side entry garage
- Slab foundation

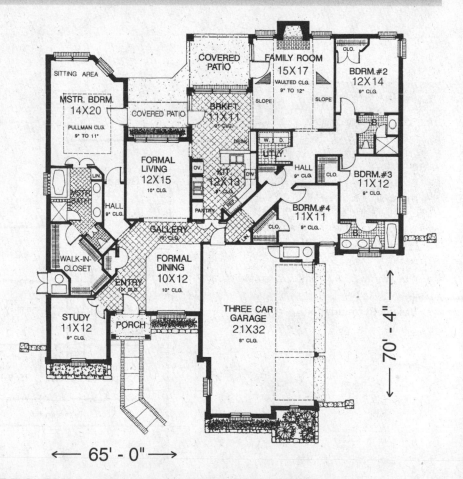

TO ORDER BLUEPRINTS USE THE FORM ON PAGE 15 OR CALL TOLL-FREE 1-877-671-6036
View thousands more home plans online at www.familyhandyman.com/homeplans

225

The Family Handyman

COUNTRY-STYLE COMFORT

Plan #710-053D-0021

2,826 total square feet of living area

Price Code E

Special features

- Wrap-around covered porch is accessible from family and breakfast rooms in addition to front entrance
- Bonus room, which is included in the square footage, has a separate entrance and is suitable for an office or private accommodations
- Large, full-windowed breakfast room
- 4 bedrooms, 2 1/2 baths, 2-car side entry garage
- Basement foundation

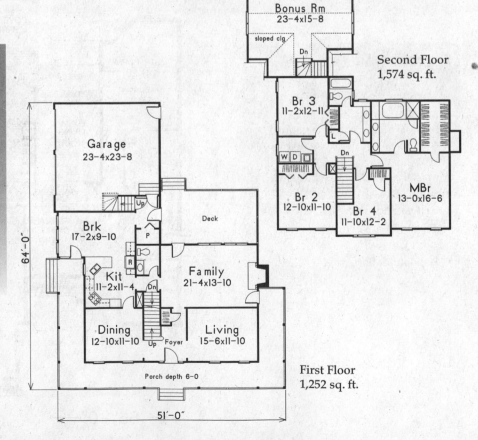

Bonus Rm
23-4x15-8

sloped clg.

Dn

Second Floor
1,574 sq. ft.

Br 3
11-2x12-11

W D

Dn

Br 2
12-10x11-10

Br 4
11-10x12-2

MBr
13-0x16-6

Garage
23-4x23-8

Up

64'-0"

Brk
17-2x9-10

Deck

P

R

Kit
11-2x11-4

Dn

Family
21-4x13-10

Dining
12-10x11-10

Up   Foyer

Living
15-6x11-10

Porch depth 6-0

51'-0"

First Floor
1,252 sq. ft.

HOME WITH FRONT ORIENTATION Plan #710-007D-0055

2,029 total square feet of living area

Price Code D

Special features

- Stonework, gables, roof dormer and double porches create a country flavor
- Kitchen enjoys extravagant cabinetry and counterspace in a bay, island snack bar, built-in pantry and cheery dining area with multiple tall windows
- Angled stair descends from large entry with wood columns and is open to vaulted great room with corner fireplace
- Master bedroom boasts two walk-in closets, double-doors leading to an opulent master bath and a private porch
- 4 bedrooms, 2 baths, 2-car side entry garage
- Basement foundation, drawings also include crawl space and slab foundations

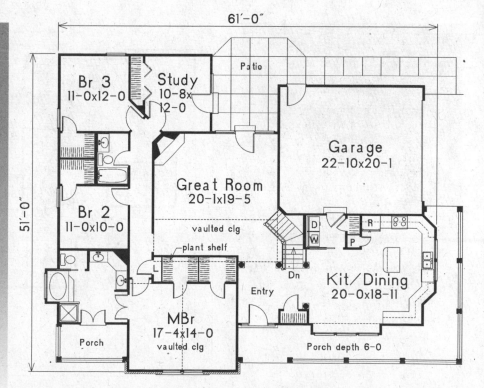

The Family Handyman

Patio And Pool For Entertaining

Plan #710-048D-0007

3,290 total square feet of living area

Price Code F

Special features

- Patio area surrounds pool with swim-up bar - both pool and spa are great options with this plan
- Formal dining room features dramatic drop down ceiling and easy access to kitchen
- Fireplace provides focal point in the master bedroom which includes a sitting room and elegant master bath
- Observation room and two bedrooms with adjoining bath on the second floor
- Varied ceiling heights throughout
- 4 bedrooms, 3 1/2 baths, 2-car side entry garage
- Slab foundation

Second Floor
621 sq. ft.

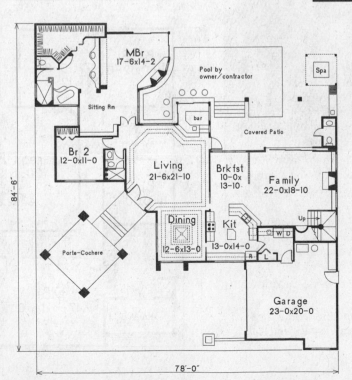

First Floor
2,669 sq. ft.

Handyman

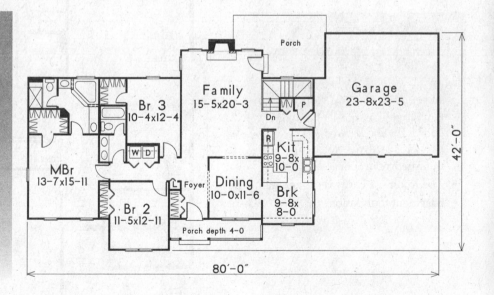

1,708 total square feet of living area

Price Code B

Special features

- Massive family room enhanced with several windows, fireplace and access to porch
- Deluxe master bath accented by step-up corner tub flanked by double vanities
- Closets throughout maintain organized living
- Bedrooms isolated from living areas
- 3 bedrooms, 2 baths, 2-car garage
- Basement foundation, drawings also include crawl space foundation

Br 3
10-4x12-4

Family
15-5x20-3

Porch

Garage
23-8x23-5

MBr
13-7x15-11

W D

Kit
9-8x
10-0

Dn

P

R

Foyer

Dining
10-0x11-6

Brk
9-8x
8-0

Br 2
11-5x12-11

Porch depth 4-0

42'-0"

80'-0"

A Ranch With All The Comforts   Plan #710-051D-0064

1,490 total square feet of living area   Price Code A

Special features

- Arch soffit frames the entrance of the kitchen
- Living room has fireplace with surrounding windows
- Bay window in master bedroom adds light and beauty
- Den can easily be converted to a third bedroom
- 2 bedrooms, 2 baths, 3-car garage
- Basement foundation

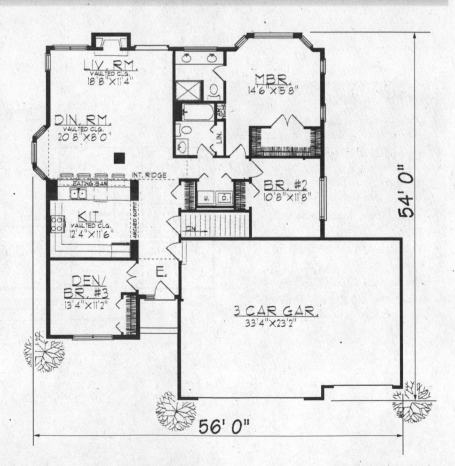

TO ORDER BLUEPRINTS USE THE FORM ON PAGE 15 OR CALL TOLL-FREE 1-877-671-6036
View thousands more home plans online at www.familyhandyman.com/homeplans

The Family **Handyman**

Wrap-Around Country-Style Home — Plan #710-037D-0004

2,449 total square feet of living area

Price Code E

Special features

- Striking living area features fireplace flanked with windows, cathedral ceiling and balcony
- First floor master bedroom has twin walk-in closets and large linen storage
- Dormers add space for desks or seats
- 3 bedrooms, 2 1/2 baths, 2-car detached garage
- Slab foundation, drawings also include crawl space foundation

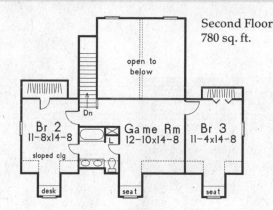

Second Floor
780 sq. ft.

open to below

Dn

Br 2
11-8x14-8

Game Rm
12-10x14-8

Br 3
11-4x14-8

sloped clg

desk

seat

seat

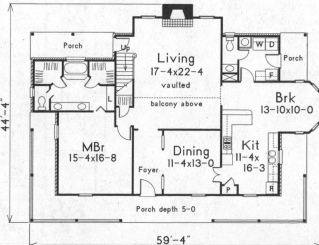

First Floor
1,669 sq. ft.

Porch

Up

Living
17-4x22-4
vaulted

W D

F.

Porch

balcony above

Brk
13-10x10-0

44'-4"

MBr
15-4x16-8

Dining
11-4x13-0

Kit
11-4x16-3

Foyer

P

R

Porch depth 5-0

59'-4"

TO ORDER BLUEPRINTS USE THE FORM ON PAGE 15 OR CALL TOLL-FREE 1-877-671-6036
View thousands more home plans online at www.familyhandyman.com/homeplans

231

Elegant Design With Many Extras   Plan #710-056D-0025

3,304 total square feet of living area   Price Code F

Special features

- First floor guest bedroom has access to bath and a walk-in closet
- Second floor has loft area at the top of the stairs
- Kitchen has center island and extra storage
- Luxurious master bedroom located on first floor for privacy
- 5 bedrooms, 4 baths, 2-car side entry garage
- Basement foundation

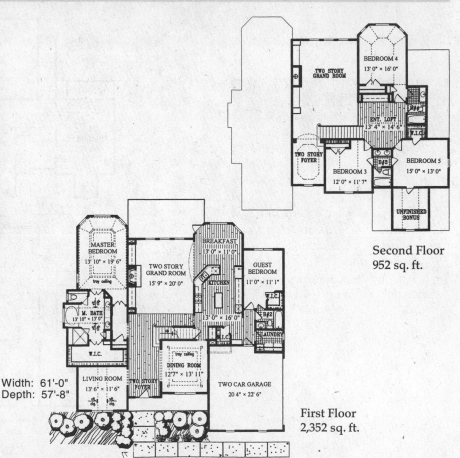

Second Floor
952 sq. ft.

Width: 61'-0"
Depth: 57'-8"

First Floor
2,352 sq. ft.

TO ORDER BLUEPRINTS USE THE FORM ON PAGE 15 OR CALL TOLL-FREE 1-877-671-6036
View thousands more home plans online at www.familyhandyman.com/homeplans

1,464 total square feet of living area

Price Code C

Special features

- Contemporary styled home has a breathtaking two-story foyer and a lovely open staircase
- U-shaped kitchen is designed for efficiency
- Elegant great room has a cozy fireplace
- 3 bedrooms, 2 1/2 baths, 2-car garage
- Crawl space foundation

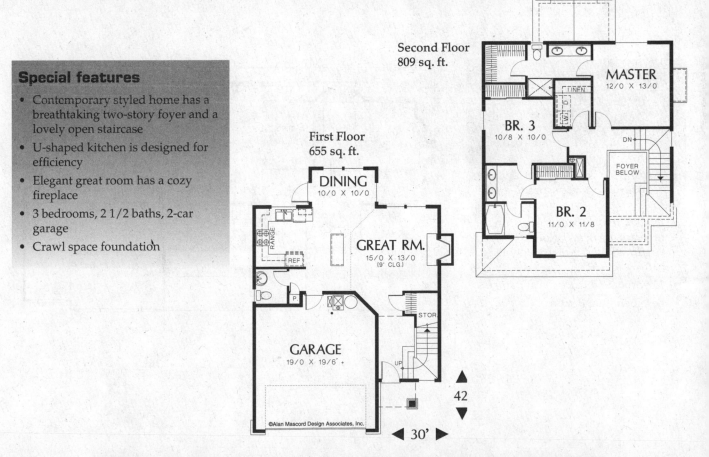

Second Floor
809 sq. ft.

First Floor
655 sq. ft.

©Alan Mascord Design Associates, Inc.

Luxurious Master Bedroom

Plan #710-007D-0007

2,523 total square feet of living area

Price Code D

Special features

- Entry with high ceiling leads to massive vaulted great room with wet bar, plant shelves, pillars and fireplace with a harmonious window trio
- Elaborate kitchen with bay and breakfast bar adjoins morning room with fireplace-in-a-bay
- Vaulted master bedroom features fireplace, book and plant shelves, large walk-in closet and double baths
- 3 bedrooms, 2 baths, 3-car garage
- Basement foundation

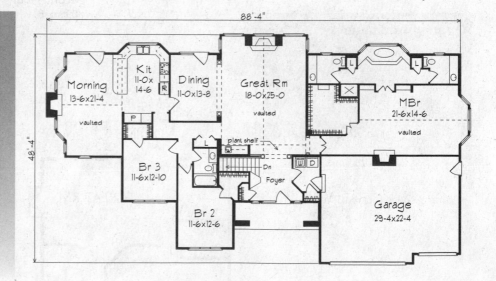

Columned Facade

Plan #710-055D-0038

2,247 total square feet of living area

Price Code D

Special features

- Enormous great room with fireplace extends into a kitchen with center island
- Formal dining area is quiet, yet convenient to kitchen
- All bedrooms located on second floor maintain privacy
- 3 bedrooms, 2 1/2 baths, 2-car side entry garage
- Basement, crawl space or slab foundation, please specify when ordering

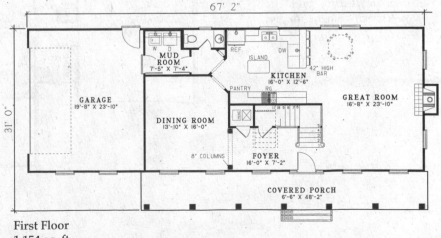

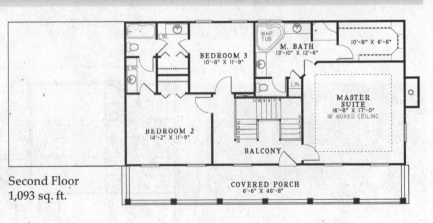

Second Floor
1,093 sq. ft.

First Floor
1,154 sq. ft.

TO ORDER BLUEPRINTS USE THE FORM ON PAGE 15 OR CALL TOLL-FREE 1-877-671-6036
View thousands more home plans online at www.familyhandyman.com/homeplans

235

Covered Porch Adds Charm

Plan #710-069D-0018

2,069 total square feet of living area

Price Code C

Special features

- 9' ceilings throughout this home
- Kitchen has many amenities including a snack bar
- Large front and rear porches
- 3 bedrooms, 2 1/2 baths, 2-car garage
- Slab or crawl space foundation, please specify when ordering

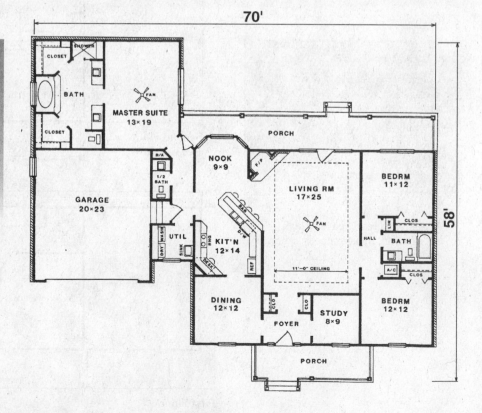

TO ORDER BLUEPRINTS USE THE FORM ON PAGE 15 OR CALL TOLL-FREE 1-877-671-6036
View thousands more home plans online at www.familyhandyman.com/homeplans

The Family Handyman

KITCHEN IS A CHEF'S DREAM — Plan #710-035D-0036

2,193 total square feet of living area

Price Code C

Special features

- Master suite includes a sitting room
- Dining room has decorative columns and overlooks family room
- Kitchen has lots of storage
- Optional bonus room with bath on second floor has an additional 400 square feet of living area
- 3 bedrooms, 3 baths, 2-car side entry garage
- Walk-out basement, crawl space or slab foundation, please specify when ordering

Optional Second Floor

First Floor 2,193 sq. ft.

TO ORDER BLUEPRINTS USE THE FORM ON PAGE 15 OR CALL TOLL-FREE 1-877-671-6036
View thousands more home plans online at www.familyhandyman.com/homeplans

237

Efficient Kitchen Layout

Plan #710-058D-0024

1,598 total square feet of living area

Price Code B

Special features

- Additional storage area in garage
- Double-door entry into master bedroom with luxurious master bath
- Entry opens into large family room with vaulted ceiling and open stairway to basement
- 3 bedrooms, 2 baths, 2-car garage
- Basement foundation

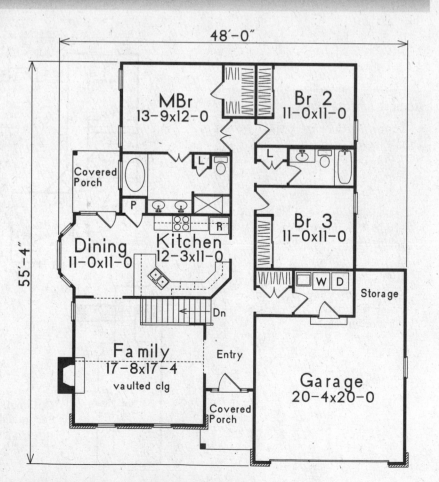

48'-0"

55'-4"

MBr
13-9x12-0

Br 2
11-0x11-0

Covered Porch

Br 3
11-0x11-0

Dining
11-0x11-0

Kitchen
12-3x11-0

W D

Storage

Family
17-8x17-4
vaulted clg

Entry

Dn

Covered Porch

Garage
20-4x20-0

Striking Arched Entry

Plan #710-033D-0002

1,859 total square feet of living area

Price Code D

Special features

- Fireplace highlights vaulted great room
- Master bedroom includes large closet and private bath
- Kitchen adjoins breakfast room providing easy access to the outdoors
- 3 bedrooms, 2 1/2 baths, 2-car garage
- Basement foundation

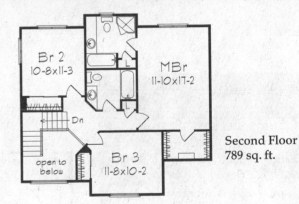

Second Floor
789 sq. ft.

Br 2
10-8x11-3

MBr
11-10x17-2

Dn

open to below

Br 3
11-8x10-2

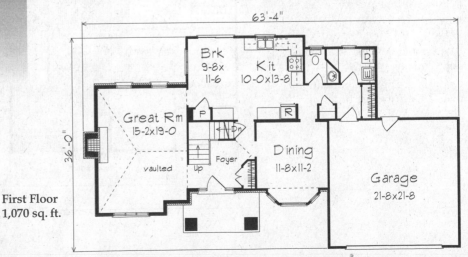

First Floor
1,070 sq. ft.

63'-4"

36'-0"

Brk
9-8x11-6

Kit
10-0x13-8

Great Rm
15-2x19-0

vaulted

Up   Foyer

Dining
11-8x11-2

Garage
21-8x21-8

TO ORDER BLUEPRINTS USE THE FORM ON PAGE 15 OR CALL TOLL-FREE 1-877-671-6036
View thousands more home plans online at www.familyhandyman.com/homeplans

239

Inviting Vaulted Entry

Plan #710-013D-0025

2,097 total square feet of living area

Price Code C

Special features

- Angled kitchen, family room and eating area adds interest to this home
- Family room includes a T.V. niche making this a cozy place to relax
- Sumptuous master bedroom includes sitting area, double walk-in closet and a full bath with double vanities
- 3 bedrooms, 3 baths, 3-car side entry garage
- Crawl space or slab foundation, please specify when ordering

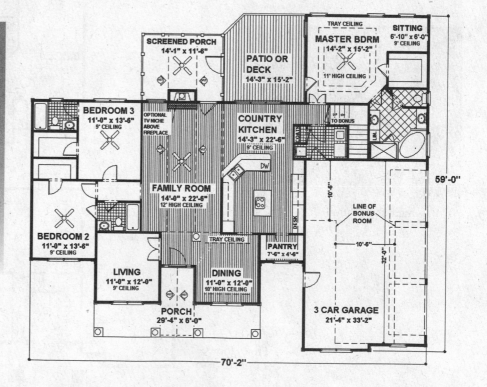

Perfect For A Small Family

Plan #710-001D-0040

864 total square feet of living area

Price Code AAA

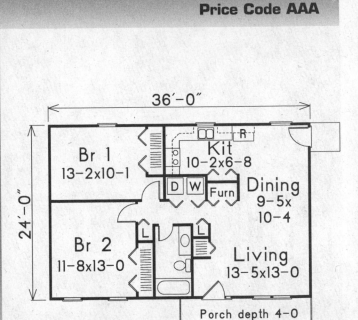

36'-0"

24'-0"

Br 1
13-2x10-1

Kit
10-2x6-8

R

D W Furn

Dining
9-5x
10-4

Br 2
11-8x13-0

Living
13-5x13-0

Porch depth 4-0

Special features

- L-shaped kitchen with convenient pantry is adjacent to dining area
- Easy access to laundry area, linen closet and storage closet
- Both bedrooms include ample closet space
- 2 bedrooms, 1 bath
- Crawl space foundation, drawings also include basement and slab foundations

Southern Styling With Porch

Plan #710-035D-0051

1,491 total square feet of living area

Price Code A

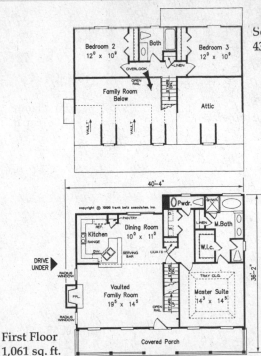

Second Floor
430 sq. ft.

Bedroom 2
12⁰ x 10⁰

Bath

Bedroom 3
12⁰ x 10⁰

OVERLOOK

OPEN RAIL

LINEN

Family Room
Below

Attic

VAULT VAULT

copyright © 1998 frank betz associates, inc.

40'-4"

36'-2"

Pwdr.

PANTRY

REF.
Kitchen
RANGE

Dining Room
10⁰ x 11⁰

LINEN

M.Bath

W.i.c.

DRIVE UNDER

RADIUS WINDOW

DW

SERVING BAR

COATS

Vaulted
Family Room
19⁵ x 14⁵

FPL.

OPEN RAIL

TRAY CLG.

Master Suite
14³ x 14⁵

RADIUS WINDOW

Covered Porch

First Floor
1,061 sq. ft.

Special features

- Two-story family room has vaulted ceiling
- Well-organized kitchen has serving bar which overlooks family and dining rooms
- First floor master suite has tray ceiling, walk-in closet and master bath
- 3 bedrooms, 2 1/2 baths, 2-car drive under garage
- Walk-out basement foundation

TO ORDER BLUEPRINTS USE THE FORM ON PAGE 15 OR CALL TOLL-FREE 1-877-671-6036
View thousands more home plans online at www.familyhandyman.com/homeplans

241

2,300 total square feet of living area

Price Code D

Special features

- Cozy fireplace in master suite
- 9' ceilings on the first floor
- Energy efficient home with 2" x 6" exterior walls
- 3 bedrooms, 2 1/2 baths, 2-car side entry garage
- Basement foundation

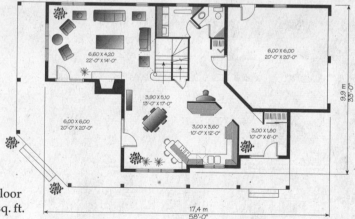

First Floor
1,067 sq. ft.

Second Floor
1,233 sq. ft.

Central Living Area

Plan #710-033D-0012

1,546 total square feet of living area

Price Code C

Special features

- Spacious, open rooms create a casual atmosphere
- Master bedroom is secluded for privacy
- Dining room features large bay window
- Kitchen and dinette combine for added space and includes access to the outdoors
- Large laundry room includes convenient sink
- 3 bedrooms, 2 baths, 2-car garage
- Basement foundation

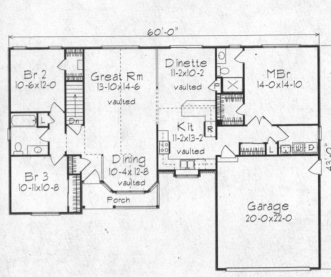

Step Up Into Master Bath Tub

Plan #710-019D-0016

2,678 total square feet of living area

Price Code E

Special features

- Elegant arched opening graces entrance
- Kitchen has double ovens, walk-in pantry and an eating bar
- Master bedroom has beautiful bath spotlighting a step-up tub
- 4 bedrooms, 2 1/2 baths, 2-car side entry garage
- Crawl space or slab foundation, please specify when ordering

TO ORDER BLUEPRINTS USE THE FORM ON PAGE 15 OR CALL TOLL-FREE 1-877-671-6036
View thousands more home plans online at www.familyhandyman.com/homeplans

See-Through Fireplace

Plan #710-043D-0018

3,502 total square feet of living area

Price Code F

Special features

- 12' ceiling in dining room
- Interior column accents and display niches
- Living and family rooms have see-through fireplace
- Master bath has double walk-in closets
- 4 bedrooms, 2 full baths, 2 half baths, 3-car side entry garage
- Basement or crawl space foundation, please specify when ordering

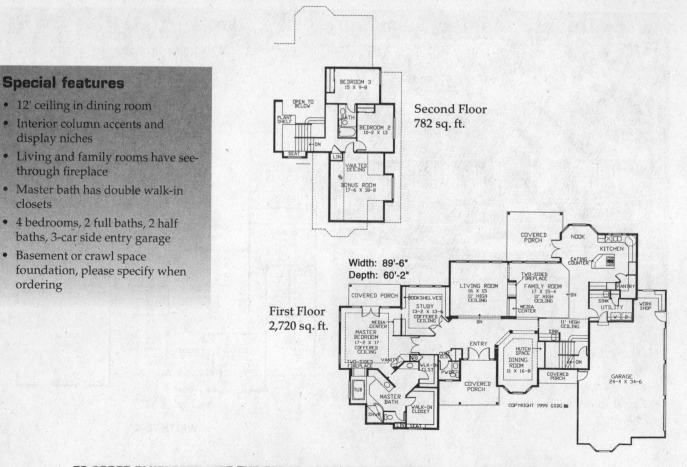

Second Floor
782 sq. ft.

Width: 89'-6"
Depth: 60'-2"

First Floor
2,720 sq. ft.

TO ORDER BLUEPRINTS USE THE FORM ON PAGE 15 OR CALL TOLL-FREE 1-877-671-6036
View thousands more home plans online at www.familyhandyman.com/homeplans

Trio Of Dormers Add Appeal

Plan #710-031D-0011

2,164 total square feet of living area

Price Code C

Width: 70'-6"
Depth: 57'-0"

© David C. Lutz

Special features

- Country-styled front porch adds charm
- Plenty of counterspace in kitchen
- Large utility area meets big families' laundry needs
- Double-doors lead to covered rear porch
- 4 bedrooms, 2 1/2 baths, 2-car side entry garage
- Slab foundation

Home Embraces Large Family

Plan #710-007D-0015

2,828 total square feet of living area

Price Code F

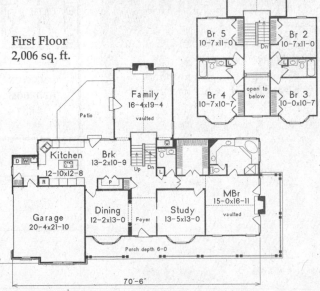

Second Floor
822 sq. ft.

First Floor
2,006 sq. ft.

Special features

- Popular wrap-around porch gives home country charm
- Secluded, oversized family room with vaulted ceiling and wet bar features many windows
- Any chef would be delighted to cook in this smartly designed kitchen with island and corner windows
- Spectacular master bedroom and bath
- 5 bedrooms, 3 1/2 baths, 2-car side entry garage
- Basement foundation, drawings also include crawl space and slab foundations

TO ORDER BLUEPRINTS USE THE FORM ON PAGE 15 OR CALL TOLL-FREE 1-877-671-6036
View thousands more home plans online at www.familyhandyman.com/homeplans

245

Cozy Country Home

Plan #710-028D-0009

2,189 total square feet of living area

Price Code C

Special features

- Study could easily be converted to a fourth bedroom
- Secluded master bedroom has all the luxuries for comfortable living
- All bedrooms include spacious walk-in closets
- 3 bedrooms, 2 1/2 baths, 2-car detached garage
- Crawl space or slab foundation, please specify when ordering

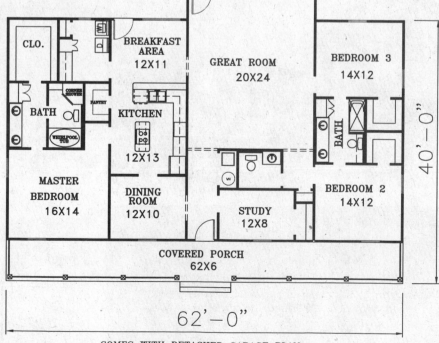

CLO.

BREAKFAST AREA 12X11

GREAT ROOM 20X24

BEDROOM 3 14X12

BATH

CORNER SHOWER

PANTRY

KITCHEN 12X13

WHIRLPOOL TUB

BATH

MASTER BEDROOM 16X14

DINING ROOM 12X10

STUDY 12X8

BEDROOM 2 14X12

COVERED PORCH 62X6

40' - 0"

62' - 0"

COMES WITH DETACHED GARAGE PLAN

246

TO ORDER BLUEPRINTS USE THE FORM ON PAGE 15 OR CALL TOLL-FREE 1-877-671-6036
View thousands more home plans online at www.familyhandyman.com/homeplans

Open Feeling In This Ranch

Plan #710-034D-0008

1,875 total square feet of living area

Price Code C

Special features

- Peninsula separating kitchen and dining room has sink, dishwasher and eating area
- Tall ceilings throughout living area create spaciousness
- Columned foyer adds style
- 3 bedrooms, 2 1/2 baths, 2-car garage
- Basement foundation

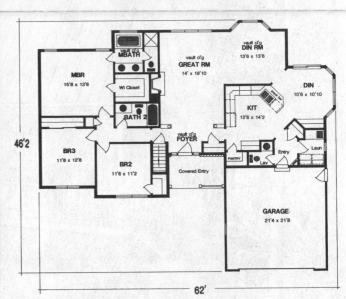

Old-Fashioned Porch

Plan #710-001D-0074

1,664 total square feet of living area

Price Code B

Special features

- L-shaped country kitchen includes pantry and cozy breakfast area
- Bedrooms located on second floor for privacy
- Master bedroom includes walk-in closet, dressing area and bath
- 3 bedrooms, 2 1/2 baths, 2-car garage
- Crawl space foundation, drawings also include basement and slab foundations

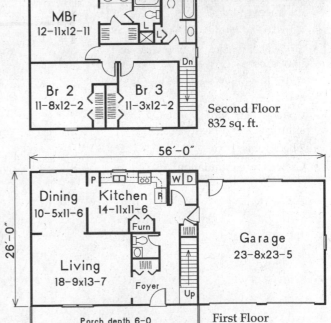

TO ORDER BLUEPRINTS USE THE FORM ON PAGE 15 OR CALL TOLL-FREE 1-877-671-6036
View thousands more home plans online at www.familyhandyman.com/homeplans

247

Cottage-Style, Appealing And Cozy   Plan #710-040D-0028

828 total square feet of living area   Price Code AAA

Special features

- Vaulted ceiling in living area enhances space
- Convenient laundry room
- Sloped ceiling creates unique style in bedroom #2
- Efficient storage space under the stairs
- Covered entry porch provides cozy sitting area and plenty of shade
- 2 bedrooms, 1 bath
- Crawl space foundation

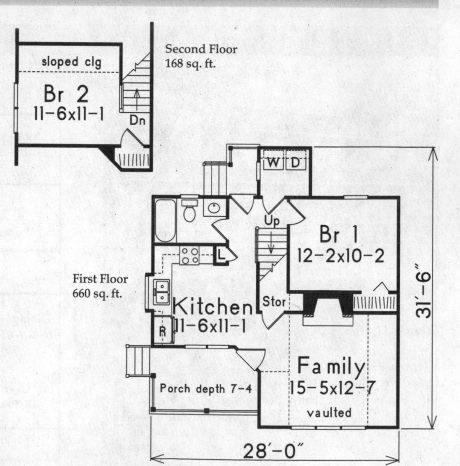

Second Floor
168 sq. ft.

sloped clg

Br 2
11-6x11-1

Dn

First Floor
660 sq. ft.

W D

Up

Br 1
12-2x10-2

Kitchen
11-6x11-1

Stor

R

31'-6"

Porch depth 7-4

Family
15-5x12-7

vaulted

28'-0"

Comfortable Country Home

Plan #710-017D-0005

1,367 total square feet of living area

Price Code B

Special features

- Neat front porch shelters the entrance
- Dining room has full wall of windows and convenient storage area
- Breakfast area leads to the rear terrace through sliding doors
- Large living room with high ceiling, skylight and fireplace
- 3 bedrooms, 2 baths, 2-car garage
- Basement foundation, drawings also include slab foundation

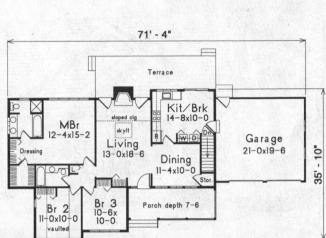

Cozy Ranch With Rustic Touches

Plan #710-056D-0003

2,272 total square feet of living area

Price Code G

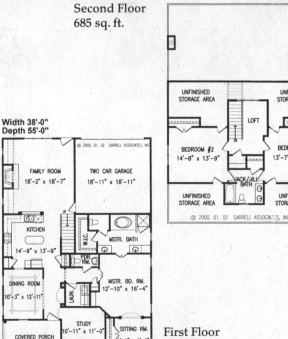

© 2003, Garrell Associates, Inc.

Second Floor 685 sq. ft.

First Floor 1,587 sq. ft.

Special features

- 10' ceilings throughout the first floor and 9' ceilings on the second floor
- Lots of storage area on the second floor
- First floor master bedroom has a lovely sitting area with an arched entry
- Second floor bedrooms share a Jack and Jill bath
- 3 bedrooms, 2 1/2 baths, 2-car rear entry garage
- Slab foundation

TO ORDER BLUEPRINTS USE THE FORM ON PAGE 15 OR CALL TOLL-FREE 1-877-671-6036
View thousands more home plans online at www.familyhandyman.com/homeplans

249

Designed For Handicap Access   **Plan #710-058D-0022**

1,578 total square feet of living area   **Price Code B**

Special features

- Plenty of closet, linen and storage space
- Covered porches in the front and rear of home add charm to this design
- Open floor plan has unique angled layout
- 3 bedrooms, 2 baths, 2-car garage
- Basement foundation

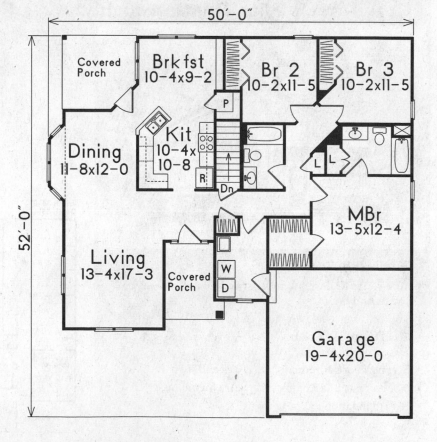

Covered Porch

Brk fst
10-4x9-2

Br 2
10-2x11-5

Br 3
10-2x11-5

Dining
11-8x12-0

Kit
10-4x
10-8

MBr
13-5x12-4

Living
13-4x17-3

Covered Porch

Garage
19-4x20-0

50'-0"

52'-0"

Raised Plantation Style

Plan #710-060D-0005

1,742 total square feet of living area

Price Code B

© COPYRIGHT MCMXC RALPH JONES

ARTIST'S CONCEPTION, ACTUAL
CONSTRUCTION MAY VARY.

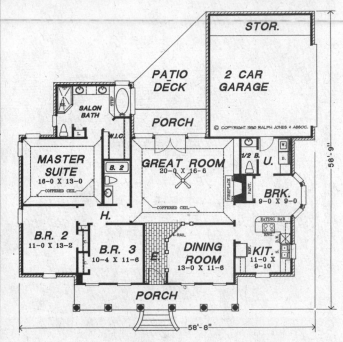

Special features

- Open formal entry with columns access dining area and great room
- Kitchen has eating bar overlooking the bayed breakfast room with separate laundry room and half bath
- Master bath has step-up tub with windows on two sides, separate shower and huge walk-in closet
- 3 bedrooms, 2 1/2 baths, 2-car side entry garage with storage
- Slab or crawl space foundation, please specify when ordering

Cozy Single-Story Home

Plan #710-041D-0004

1,195 total square feet of living area

Price Code AA

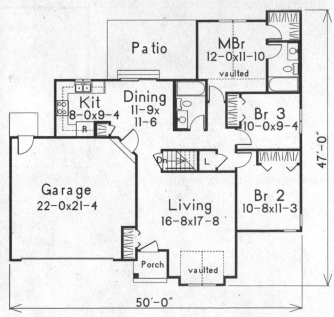

Special features

- Dining room opens onto the patio
- Master bedroom features vaulted ceiling, private bath and walk-in closet
- Coat closets located by both the entrances
- Convenient secondary entrance at the back of the garage
- 3 bedrooms, 2 baths, 2-car garage
- Basement foundation

COVERED REAR PORCH

Plan #710-039D-0001

1,253 total square feet of living area

Price Code A

Special features

- Sloped ceiling and fireplace in family room add drama
- U-shaped kitchen is efficiently designed
- Large walk-in closets are found in all the bedrooms
- 3 bedrooms, 2 baths, 2-car garage
- Crawl space or slab foundation, please specify when ordering

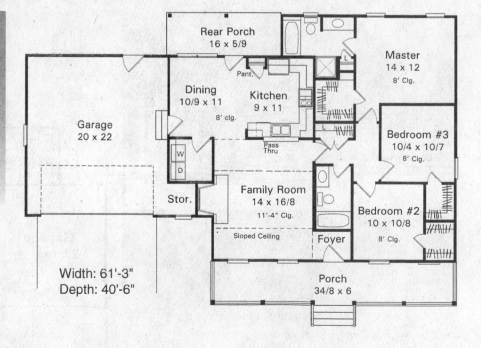

Rear Porch
16 x 5/9

Pant.

Dining
10/9 x 11
8' clg.

Kitchen
9 x 11

Pass Thru

Master
14 x 12
8' Clg.

Bedroom #3
10/4 x 10/7
8' Clg.

Garage
20 x 22

W
D

Stor.

Family Room
14 x 16/8
11'-4" Clg.

Sloped Ceiling

Foyer

Bedroom #2
10 x 10/8
8' Clg.

Width: 61'-3"
Depth: 40'-6"

Porch
34/8 x 6

Open Living Space

Plan #710-001D-0041

1,000 total square feet of living area

Price Code AA

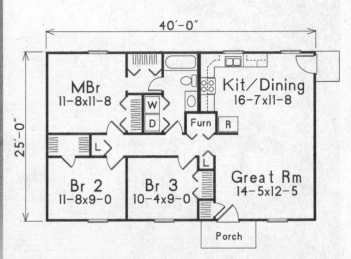

40'-0"

25'-0"

MBr
11-8x11-8

W
D

L

Kit/Dining
16-7x11-8

Furn R

Br 2
11-8x9-0

Br 3
10-4x9-0

L

Great Rm
14-5x12-5

Porch

Special features

- Bath includes convenient closeted laundry area
- Master bedroom includes double closets and private access to bath
- Foyer features handy coat closet
- L-shaped kitchen provides easy access outdoors
- 3 bedrooms, 1 bath
- Crawl space foundation, drawings also include basement and slab foundations

Stone Accents The Front Facade

Plan #710-032D-0025

2,089 total square feet of living area

Price Code C

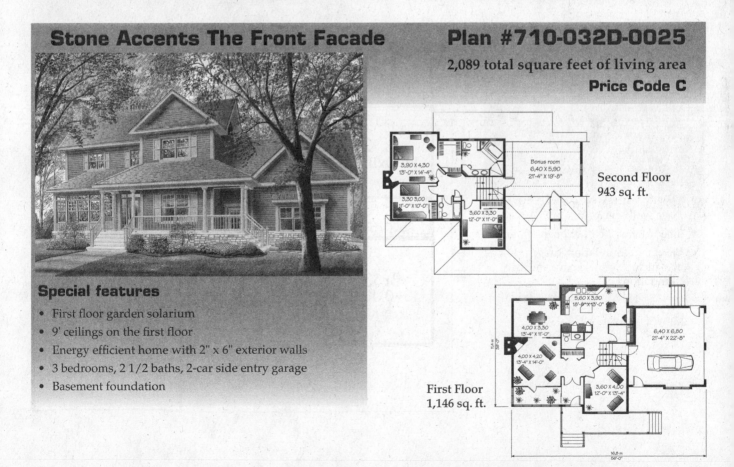

3,90 X 4,30
13'-0" X 14'-4"

3,30 3,00
11'-0" X 10'-0"

3,60 X 3,30
12'-0" X 11'-0"

Bonus room
6,40 X 5,90
21'-4" X 19'-8"

Second Floor
943 sq. ft.

5,60 X 3,90
18'-9" X 13'-0"

4,00 X 3,30
13'-4" X 11'-0"

4,00 X 4,20
13'-4" X 14'-0"

3,60 X 4,00
12'-0" X 13'-4"

6,40 X 6,80
21'-4" X 22'-8"

First Floor
1,146 sq. ft.

Special features

- First floor garden solarium
- 9' ceilings on the first floor
- Energy efficient home with 2" x 6" exterior walls
- 3 bedrooms, 2 1/2 baths, 2-car side entry garage
- Basement foundation

Spacious Living In This Ranch

Plan #710-068D-0005

1,433 total square feet of living area

Price Code A

Special features

- Vaulted living room includes cozy fireplace and an oversized entertainment center
- Bedrooms #2 and #3 share a full bath
- Master bedroom has a full bath and large walk-in closet
- 3 bedrooms, 2 baths, 2-car garage
- Basement foundation, drawings also include crawl space and slab foundations

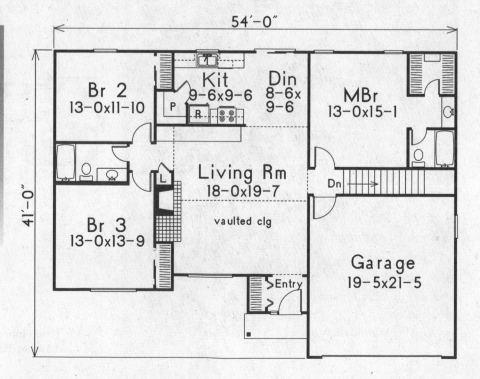

54'-0"

41'-0"

Br 2
13-0x11-10

Kit
9-6x9-6

Din
8-6x
9-6

MBr
13-0x15-1

P

R

Living Rm
18-0x19-7

Dn

vaulted clg

Br 3
13-0x13-9

L

Entry

Garage
19-5x21-5

Exterior Boasts Exciting Interior

Plan #710-007D-0004

2,531 total square feet of living area

Price Code D

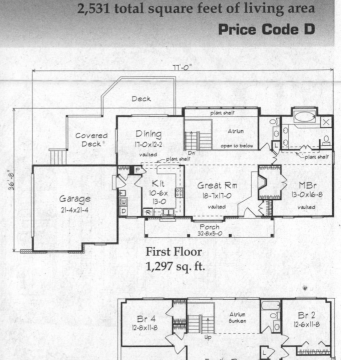

First Floor
1,297 sq. ft.

Lower Level
1,234 sq. ft.

Special features

- Charming porch with dormers leads into vaulted great room with atrium
- Well-designed kitchen and breakfast bar adjoin extra large laundry/mud room
- Double sinks, tub with window above and plant shelf complete vaulted master bath
- 4 bedrooms, 2 1/2 baths, 2-car side entry garage
- Walk-out basement foundation

Convenient Wet Bar

Plan #710-026D-0122

1,850 total square feet of living area

Price Code C

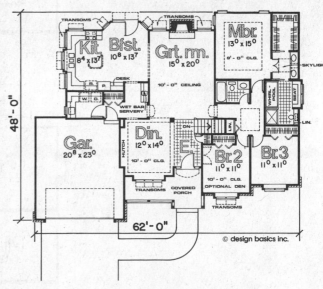

© design basics inc.

Special features

- Oversized rooms throughout
- Great room spotlights fireplace with sunny windows on both sides
- Master bedroom has private skylighted bath
- Interesting wet bar between kitchen and dining area is an added bonus when entertaining
- 3 bedrooms, 2 baths, 2-car garage
- Basement foundation

TO ORDER BLUEPRINTS USE THE FORM ON PAGE 15 OR CALL TOLL-FREE 1-877-671-6036
View thousands more home plans online at www.familyhandyman.com/homeplans

255

GRAND CURVED STAIRWAY

Plan #710-001D-0038

3,144 total square feet of living area

Price Code E

Special features

- 9' ceilings on first floor
- Kitchen offers large pantry, island cooktop and close proximity to laundry and dining rooms
- Expansive family room includes wet bar, fireplace and attractive bay window
- 4 bedrooms, 4 1/2 baths, 3-car side entry garage
- Basement foundation

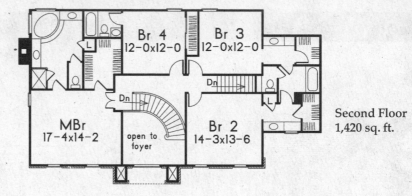

Second Floor
1,420 sq. ft.

Br 4
12-0x12-0

Br 3
12-0x12-0

MBr
17-4x14-2

open to foyer

Br 2
14-3x13-6

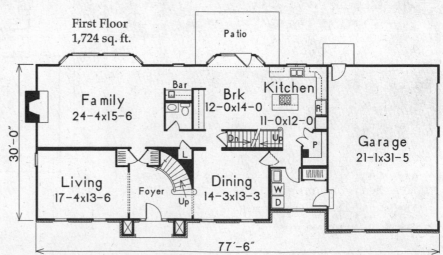

First Floor
1,724 sq. ft.

Patio

Family
24-4x15-6

Bar

Brk
12-0x14-0

Kitchen
11-0x12-0

Garage
21-1x31-5

Living
17-4x13-6

Foyer

Dining
14-3x13-3

30'-0"

77'-6"

Luxurious Bay-Shaped Master Bath   Plan #710-047D-0051

2,962 total square feet of living area

Price Code E

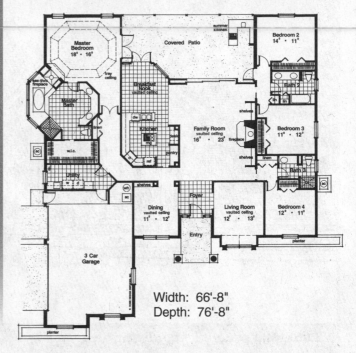

Width: 66'-8"
Depth: 76'-8"

Special features

- Vaulted breakfast nook is adjacent to the kitchen for convenience
- Bedroom #4 is an ideal guest suite with private bath
- Master bedroom includes see-through fireplace, bayed vanity and massive walk-in closet
- 4 bedrooms, 3 baths, 3-car side entry garage
- Slab foundation

Elaborate Stonework Adds Charm   Plan #710-031D-0016

2,560 total square feet of living area

Price Code D

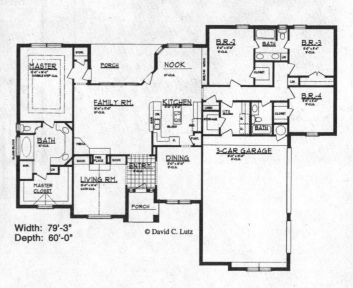

Width: 79'-3"
Depth: 60'-0"

© David C. Lutz

Special features

- See-through fireplace surrounded with shelving warms both family and living rooms
- Tall ceilings in living areas
- Bedrooms maintain privacy
- 4 bedrooms, 3 baths, 3-car side entry garage
- Slab foundation

TO ORDER BLUEPRINTS USE THE FORM ON PAGE 15 OR CALL TOLL-FREE 1-877-671-6036
View thousands more home plans online at www.familyhandyman.com/homeplans

257

Covered Patio For Outdoor Dining — Plan #710-036D-0040

2,061 total square feet of living area

Price Code C

Special features

- Charming stone facade entry
- Centrally located great room
- Private study in the front of the home is ideal as a home office
- Varied ceiling heights throughout this home
- 3 bedrooms, 2 1/2 baths, 2-car garage
- Crawl space or slab foundation, please specify when ordering

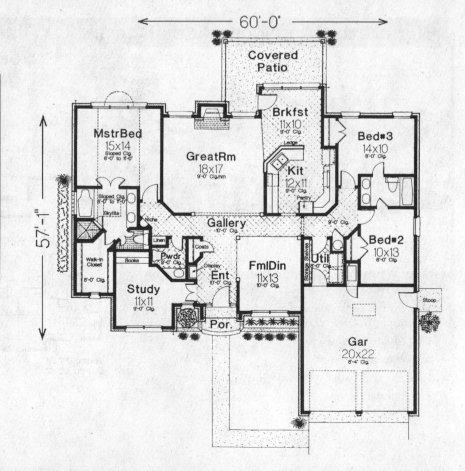

Corner Fireplace In Grand Room

Plan #710-056D-0009

1,606 total square feet of living area

Price Code B

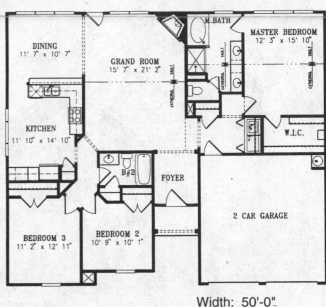

Special features

- Kitchen has snack bar which overlooks dining area for convenience
- Master bedroom has lots of windows with a private bath and large walk-in closet
- Cathedral vault in great room adds spaciousness
- 3 bedrooms, 2 baths, 2-car garage
- Slab foundation

Width: 50'-0"
Depth: 42'-0"

Traditional Ranch With Extras

Plan #710-038D-0039

1,771 total square feet of living area

Price Code B

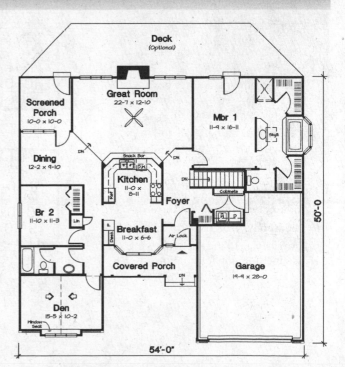

Special features

- Den has a sloped ceiling and charming window seat
- Private master bedroom has access to the outdoors
- Central kitchen allows for convenient access when entertaining
- 2 bedrooms, 2 baths, 2-car garage
- Basement, crawl space or slab foundation, please specify when ordering

TO ORDER BLUEPRINTS USE THE FORM ON PAGE 15 OR CALL TOLL-FREE 1-877-671-6036
View thousands more home plans online at www.familyhandyman.com/homeplans

259

CENTRAL Fireplace

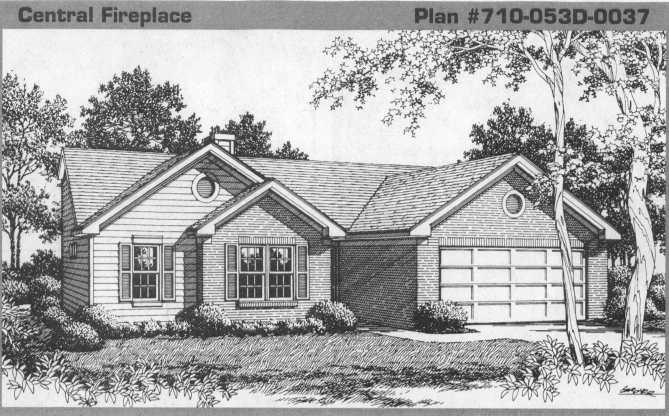

1,408 total square feet of living area

Price Code A

Special features

- Handsome see-through fireplace offers a gathering point for the family room, breakfast area and kitchen
- Vaulted ceiling and large bay window in the master bedroom add charm to this room
- A dramatic angular wall and large windows add brightness to the kitchen and breakfast area
- Kitchen, breakfast and family rooms have vaulted ceilings, adding to this central living area
- 3 bedrooms, 2 baths, 2-car garage
- Crawl space foundation, drawings also include slab foundation

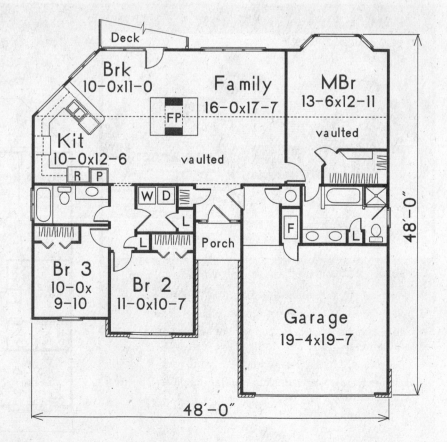

Deck

Brk
10-0x11-0

Family
16-0x17-7

MBr
13-6x12-11

vaulted

FP

Kit
10-0x12-6

vaulted

R P

W D

L

L

Porch

F

L

Br 3
10-0x
9-10

Br 2
11-0x10-7

Garage
19-4x19-7

48'-0"

48'-0"

Full-Length Front Porch

Plan #710-024D-0004

1,500 total square feet of living area

Price Code B

Special features

- Living room features corner fireplace adding warmth
- Master bedroom has all the amenities like walk-in closet, private bath and porch access
- Sunny bayed breakfast room is cheerful and bright
- 3 bedrooms, 2 baths, 2-car garage
- Slab foundation

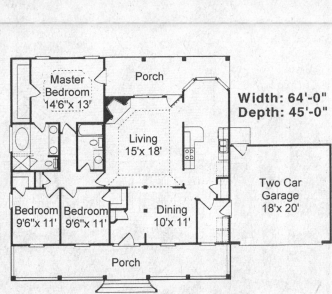

Width: 64'-0"
Depth: 45'-0"

Master Bedroom 14'6"x 13'
Porch
Living 15'x 18'
Two Car Garage 18'x 20'
Bedroom 9'6"x 11'
Bedroom 9'6"x 11'
Dining 10'x 11'
Porch

Scalloped Front Porch

Plan #710-030D-0001

1,374 total square feet of living area

Price Code A

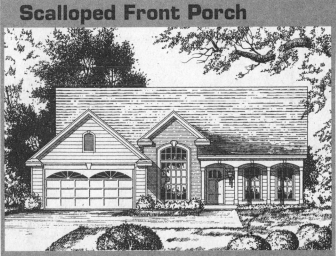

Special features

- Garage has extra storage space
- Spacious living room has fireplace
- Well-designed kitchen with adjacent breakfast nook
- Separated master suite maintains privacy
- 3 bedrooms, 2 baths, 2-car garage
- Slab or crawl space foundation, please specify when ordering

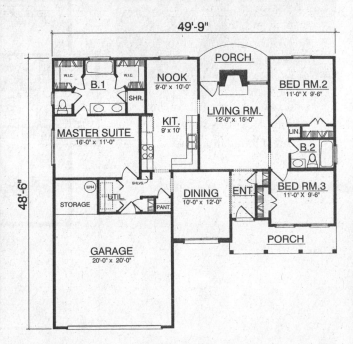

49'-9"
48'-6"

B.1
W.I.C.
W.I.C.
SHR.
NOOK 9'-0" x 10'-0"
PORCH
BED RM.2 11'-0" X 9'-6"
LIVING RM. 12'-0" x 15'-0"
MASTER SUITE 16'-0" x 11'-0"
KIT. 9' x 10'
LIN.
B.2
STORAGE
UTIL.
SHLVS.
DINING 10'-0" x 12'-0"
ENT.
PANT.
BED RM.3 11'-0" X 9'-6"
GARAGE 20'-0" x 20'-0"
PORCH

TO ORDER BLUEPRINTS USE THE FORM ON PAGE 15 OR CALL TOLL-FREE 1-877-671-6036
View thousands more home plans online at www.familyhandyman.com/homeplans

261

Spacious Country Ranch

Plan #710-051D-0056

1,806 total square feet of living area

Price Code C

Special features

- Two additional bedrooms share a full bath and linen closet
- Kitchen has direct access to the dining room and nook areas
- Large great room has vaulted ceiling, centered fireplace and large windows to let in plenty of light
- 3 bedrooms, 2 baths, 2-car garage
- Basement foundation

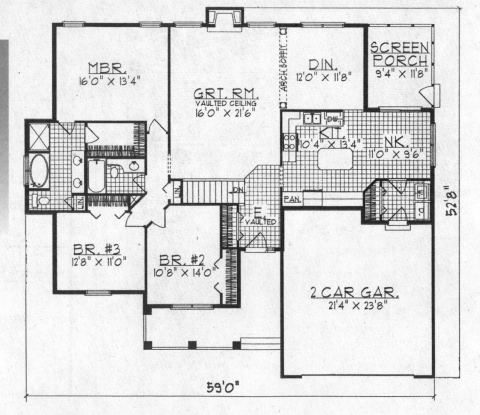

Dramatic Expanse Of Windows

Plan #710-017D-0010

1,660 total square feet of living area

Price Code C

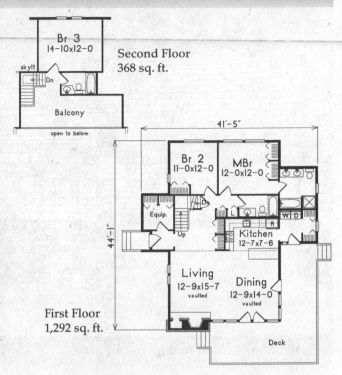

Br 3
14-10x12-0

Second Floor
368 sq. ft.

skylt

Dn

Balcony

open to below

41'-5"

Br 2
11-0x12-0

MBr
12-0x12-0

44'-1"

Equip.

Up

L

W D

R

Kitchen
12-7x7-6

Living
12-9x15-7
vaulted

Dining
12-9x14-0
vaulted

First Floor
1,292 sq. ft.

Deck

Special features

- Convenient gear and equipment room
- Spacious living and dining rooms look even larger with the openness of the foyer and kitchen
- Large wrap-around deck is a great plus for outdoor living
- Broad balcony overlooks living and dining rooms
- 3 bedrooms, 3 baths
- Partial basement/crawl space foundation, drawings also include slab foundation

Stately Covered Front Entry

Plan #710-048D-0008

2,089 total square feet of living area

Price Code C

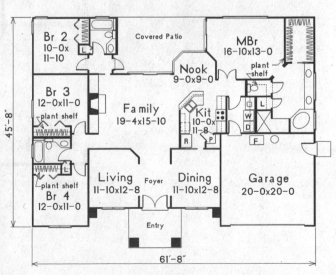

Br 2
10-0x
11-10

L

Covered Patio

MBr
16-10x13-0

plant
shelf

Nook
9-0x9-0

Br 3
12-0x11-0

plant shelf

Family
19-4x15-10

Kit
10-0x
11-8

W D

L

R

P

F

45'-8"

plant shelf

Br 4
12-0x11-0

Living
11-10x12-8

Foyer

Dining
11-10x12-8

Garage
20-0x20-0

Entry

61'-8"

Special features

- Family room features fireplace, built-in bookshelves and triple sliders opening to covered patio
- Kitchen overlooks family room and has pantry and desk
- Separated from the three secondary bedrooms, the master bedroom becomes a quiet retreat with patio access
- Master bedroom features an oversized bath with walk-in closet and corner tub
- 4 bedrooms, 3 baths, 2-car garage
- Slab foundation

TO ORDER BLUEPRINTS USE THE FORM ON PAGE 15 OR CALL TOLL-FREE 1-877-671-6036
View thousands more home plans online at www.familyhandyman.com/homeplans

263

Vaults Add Spaciousness — Plan #710-062D-0050

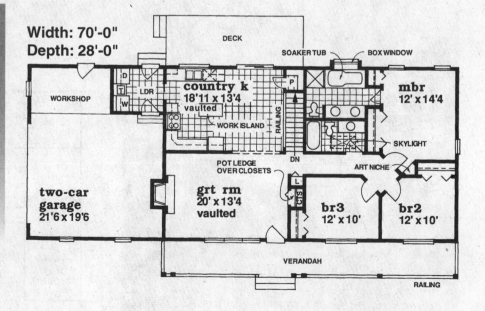

1,408 total square feet of living area

Price Code A

Special features

- A bright country kitchen boasts an abundance of counterspace and cupboards
- The front entry is sheltered by a broad verandah
- A spa tub is brightened by a box bay window in the master bath
- 3 bedrooms, 2 baths, 2-car side entry garage
- Basement or crawl space foundation, please specify when ordering

Width: 70'-0"
Depth: 28'-0"

DECK

SOAKER TUB | BOX WINDOW

WORKSHOP

D T W | LDR

country k 18'11 x 13'4 vaulted

WORK ISLAND

RAILING | P

mbr 12' x 14'4

SKYLIGHT

ART NICHE

POT LEDGE OVER CLOSETS

DN

two-car garage 21'6 x 19'6

grt rm 20' x 13'4 vaulted

L CTS

br3 12' x 10'

br2 12' x 10'

VERANDAH

RAILING

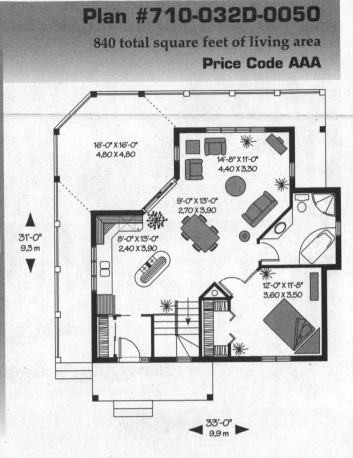

Casual Open Living

Plan #710-032D-0050

840 total square feet of living area

Price Code AAA

Special features

- Energy efficient home with 2" x 6" exterior walls
- Prominent gazebo located in the rear of the home for superb outdoor living
- Enormous bath has a corner oversized tub
- Lots of windows create a cheerful and sunny atmosphere throughout this home
- 1 bedroom, 1 bath
- Walk-out basement foundation

16'-0" X 16'-0"
4,80 X 4,80

14'-8" X 11'-0"
4,40 X 3,30

9'-0" X 13'-0"
2,70 X 3,90

8'-0" X 13'-0"
2,40 X 3,90

12'-0" X 11'-8"
3,60 X 3,50

31'-0"
9,3 m

33'-0"
9,9 m

Surprisingly Spacious

Plan #710-034D-0013

1,493 total square feet of living area

Price Code A

Special features

- First floor master bedroom maintains privacy
- Dining and great rooms have a feeling of spaciousness with two-story high ceilings
- Utilities are conveniently located near garage entrance
- 3 bedrooms, 2 1/2 baths, 2-car garage
- Basement foundation

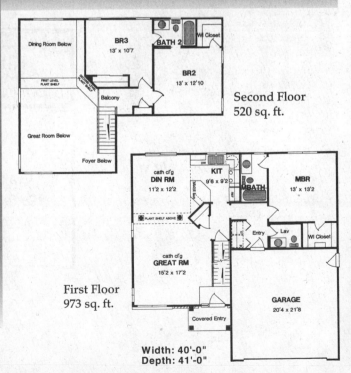

Dining Room Below

BR3
13' x 10'7

BATH 2

W/ Closet

FIRST LEVEL PLANT SHELF

Balcony

BR2
13' x 12'10

Great Room Below

Foyer Below

Second Floor
520 sq. ft.

cath cl'g
DIN RM
11'2 x 12'2

KIT
9'6 x 9'2

MBATH

MBR
13' x 13'2

PLANT SHELF ABOVE

Entry

Lav

W/ Closet

cath cl'g
GREAT RM
15'2 x 17'2

GARAGE
20'4 x 21'8

Covered Entry

First Floor
973 sq. ft.

Width: 40'-0"
Depth: 41'-0"

Vaulted Ceilings

Plan #710-014D-0008

1,135 total square feet of living area

Price Code AA

Special features

- Living and dining rooms feature vaulted ceilings and a corner fireplace
- Energy efficient home with 2" x 6" exterior walls
- Master bedroom offers a vaulted ceiling, private bath and generous closet space
- Compact but functional kitchen complete with pantry and adjacent utility room
- 3 bedrooms, 2 baths, 2-car garage
- Basement foundation, drawings also include crawl space foundation

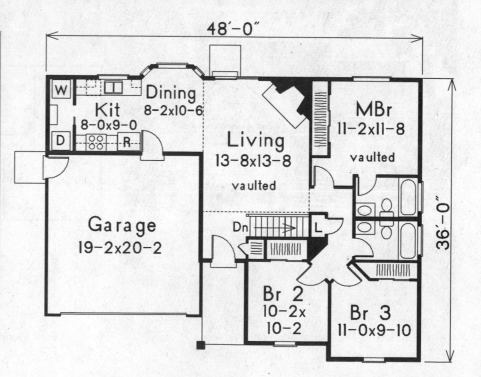

48'-0"

36'-0"

W

Kit
8-0x9-0

D

R

Dining
8-2x10-6

Living
13-8x13-8
vaulted

MBr
11-2x11-8
vaulted

Garage
19-2x20-2

Dn

L

Br 2
10-2x10-2

Br 3
11-0x9-10

10' Ceilings

Special features

- Comfortable traditional has all the amenities of a larger plan in a compact layout
- Angled eating bar separates kitchen and great room while leaving these areas open to one another for entertaining
- 3 bedrooms, 2 baths, 2-car garage
- Crawl space or slab foundation, please specify when ordering

Plan #710-019D-0009

1,862 total square feet of living area

Price Code C

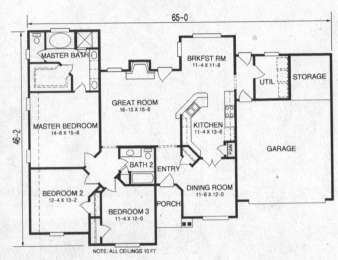

Cozy Corner Patio

Special features

- Box window and inviting porch with dormers create a charming facade
- Eat-in kitchen offers a pass-through breakfast bar, corner window wall to patio, pantry and convenient laundry with half bath
- Master bedroom features double entry doors and walk-in closet
- 3 bedrooms, 1 1/2 baths, 1-car garage
- Basement foundation

Plan #710-007D-0031

1,092 total square feet of living area

Price Code AA

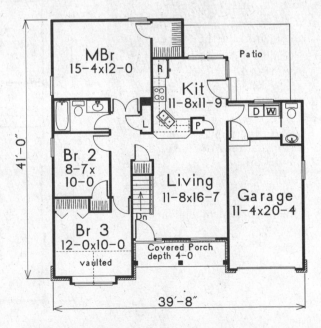

TO ORDER BLUEPRINTS USE THE FORM ON PAGE 15 OR CALL TOLL-FREE 1-877-671-6036
View thousands more home plans online at www.familyhandyman.com/homeplans

267

Appealing Gabled Front Facade   Plan #710-058D-0017

2,412 total square feet of living area

Price Code D

Special features

- Coffered ceiling in dining room adds character and spaciousness
- Great room enhanced by vaulted ceiling and an atrium window wall
- Spacious well-planned kitchen includes counterspace dining and overlooks breakfast room and beyond to deck
- Luxurious master bedroom features enormous walk-in closet, private bath and easy access to laundry area
- 4 bedrooms, 2 baths, 3-car side entry garage
- Walk-out basement foundation

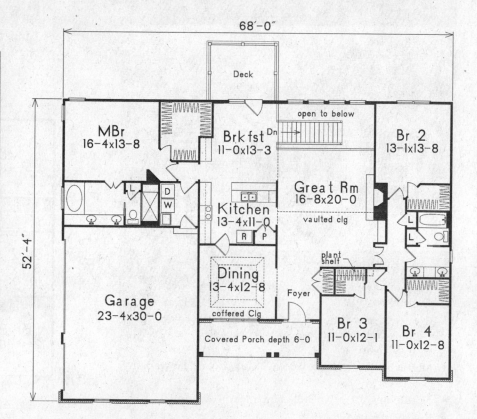

268

TO ORDER BLUEPRINTS USE THE FORM ON PAGE 15 OR CALL TOLL-FREE 1-877-671-6036
View thousands more home plans online at www.familyhandyman.com/homeplans

Porch Adds Farmhouse Style

Plan #710-016D-0049

1,793 total square feet of living area

Price Code B

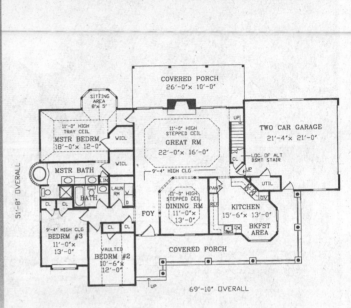

Special features

- Beautiful foyer leads into the great room that has a fireplace flanked by two sets of beautifully transomed doors both leading to a large covered porch
- Kitchen has an abundance of cabinets and workspace
- Delightful master bedroom has many amenities
- Optional bonus room above the garage has an additional 779 square feet of living area
- 3 bedrooms, 2 baths, 2-car side entry garage
- Basement, crawl space or slab foundation, please specify when ordering

Compact And Charming

Plan #710-021D-0008

1,266 total square feet of living area

Price Code A

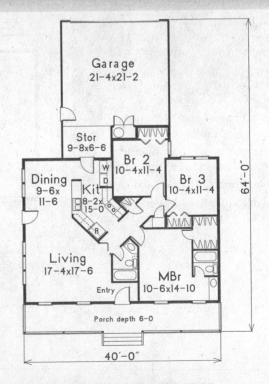

Special features

- Narrow frontage is perfect for small lots
- Energy efficient home with 2" x 6" exterior walls
- Prominent central hall connects all main rooms
- Design incorporates full-size master bedroom complete with dressing room, bath and walk-in closet
- Angled kitchen includes handy laundry facilities
- 3 bedrooms, 2 baths, 2-car rear entry garage
- Crawl space foundation, drawings also include slab foundation

Distinctive Turret

Plan #710-018D-0006

1,742 total square feet of living area

Price Code B

Special features

- Efficient kitchen combines with breakfast area and great room creating a spacious living area
- Master bedroom includes private bath with huge walk-in closet, shower and corner tub
- Great room boasts a fireplace and access outdoors
- Laundry room conveniently located near kitchen and garage
- 3 bedrooms, 2 baths, 2-car garage
- Slab foundation, drawings also include crawl space foundation

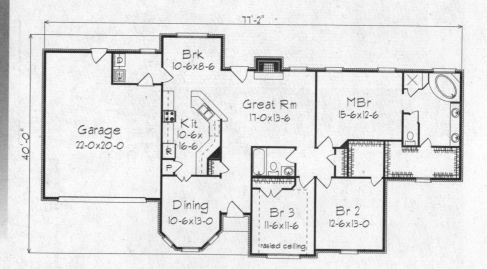

Kitchen Designed For Efficiency

Plan #710-047D-0036

2,140 total square feet of living area

Price Code C

Special features

- Living and dining areas traditionally separated by foyer
- Media wall and fireplace are located in cozy family room
- Generous master suite has sliding glass doors onto patio, walk-in closet and a private bath
- 4 bedrooms, 3 baths, 2-car side entry garage
- Slab foundation

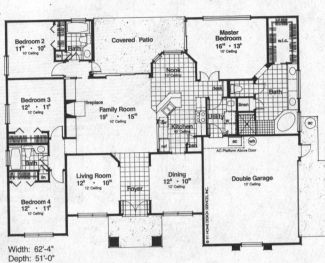

Width: 62'-4"
Depth: 51'-0"

Open Layout Ensures Easy Living

Plan #710-045D-0012

976 total square feet of living area

Price Code AA

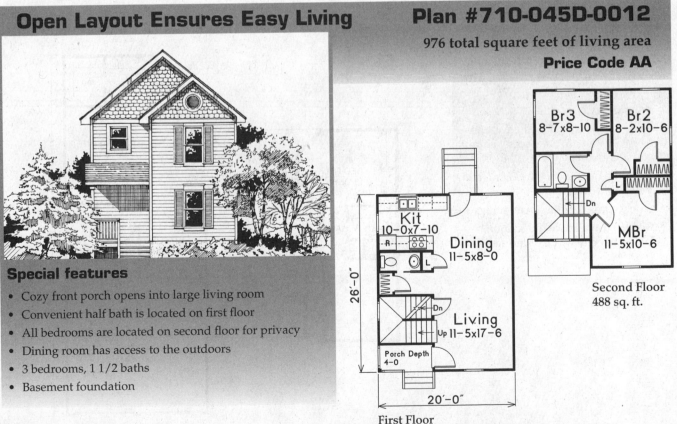

Special features

- Cozy front porch opens into large living room
- Convenient half bath is located on first floor
- All bedrooms are located on second floor for privacy
- Dining room has access to the outdoors
- 3 bedrooms, 1 1/2 baths
- Basement foundation

Second Floor
488 sq. ft.

First Floor
488 sq. ft.

TO ORDER BLUEPRINTS USE THE FORM ON PAGE 15 OR CALL TOLL-FREE 1-877-671-6036
View thousands more home plans online at www.familyhandyman.com/homeplans

271

The Family **Handyman**

CENTRAL Living Room

Plan #710-020D-0003

1,420 total square feet of living area

Price Code A

Special features

- Energy efficient home with 2" x 6" exterior walls
- Living room has 12' ceiling, corner fireplace and atrium doors leading to covered porch
- Separate master suite has garden bath and walk-in closet
- 3 bedrooms, 2 baths, 2-car garage
- Slab or crawl space foundation, please specify when ordering

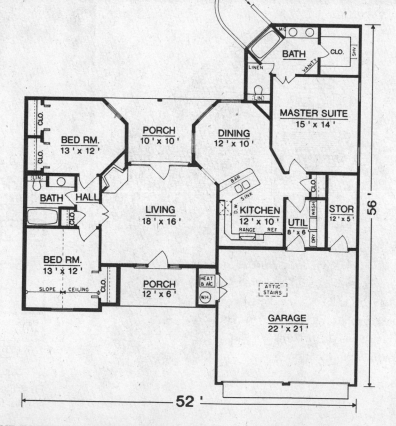

A GREAT COUNTRY FARMHOUSE

Plan #710-049

1,669 total square feet of living area

Price Code B

Special features

- Generous use of windows add exciting visual elements to the exterior as well as plenty of natural light to the interior
- Two-story great room has a raised hearth
- Second floor loft/study would easily make a terrific home office
- 3 bedrooms, 2 baths
- Crawl space foundation

Second Floor
576 sq. ft.

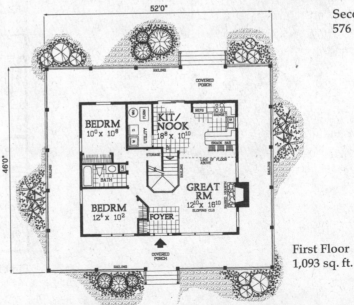

First Floor
1,093 sq. ft.

TO ORDER BLUEPRINTS USE THE FORM ON PAGE 15 OR CALL TOLL-FREE 1-877-671-6036
View thousands more home plans online at www.familyhandyman.com/homeplans

273

1,039 total square feet of living area

Price Code AA

Special features

- Cathedral construction provides the maximum in living area openness
- Expansive glass viewing walls
- Two decks, front and back
- Charming second story loft arrangement
- Simple, low-maintenance construction
- 2 bedrooms, 1 1/2 baths
- Crawl space foundation

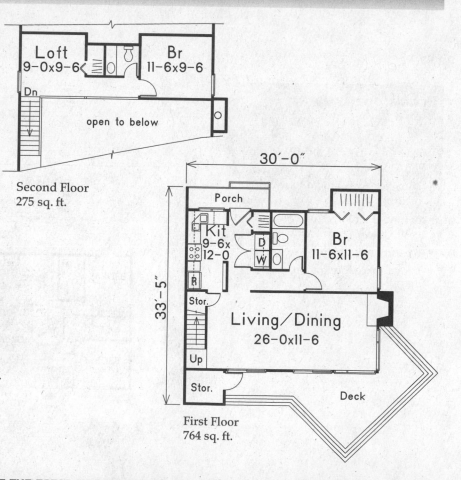

Loft 9-0x9-6

Br 11-6x9-6

Dn

open to below

Second Floor
275 sq. ft.

30'-0"

33'-5"

Porch

Kit 9-6x 12-0

R

Stor.

Up

Stor.

Br 11-6x11-6

Living/Dining 26-0x11-6

Deck

First Floor
764 sq. ft.

COUNTRY Home With Plenty Of Style   Plan #710-040D-0033

1,829 total square feet of living area

Price Code C

Special features

- Entry foyer with coat closet opens to large family room with fireplace
- Two second floor bedrooms share a full bath
- Optional bedroom #4 on second floor can be finished as your family grows
- Cozy porch provides convenient side entrance into home
- 3 bedrooms, 2 1/2 baths, 2-car side entry garage
- Partial basement/crawl space foundation

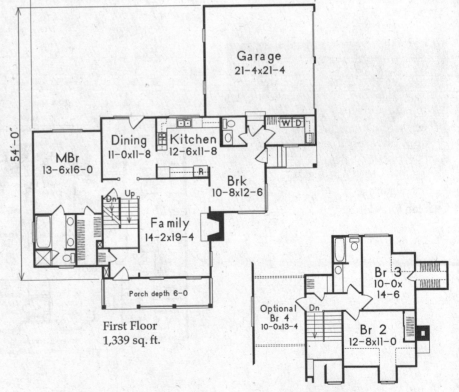

56'-8"

54'-0"

Garage
21-4x21-4

Dining
11-0x11-8

Kitchen
12-6x11-8

W D

MBr
13-6x16-0

Brk
10-8x12-6

Dn   Up

Family
14-2x19-4

Porch depth 6-0

First Floor
1,339 sq. ft.

Br 3
10-0x
14-6

Optional
Br 4
10-0x13-4

Dn

Br 2
12-8x11-0

Second Floor
490 sq. ft.

TO ORDER BLUEPRINTS USE THE FORM ON PAGE 15 OR CALL TOLL-FREE 1-877-671-6036
View thousands more home plans online at www.familyhandyman.com/homeplans

275

Double Bays Accent Front
Plan #710-036D-0058

2,529 total square feet of living area

Price Code D

Special features

- Kitchen and breakfast area are located between the family and living rooms for easy access
- Master bedroom includes sitting area, private bath and access to covered patio
- 4 bedrooms, 3 baths, 3-car side entry garage
- Slab foundation

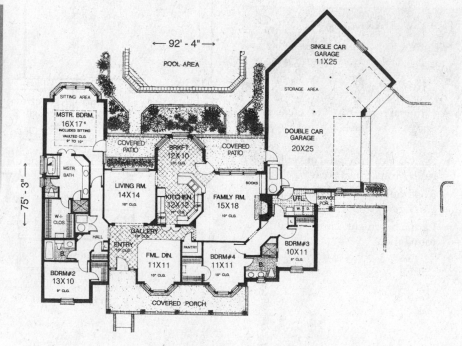

Quiet Retreat In Parlor

Plan #710-047D-0058

3,436 total square feet of living area

Price Code F

Special features

- Unique angled rooms create an exciting feel
- Well-organized kitchen with island is adjacent to family room
- Beautiful sculptured ceilings in master suite
- Guest house is ideal as an in-law suite or secluded home office
- Bonus room on the second floor is included in the square footage
- 4 bedrooms, 4 baths, 2-car and 1-car garage
- Slab foundation

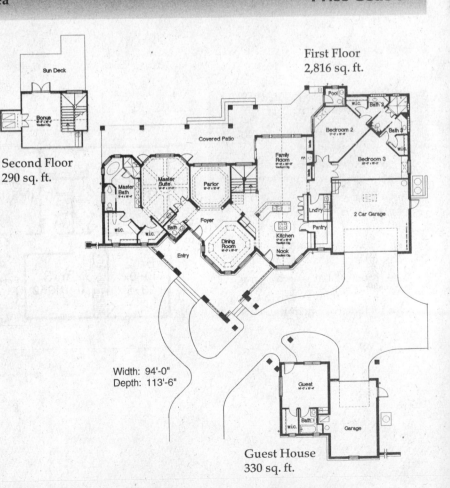

First Floor
2,816 sq. ft.

Second Floor
290 sq. ft.

Width: 94'-0"
Depth: 113'-6"

Guest House
330 sq. ft.

TO ORDER BLUEPRINTS USE THE FORM ON PAGE 15 OR CALL TOLL-FREE 1-877-671-6036
View thousands more home plans online at www.familyhandyman.com/homeplans

277

Roomy Ranch For Easy Living   Plan #710-001D-0023

1,343 total square feet of living area

Price Code A

Special features

- Separate and convenient family and living/dining areas
- Nice-sized master bedroom suite with large closet and private bath
- Foyer with convenient coat closet opens into combined living and dining rooms
- Kitchen has access to the outdoors through sliding glass doors
- 3 bedrooms, 2 baths, 2-car garage
- Crawl space foundation, drawings also include basement foundation

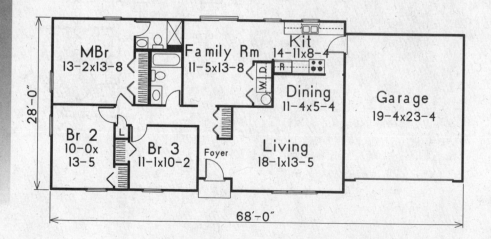

MBr 13-2x13-8

Family Rm 11-5x13-8

Kit 14-11x8-4

Dining 11-4x5-4

Garage 19-4x23-4

Br 2 10-0x13-5

Br 3 11-1x10-2

Foyer

Living 18-1x13-5

28'-0"

68'-0"

Double Atrium Embraces The Sun — Plan #710-007D-0056

3,199 total square feet of living area

Price Code E

Special features

- Grand scale kitchen features bay-shaped cabinetry built over atrium that overlooks two-story window wall
- A second atrium dominates the master bedroom which boasts a sitting area with bay window as well as a luxurious bath which has a whirlpool tub open to the garden atrium and lower level study
- 3 bedrooms, 2 1/2 baths, 3-car side entry garage
- Walk-out basement foundation

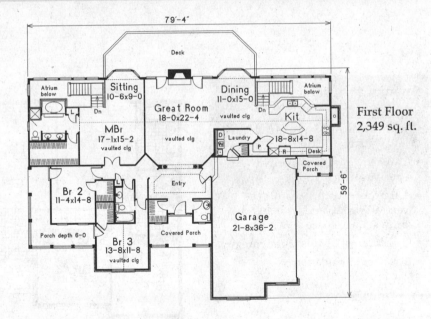

First Floor
2,349 sq. ft.

79'-4"

59'-6"

Deck
Atrium below
Sitting 10-6x9-0
Great Room 18-0x22-4 vaulted clg
Dining 11-0x15-0 vaulted clg
Atrium below
Kit 18-8x14-8
MBr 17-1x15-2 vaulted clg
Laundry
Desk
Covered Porch
Br 2 11-4x14-8
Entry
Porch depth 6-0
Br 3 13-8x11-8 vaulted clg
Covered Porch
Garage 21-8x36-2

Rear View

Lower Level
850 sq. ft.

Study 16-7x21-4
Unfinished Basement
Family Room 18-4x19-4

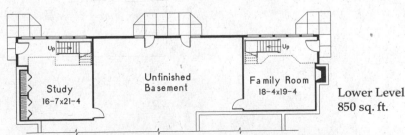

TO ORDER BLUEPRINTS USE THE FORM ON PAGE 15 OR CALL TOLL-FREE 1-877-671-6036
View thousands more home plans online at www.familyhandyman.com/homeplans

279

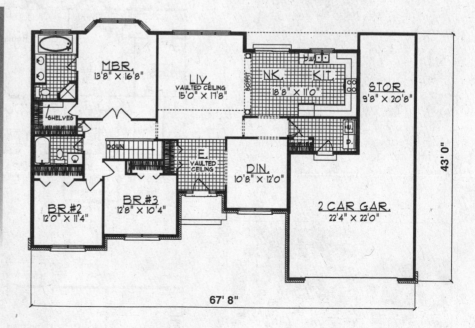

The Family Handyman

Triple Tandem Garage

Plan #710-051D-0013

1,763 total square feet of living area

Price Code B

Special features

- Master suite features a private master bath and bay-shaped sitting area with French doors
- Large foyer leads to a bright spacious living room
- Large open kitchen features a central work island with lots of extra storage space
- 3 bedrooms, 2 baths, 2-car garage
- Basement foundation

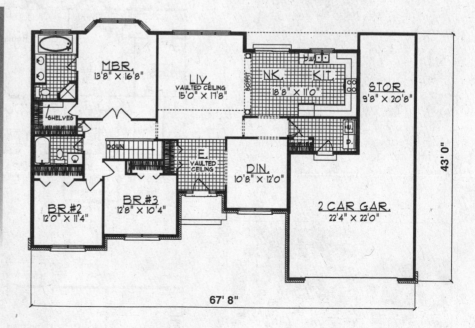

Circle-Top Windows

Plan #710-021D-0012

1,672 total square feet of living area

Price Code C

Special features

- Vaulted master bedroom features walk-in closet and adjoining bath with separate tub and shower
- Energy efficient home with 2" x 6" exterior walls
- Covered front and rear porches
- 12' ceilings in living room, kitchen and bedroom #2
- Kitchen complete with pantry, angled bar and adjacent eating area
- Sloped ceiling in dining room
- 3 bedrooms, 2 baths, 2-car side entry garage
- Crawl space foundation, drawings also include basement and slab foundations

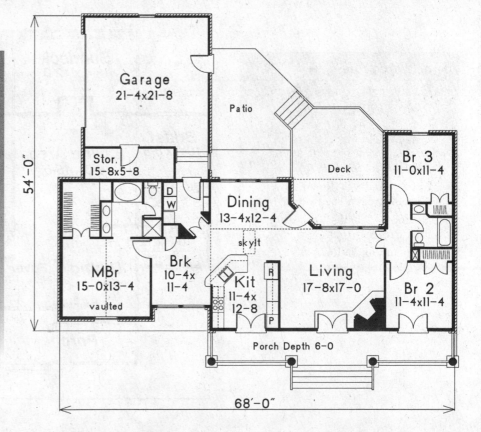

Scalloped Porch Cornice Adds Flair   Plan #710-052D-0036

1,772 total square feet of living area

Price Code B

Special features

- Dramatic palladian window and scalloped porch are attention grabbers
- Island kitchen sink allows for easy access and views into the living and breakfast areas
- Washer and dryer closet easily accessible from all bedrooms
- 3 bedrooms, 2 baths, 3-car drive under garage
- Basement foundation

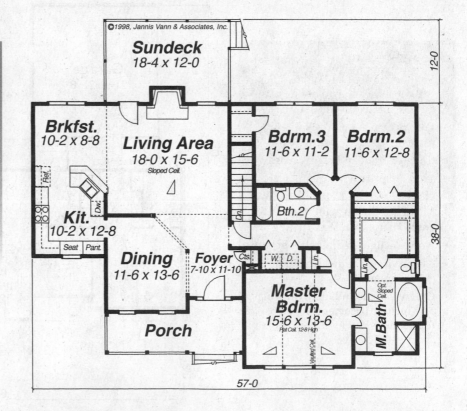

©1998, Jannis Vann & Associates, Inc.

Sundeck 18-4 x 12-0

Brkfst. 10-2 x 8-8

Living Area 18-0 x 15-6 Sloped Ceil.

Bdrm.3 11-6 x 11-2

Bdrm.2 11-6 x 12-8

Kit. 10-2 x 12-8

Seat Pant.

Bth.2

Dining 11-6 x 13-6

Foyer 7-10 x 11-10

W.D.

Master Bdrm. 15-6 x 13-6 Flat Ceil. 12-8 High

M. Bath

Opt. Sloped Ceil.

Porch

12-0

38-0

57-0

282

TO ORDER BLUEPRINTS USE THE FORM ON PAGE 15 OR CALL TOLL-FREE 1-877-671-6036
View thousands more home plans online at www.familyhandyman.com/homeplans

Vaulted Ceilings Add Dimension — Plan #710-003D-0002

1,676 total square feet of living area

Price Code B

Special features

- The living area skylights and large breakfast room with bay window provide plenty of sunlight
- The master bedroom has a walk-in closet and both the secondary bedrooms have large closets
- Vaulted ceilings, plant shelving and a fireplace provide a quality living area
- 3 bedrooms, 2 baths, 2-car garage
- Basement foundation, drawings also include crawl space and slab foundations

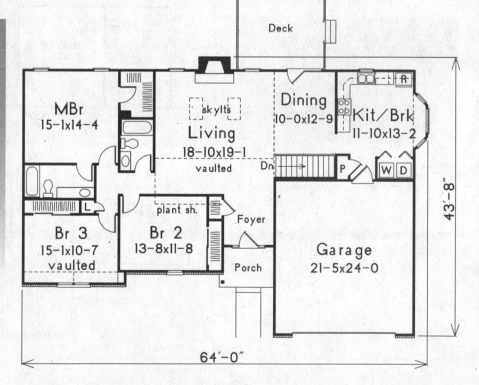

TO ORDER BLUEPRINTS USE THE FORM ON PAGE 15 OR CALL TOLL-FREE 1-877-671-6036
View thousands more home plans online at www.familyhandyman.com/homeplans

283

The Family Handyman

Garage With Two Storage Areas — Plan #710-060D-0008

2,281 total square feet of living area

© Copyright MCMXCVIII – Ralph Jones

Price Code D

Special features

- Formal dining room features coffered ceilings
- Great room with fireplace and coffered ceiling overlooks covered back porch
- Kitchen with angled eating bar adjoins angled morning room with bay window
- Salon bath has double walk-in closets and vanities, step-up tub and separate shower
- 3 bedrooms, 2 baths, 2-car side entry garage
- Slab or crawl space foundation, please specify when ordering

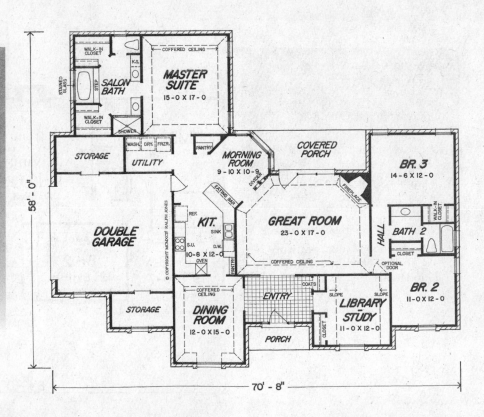

Handyman

1,674 total square feet of living area   **Price Code B**

Special features

- Vaulted great room, dining area and kitchen all enjoy central fireplace and log bin
- Convenient laundry/mud room located between garage and family area with handy stairs to basement
- Easily expandable screened porch and adjacent patio with access from dining area
- Master bedroom features full bath with tub, separate shower and walk-in closet
- 3 bedrooms, 2 baths, 2-car garage
- Basement foundation, drawings also include crawl space and slab foundations

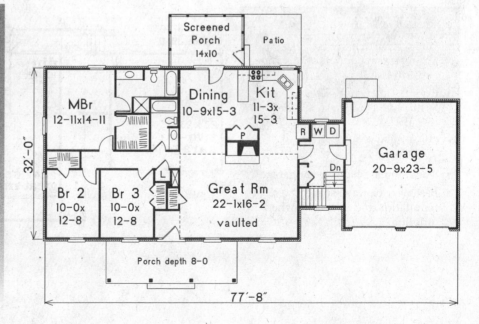

TO ORDER BLUEPRINTS USE THE FORM ON PAGE 15 OR CALL TOLL-FREE 1-877-671-6036
View thousands more home plans online at www.familyhandyman.com/homeplans

285

Spacious Wrap-Around Porch — Plan #710-062D-0041

1,541 total square feet of living area

Price Code B

Special features

- Dining area offers access to a screened porch for outdoor dining and entertaining
- Country kitchen features a center island and a breakfast bay for casual meals
- Great room is warmed by a woodstove
- 3 bedrooms, 2 baths, 2-car garage
- Basement or crawl space foundation, please specify when ordering

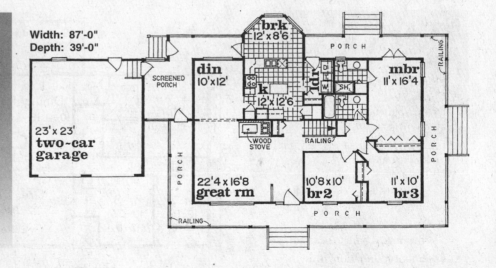

Width: 87'-0"
Depth: 39'-0"

SCREENED PORCH

23' x 23' **two-car garage**

PORCH

din 10'x12'

k 12'x12'6

brk 12'x8'6

WOOD STOVE

RAILING

PORCH

mbr 11'x16'4

RAILING

PORCH

great rm 22'4 x 16'8

br2 10'8 x 10'

br3 11'x 10'

RAILING

PORCH

1,127 total square feet of living area   **Price Code AA**

Special features

- Plant shelf joins kitchen and dining room
- Vaulted master bedroom has double walk-in closets, deck access and private bath
- Great room features vaulted ceiling, fireplace and sliding doors to covered deck
- Ideal home for a narrow lot
- 2 bedrooms, 2 baths, 2-car garage
- Basement foundation

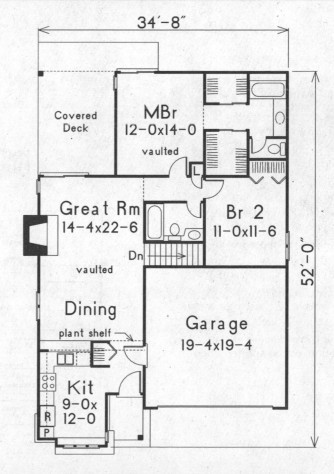

TO ORDER BLUEPRINTS USE THE FORM ON PAGE 15 OR CALL TOLL-FREE 1-877-671-6036
View thousands more home plans online at www.familyhandyman.com/homeplans

287

Unique Octagon-Shaped Porch   Plan #710-038D-0045

2,044 total square feet of living area   **Price Code C**

Special features

- Formal dining area easily accesses kitchen through double-doors
- Two-car garage features a workshop area for projects or extra storage
- Second floor includes loft space ideal for office area and a handy computer center
- Colossal master bedroom with double walk-in closets and a private bath with a bay window seat
- 3 bedrooms, 2 1/2 baths, 2-car side entry garage
- Basement, crawl space or slab foundation, please specify when ordering

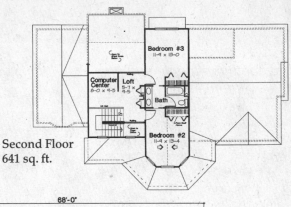

Second Floor
641 sq. ft.

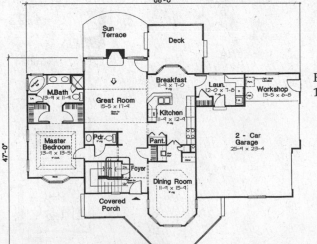

First Floor
1,403 sq. ft.

Design Features Home Office

Plan #710-007D-0008

2,452 total square feet of living area

Price Code D

Special features

- Cheery and spacious home office room with private entrance and bath, two closets, vaulted ceiling and transomed window perfect shown as a home office or a fourth bedroom
- Delightful great room with vaulted ceiling, fireplace, extra storage closets and patio doors to sundeck
- Extra-large kitchen features walk-in pantry, cooktop island and bay window
- Vaulted master bedroom includes transomed windows, walk-in closet and luxurious bath
- 4 bedrooms, 2 1/2 baths, 3-car garage
- Basement foundation

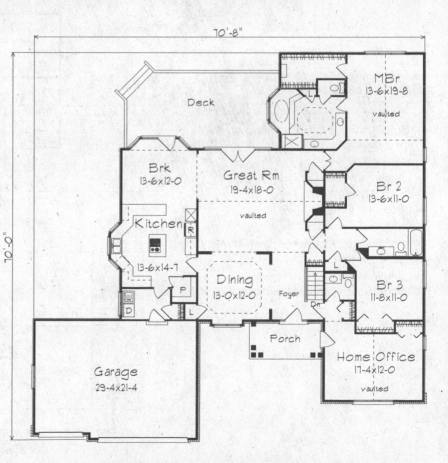

Attractive Full-Length Porch

Plan #710-023D-0006

2,357 total square feet of living area

Price Code D

Special features

- 9' ceilings on the first floor
- Secluded master bedroom includes private bath with double walk-in closets and vanity
- Balcony overlooks living room with large fireplace
- Second floor has three bedrooms and an expansive game room
- 4 bedrooms, 3 1/2 baths, 2-car side entry garage
- Slab foundation, drawings also include crawl space foundation

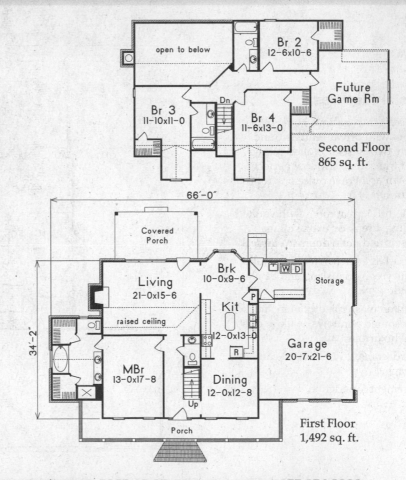

open to below

Br 2
12-6x10-6

Br 3
11-10x11-0

Dn

Br 4
11-6x13-0

Future
Game Rm

Second Floor
865 sq. ft.

66'-0"

Covered
Porch

34'-2"

Living
21-0x15-6

Brk
10-0x9-6

W D

Storage

raised ceiling

Kit
12-0x13-0

P

R

Garage
20-7x21-6

MBr
13-0x17-8

Dining
12-0x12-8

Up

Porch

First Floor
1,492 sq. ft.

Small Home Is Remarkably Spacious   Plan #710-007D-0042

914 total square feet of living area

Price Code AA

Special features

- Large porch for leisure evenings
- Dining area with bay window, open stair and pass-through kitchen creates openness
- Basement includes generous garage space, storage area, finished laundry and mechanical room
- 2 bedrooms, 1 bath, 2-car drive under garage
- Basement foundation

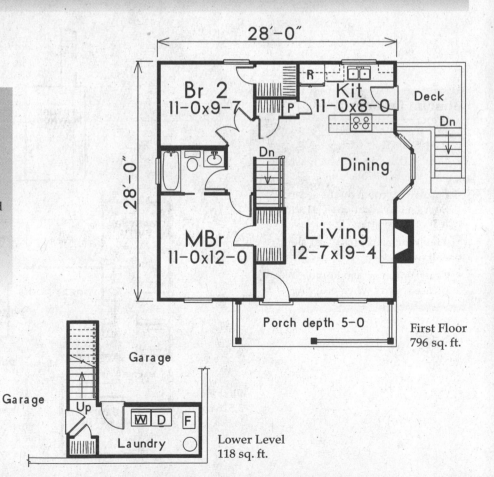

28'-0"

28'-0"

Br 2
11-0x9-7

Kit
11-0x8-0

Deck

Dn

Dn

Dining

MBr
11-0x12-0

Living
12-7x19-4

Porch depth 5-0

First Floor
796 sq. ft.

Garage

Garage

Up

W D F

Laundry

Lower Level
118 sq. ft.

TO ORDER BLUEPRINTS USE THE FORM ON PAGE 15 OR CALL TOLL-FREE 1-877-671-6036
View thousands more home plans online at www.familyhandyman.com/homeplans

291

Great Curb Appeal With Gables — Plan #710-025D-0048

2,526 total square feet of living area

Price Code D

Special features

- Sunroom brightens dining areas near kitchen
- Corner whirlpool tub in master bath is a luxurious touch
- Future playroom on the second floor has an additional 341 square feet of living area
- 4 bedrooms, 3 baths, 2-car side entry garage
- Crawl space or slab foundation, please specify when ordering

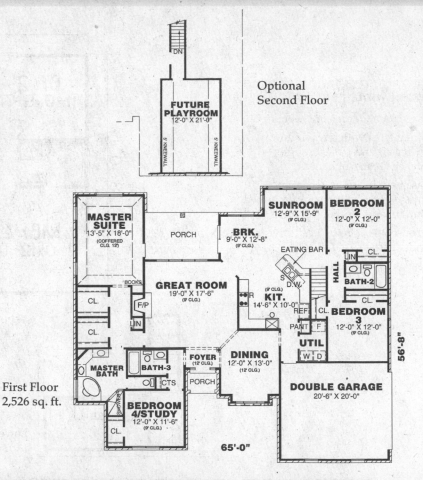

Optional Second Floor

First Floor
2,526 sq. ft.

292

TO ORDER BLUEPRINTS USE THE FORM ON PAGE 15 OR CALL TOLL-FREE 1-877-671-6036
View thousands more home plans online at www.familyhandyman.com/homeplans

Sophisticated Southern Style   Plan #710-011D-0042

2,561 total square feet of living area   **Price Code F**

Special features

- Sunny vaulted breakfast nook
- Dormers are a charming touch in the second floor bedrooms
- Columns throughout the first floor help separate rooms while creating a feeling of openness
- Bonus room on the second floor has an additional 232 square feet of living area
- 4 bedrooms, 2 1/2 baths, 2-car side entry garage
- Crawl space foundation

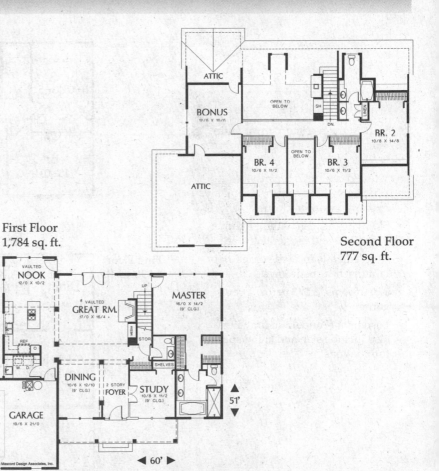

First Floor
1,784 sq. ft.

Second Floor
777 sq. ft.

©Alan Mascord Design Associates, Inc.

TO ORDER BLUEPRINTS USE THE FORM ON PAGE 15 OR CALL TOLL-FREE 1-877-671-6036
View thousands more home plans online at www.familyhandyman.com/homeplans

293

2,058 total square feet of living area   **Price Code C**

Special features

- Handsome two-story foyer with balcony creates a spacious entrance area
- Vaulted ceiling in the master bedroom with private dressing area and large walk-in closet
- Skylights furnish natural lighting in the hall and master bath
- Conveniently located second floor laundry near bedrooms
- 3 bedrooms, 2 1/2 baths, 2-car garage
- Basement foundation, drawings also include slab and crawl space foundations

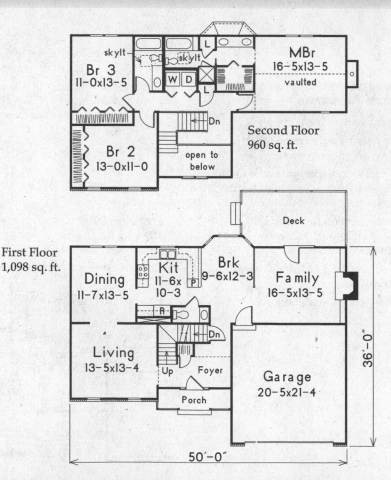

Br 3
11-0x13-5

MBr
16-5x13-5
vaulted

Br 2
13-0x11-0

Second Floor
960 sq. ft.

First Floor
1,098 sq. ft.

Dining
11-7x13-5

Kit
11-6x
10-3

Brk
9-6x12-3

Family
16-5x13-5

Deck

Living
13-5x13-4

Foyer

Garage
20-5x21-4

Porch

36'-0"

50'-0"

Spacious Country Home   Plan #710-028D-0011

2,123 total square feet of living area

Price Code C

Special features

- L-shaped porch extends the entire length of this home creating lots of extra space for outdoor living
- Master bedroom is secluded for privacy and has two closets, double vanity in bath and a double-door entry onto covered porch
- Efficiently designed kitchen
- 3 bedrooms, 2 1/2 baths
- Crawl space foundation

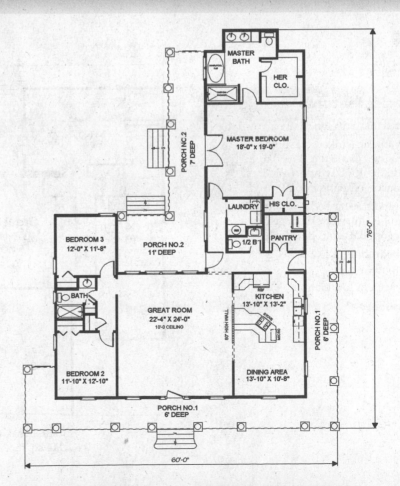

TO ORDER BLUEPRINTS USE THE FORM ON PAGE 15 OR CALL TOLL-FREE 1-877-671-6036
View thousands more home plans online at www.familyhandyman.com/homeplans

295

The Family Handyman

Symmetrical Great Room

Plan #710-007D-0014

1,985 total square feet of living area

Price Code C

Special features

- Charming design for a narrow lot
- Dramatic sunken great room features vaulted ceiling, large double-hung windows and transomed patio doors
- Grand master bedroom includes double entry doors, large closet, elegant bath and patio access
- 4 bedrooms, 3 1/2 baths, 2-car garage
- Basement foundation

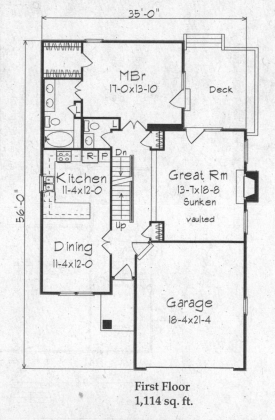

35'-0"

56'-0"

MBr
17-0x13-10

Deck

Dn

Kitchen
11-4x12-0

Up

R   P

Dining
11-4x12-0

Great Rm
13-7x18-8
Sunken

vaulted

Garage
18-4x21-4

First Floor
1,114 sq. ft.

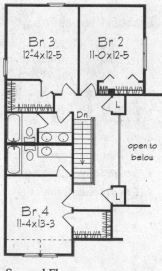

Br 3
12-4x12-5

Br 2
11-0x12-5

Dn

open to below

Br 4
11-4x13-3

Second Floor
871 sq. ft.

296

TO ORDER BLUEPRINTS USE THE FORM ON PAGE 15 OR CALL TOLL-FREE 1-877-671-6036
View thousands more home plans online at www.familyhandyman.com/homeplans

Floridian Architecture

Plan #710-007D-0066

2,408 total square feet of living area

Price Code D

Special features

- Large vaulted great room overlooks atrium and window wall, adjoins dining room, spacious breakfast room with bay and pass-through kitchen

- A special private bedroom with bath, separate from other bedrooms, is perfect for mother-in-law suite or children home from college

- Atrium opens to 1,100 square feet of optional living area below

- 4 bedrooms, 3 baths, 3-car side entry garage

- Walk-out basement foundation

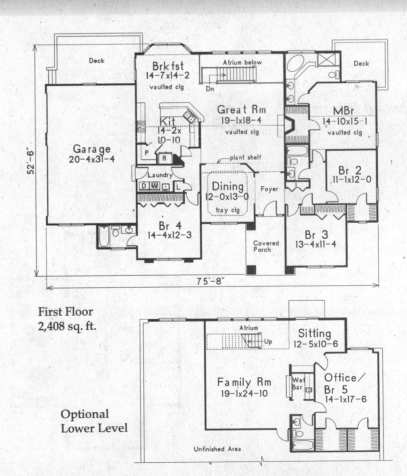

First Floor
2,408 sq. ft.

Optional
Lower Level

TO ORDER BLUEPRINTS USE THE FORM ON PAGE 15 OR CALL TOLL-FREE 1-877-671-6036
View thousands more home plans online at www.familyhandyman.com/homeplans

297

COVERED PORCH ADDS APPEAL

Plan #710-032D-0040

1,480 total square feet of living area

Price Code A

Special features

- Energy efficient home with 2" x 6" exterior walls
- Cathedral ceilings in family and dining rooms
- Master bedroom has a walk-in closet and access to bath
- 2 bedrooms, 2 baths
- Basement foundation

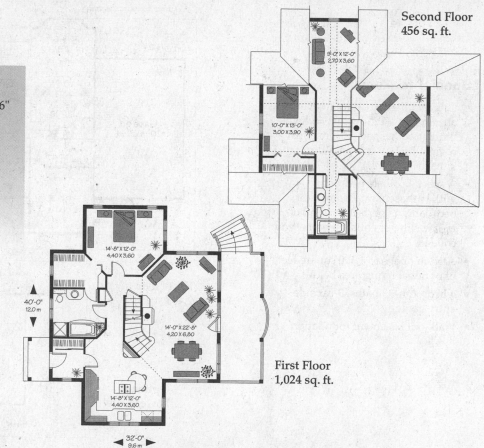

Second Floor
456 sq. ft.

First Floor
1,024 sq. ft.

TO ORDER BLUEPRINTS USE THE FORM ON PAGE 15 OR CALL TOLL-FREE 1-877-671-6036

View thousands more home plans online at www.familyhandyman.com/homeplans

Home Made For Country Living   Plan #710-062D-0051

1,578 total square feet of living area   **Price Code B**

Special features

- A fireplace warms the great room and is flanked by windows overlooking the rear deck
- Bedrooms are clustered on one side of the home for privacy from living areas
- Master bedroom has unique art niche at its entry and a private bath with separate tub and shower
- 3 bedrooms, 2 baths, 2-car side entry garage
- Basement or crawl space foundation, please specify when ordering

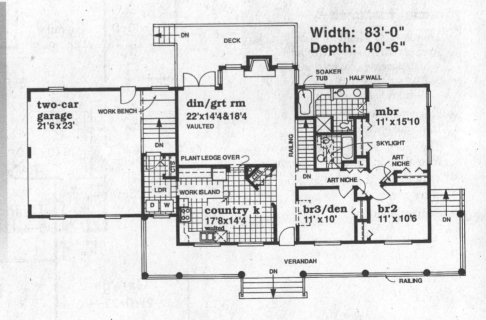

Width: 83'-0"
Depth: 40'-6"

TO ORDER BLUEPRINTS USE THE FORM ON PAGE 15 OR CALL TOLL-FREE 1-877-671-6036
View thousands more home plans online at www.familyhandyman.com/homeplans

299

Impressive Master Suite

Plan #710-048D-0005

2,287 total square feet of living area

Price Code E

Special features

- Double-doors lead into an impressive master bedroom which accesses covered porch and features deluxe bath with double closets and step-up tub
- Kitchen easily serves formal and informal areas of home
- The spacious foyer opens into formal dining and living rooms
- 4 bedrooms, 2 1/2 baths, 2-car side entry garage
- Slab foundation

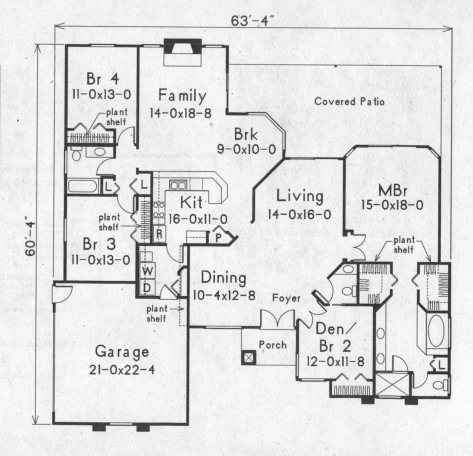

Compact Home For Functional Living   Plan #710-053D-002

1,220 total square feet of living area

Price Code A

Special features

- Vaulted ceilings add luxury to the living room and master bedroom
- Spacious living room is accented with a large fireplace and hearth
- Gracious dining area is adjacent to the convenient wrap-around kitchen
- Washer and dryer is handy to the bedrooms
- Covered porch entry adds appeal
- Rear deck adjoins dining area
- 3 bedrooms, 2 baths, 2-car drive under garage
- Basement foundation

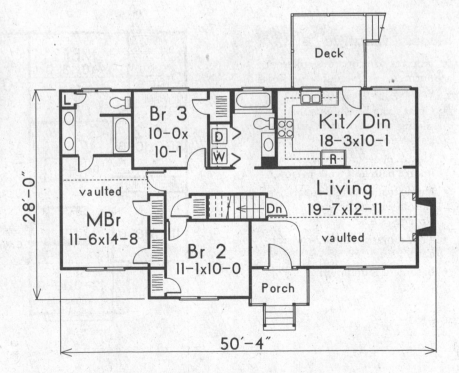

TO ORDER BLUEPRINTS USE THE FORM ON PAGE 15 OR CALL TOLL-FREE 1-877-671-6036
View thousands more home plans online at www.familyhandyman.com/homeplans

301

1,761 total square feet of living area

Price Code B

Special features

- Exterior window dressing, roof dormers and planter boxes provide visual warmth and charm
- Great room boasts a vaulted ceiling, fireplace and opens to a pass-through kitchen
- Master bedroom is vaulted with luxury bath and walk-in closet
- Home features eight separate closets with an abundance of storage
- 4 bedrooms, 2 baths, 2-car side entry garage
- Basement foundation

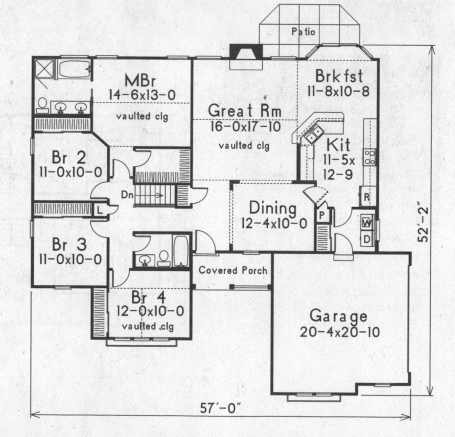

Ranch With Traditional Feel   Plan #710-056D-0007

© 2003, Garrell Associates, Inc.

1,985 total square feet of living area   **Price Code G**

Special features

- 9' ceilings throughout home
- Master suite has direct access into sunroom
- Sunny breakfast room features bay window
- Bonus room on the second floor has an additional 191 square feet of living area
- 3 bedrooms, 3 baths, 2-car side entry garage
- Slab foundation

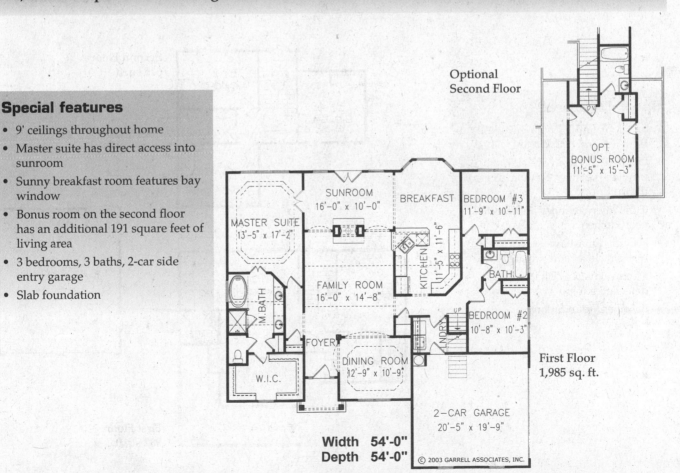

Optional Second Floor

OPT. BONUS ROOM 11'-5" x 15'-3"

SUNROOM 16'-0" x 10'-0"

BREAKFAST

BEDROOM #3 11'-9" x 10'-11"

MASTER SUITE 13'-5" x 17'-2"

KITCHEN 11'-5" x 11'-6"

BATH

FAMILY ROOM 16'-0" x 14'-8"

M.BATH

BEDROOM #2 10'-8" x 10'-3"

FOYER

DINING ROOM 12'-9" x 10'-9"

W.I.C.

First Floor 1,985 sq. ft.

2-CAR GARAGE 20'-5" x 19'-9"

Width 54'-0"
Depth 54'-0"

© 2003 GARRELL ASSOCIATES, INC.

TO ORDER BLUEPRINTS USE THE FORM ON PAGE 15 OR CALL TOLL-FREE 1-877-671-6036
View thousands more home plans online at www.familyhandyman.com/homeplans

303

Country-Style Wrap-Around Porch   Plan #710-040D-0027

1,597 total square feet of living area

Price Code C

Special features

- Spacious family room includes fireplace and coat closet
- Open kitchen and dining room provide breakfast bar and access to the outdoors
- Convenient laundry area located near kitchen
- Secluded master bedroom with walk-in closet and private bath
- 4 bedrooms, 2 1/2 baths, 2-car detached garage
- Basement foundation

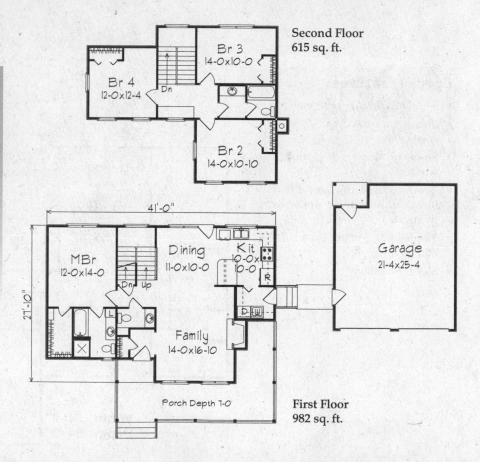

Second Floor
615 sq. ft.

Br 3
14-0x10-0

Br 4
12-0x12-4

Br 2
14-0x10-10

41'-0"

MBr
12-0x14-0

Dining
11-0x10-0

Kit
10-0x10-0

27'-10"

Family
14-0x16-10

Garage
21-4x25-4

Porch Depth 1-0

First Floor
982 sq. ft.

Secluded Master Bedroom   Plan #710-058D-0026

1,819 total square feet of living area   **Price Code C**

Special features

- Master bedroom features access to the outdoors, large walk-in closet and private bath
- 9' ceilings throughout
- Formal foyer with coat closet opens into vaulted great room with fireplace and formal dining room
- Kitchen and breakfast room create a cozy and casual area
- 3 bedrooms, 2 baths, 2-car side entry garage
- Basement foundation

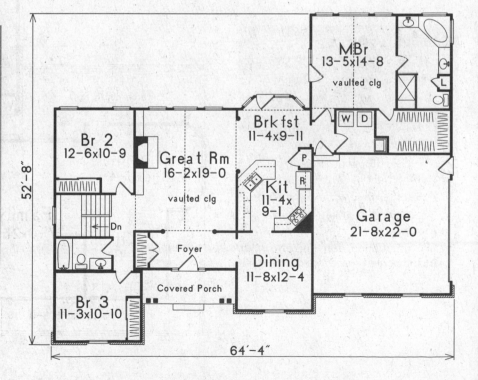

TO ORDER BLUEPRINTS USE THE FORM ON PAGE 15 OR CALL TOLL-FREE 1-877-671-6036
View thousands more home plans online at www.familyhandyman.com/homeplans

305

Old-Fashioned Comfort And Privacy   Plan #710-037D-0006

1,772 total square feet of living area   Price Code C

Special features

- Extended porches in front and rear provide a charming touch
- Large bay windows lend distinction to dining room and bedroom #3
- Efficient U-shaped kitchen
- Master bedroom includes two walk-in closets
- Full corner fireplace in family room
- 3 bedrooms, 2 baths, 2-car detached garage
- Slab foundation, drawings also include crawl space foundation

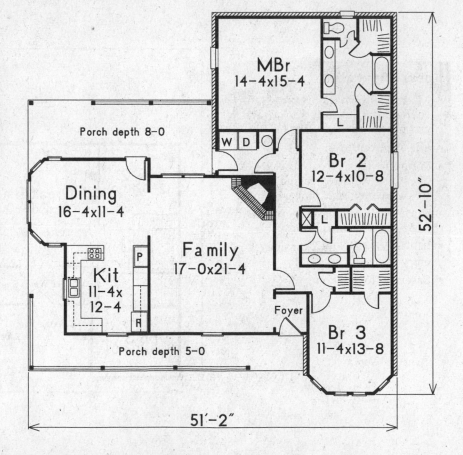

Porch depth 8-0

MBr
14-4x15-4

W D

Dining
16-4x11-4

Br 2
12-4x10-8

L

Kit
11-4x
12-4

P

Family
17-0x21-4

R

Foyer

Br 3
11-4x13-8

Porch depth 5-0

52'-10"

51'-2"

Handyman The Family

Fireplace Warms Great Room   Plan #710-036D-0057

2,578 total square feet of living area

Price Code D

Special features

- Enormous entry has an airy feel with gallery area nearby
- Living room with bay window is tucked away from traffic areas
- Large kitchen and breakfast area both access covered patio
- Great room has entertainment center, fireplace and cathedral ceiling
- 4 bedrooms, 3 1/2 baths, 3-car side entry garage
- Slab foundation

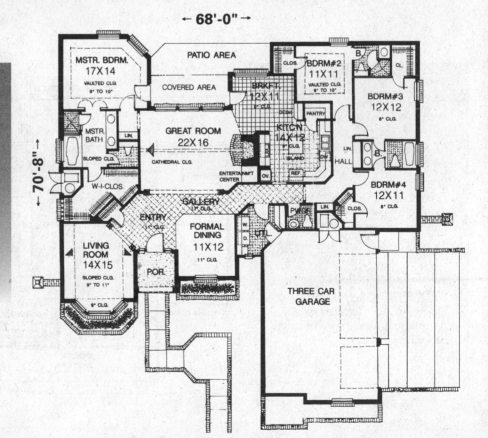

TO ORDER BLUEPRINTS USE THE FORM ON PAGE 15 OR CALL TOLL-FREE 1-877-671-6036
View thousands more home plans online at www.familyhandyman.com/homeplans

307

Spacious Country Kitchen

Plan #710-013D-0027

2,184 total square feet of living area

Price Code C

Special features

- Delightful family room has access to the screened porch for enjoyable outdoor living
- Secluded master suite is complete with a sitting area and luxurious bath
- Formal living room has double-door entry easily converting it to a study or home office
- Two secondary bedrooms share a full bath
- 3 bedrooms, 3 baths, 2-car side entry garage
- Basement, crawl space or slab foundation, please specify when ordering

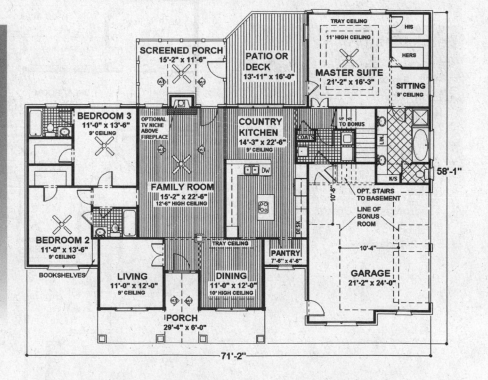

Bayed Breakfast Room

Plan #710-035D-0048

1,915 total square feet of living area

Price Code C

Special features

- Large breakfast area overlooks vaulted great room
- Master suite has cheerful sitting room and a private bath
- Plan features unique in-law suite with private bath and walk-in closet
- 4 bedrooms, 3 baths, 2-car garage
- Walk-out basement, slab or crawl space foundation, please specify when ordering

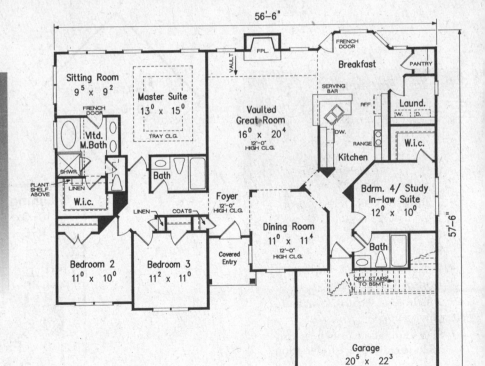

56'-6"

Sitting Room
9⁵ x 9²

Master Suite
13⁰ x 15⁰
TRAY CLG.

FPL.

VAULT

FRENCH DOOR

Breakfast

PANTRY

SERVING BAR

Vaulted Great Room
16⁰ x 20⁴
12'-0" HIGH CLG.

Laund.
W. D.

W.i.c.

FRENCH DOOR

Vltd. M.Bath

Bath

Kitchen

RANGE

DW.

REF.

PLANT SHELF ABOVE

SHWR.

LINEN

W.i.c.

LINEN

COATS

Foyer
12'-0" HIGH CLG.

Dining Room
11⁰ x 11⁴
12'-0" HIGH CLG.

Bdrm. 4/ Study In-law Suite
12⁰ x 10⁰

Bath

Covered Entry

Bedroom 2
11⁰ x 10⁰

Bedroom 3
11² x 11⁰

OPT. STAIRS TO BSMT.

57'-6"

Garage
20⁵ x 22³

copyright © 1997 frank betz associates, inc.

GARAGE LOCATION WITH BASEMENT

TO ORDER BLUEPRINTS USE THE FORM ON PAGE 15 OR CALL TOLL-FREE 1-877-671-6036
View thousands more home plans online at www.familyhandyman.com/homeplans

309

Rambling Country Bungalow   Plan #710-040D-0003

1,475 total square feet of living area

Price Code B

Special features

- Family room features a high ceiling and prominent corner fireplace
- Kitchen with island counter and garden window makes a convenient connection between the family and dining rooms
- Hallway leads to three bedrooms all with large walk-in closets
- Covered breezeway joins main house and garage
- Full-width covered porch entry lends a country touch
- 3 bedrooms, 2 baths, 2-car side entry garage
- Slab foundation, drawings also include crawl space foundation

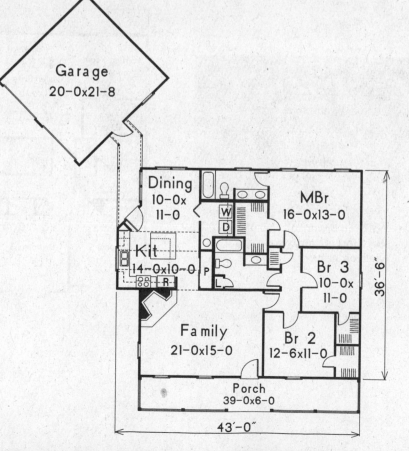

Garage
20-0x21-8

Dining
10-0x
11-0

MBr
16-0x13-0

Kit
14-0x10-0

Br 3
10-0x
11-0

Family
21-0x15-0

Br 2
12-6x11-0

Porch
39-0x6-0

36'-6"

43'-0"

3 Car Garage Apartment

Plan #710-15507

974 square feet

Price Code P12

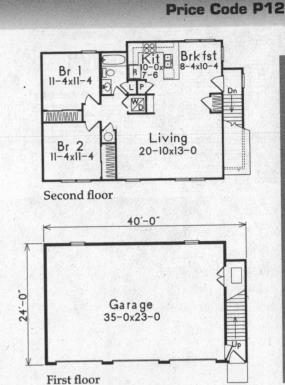

Br 1
11-4x11-4

Kit
10-0x
7-6

Brk fst
8-4x10-4

Dn

Br 2
11-4x11-4

Living
20-10x13-0

Second floor

40'-0"

24'-0"

Garage
35-0x23-0

Up

First floor

Apartment Garages

Special features

- Building height - 23'-2"
- Roof pitch - 5/12
- Ceiling height - 8'-0"
- 2 bedrooms, 1 bath
- Three 9' x 7' overhead doors
- Efficiently designed kitchen and breakfast room combine with living area for spaciousness
- Complete list of materials

2 Car Garage Apartment

Plan #710-15504

840 square feet

Price Code P11

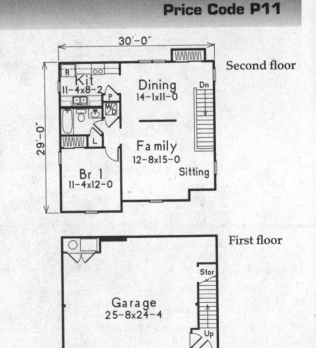

30'-0"

29'-0"

Kit
11-4x8-2

Dining
14-1x11-0

Dn

Second floor

Family
12-8x15-0

Br 1
11-4x12-0

Sitting

Stor

First floor

Garage
25-8x24-4

Up

Special features

- Building height - 25'-8"
- Roof pitch - 7/12
- Ceiling heights - First floor - 9'-0" Second floor - 8'-0"
- 1 bedroom, 1 bath
- Two 9' x 7' overhead doors
- Cozy covered entry
- Complete list of materials

TO ORDER BLUEPRINTS USE THE FORM ON PAGE 320 OR CALL TOLL-FREE 1-877-671-6036
View thousands more home plans online at www.familyhandyman.com/homeplans

311

3 Car Garage Apartment

Plan #710-15515
676 square feet
Price Code P11

Special features

- Building height - 22'-0"
- Roof pitch - 12/12
- Ceiling height - 8'-0"
- 1 bedroom, 1 bath
- Complete list of materials

WIC · F · k 11'2x8' · L · br 10'x12' · W/D · HWT · liv 12'4x15' · DN · **Second floor**

34' (10.3 m) · UP · 24' (7.3 m) · **three car garage** · **First floor**

3 Car Apartment Garage With Flair

Plan #710-15040
929 square feet
Price Code P13

Special features

- Size - 31' x 35'
- Building height - 27'-0"
- Roof pitch - 6.5/12, 10/12
- Ceiling heights - First floor - 9'-0" Second floor - 8'-0"
- 16' x 8', 9' x 8' overhead doors
- 2 bedrooms, 1 bath, 3-car side entry garage
- Slab foundation
- Living room with dining area has access to 8' x 12' deck
- Complete list of materials

Deck · **Second Floor** · Dn · Living 16-0x18-4 · Br 2 10-1x11-0 · Dining · L · Kit 9-0x 11-0 · R · MBr 14-0x11-1 · vaulted clg

Patio · Util · Sto · Up · W/D · Entry · Garage 23-4x29-4 · 35'-0" · **First Floor** · Covered porch depth 5-0 · 31'-0"

THE FAMILY Handyman

2 Car Garage Apartment

Plan #710-15513
588 square feet
Price Code P11

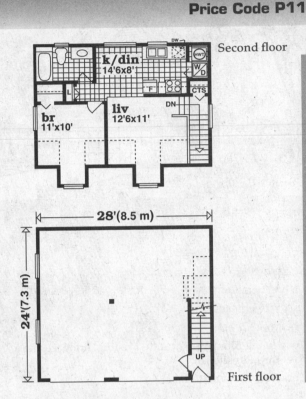

Second floor

k/din
14'6x8'

br
11'x10'

liv
12'6x11'

28'(8.5 m)

24'(7.3 m)

UP

First floor

Special features

- Building height - 23'-0"
- Roof pitch - 12/12 and 4/12
- Ceiling heights - First floor - 8'-0" Second floor - 8'-0"
- Charming dormers add character to exterior
- 1 bedroom, 1 bath
- Complete list of materials

2 Car Garage Apartment

Plan #710-15514
652 square feet
Price Code P11

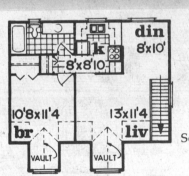

din
8'x10'

k
8'x8'10

10'8x11'4
br
VAULT

13x11'4
liv
VAULT

Second Floor

Special features

- Building height - 23'-0"
- Ceiling height - 8'-0"
- Roof pitch - 3 1/2/12, 11/12
- 1 bedroom, 1 bath
- Complete list of materials

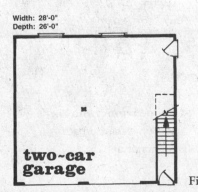

Width: 28'-0"
Depth: 26'-0"

two-car garage

First Floor

TO ORDER BLUEPRINTS USE THE FORM ON PAGE 320 OR CALL TOLL-FREE 1-877-671-6036
View thousands more home plans online at www.familyhandyman.com/homeplans

313

The Family Handyman

2 Car Garage Apartment

Special features

- Size - 28' x 26'
- Building height - 26'-6"
- Roof pitch - 8/12, 9/12
- Ceiling heights - First floor 9'-0" Second floor 8'-0"
- 16' x 7' overhead door
- 1 bedroom, 1 bath
- Cozy living room offers vaulted ceiling, fireplace and a pass-through kitchen
- Complete list of materials

Plan #710-15037

628 square feet

Price Code P13

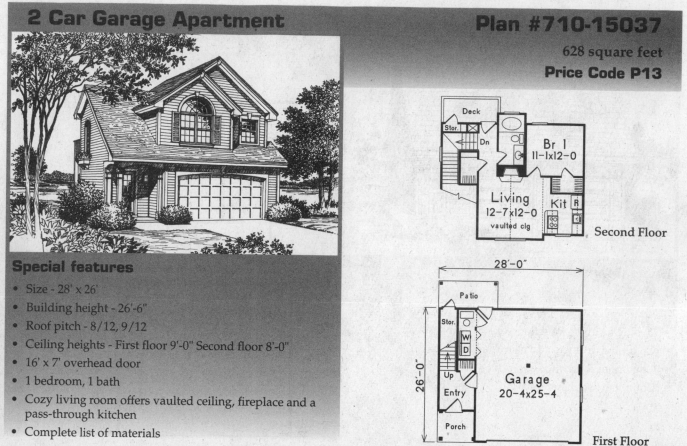

Deck

Stor.

Dn

Br 1
11-1x12-0

Living
12-7x12-0
vaulted clg

Kit R

Second Floor

28'-0"

Patio

Stor.

W D

Up

Entry

Porch

Garage
20-4x25-4

26'-0"

First Floor

3 Car Garage Apartment

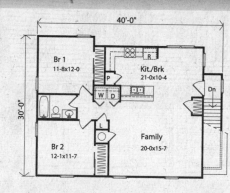

Special features

- Building height - 24'-0"
- Roof pitch - 5/12, 10/12
- Ceiling height - 8'-0"
- 2 bedrooms, 1 bath
- Spacious family room flows into kitchen/breakfast area
- Two sunny bedrooms share a bath
- Complete list of materials

Plan #710-15519

1,032 square feet

Price Code P12

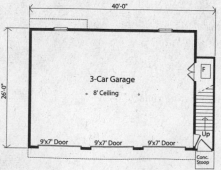

40'-0"

Br 1
11-8x12-0

Kit./Brk
21-0x10-4

P

W D

Dn

Br 2
12-1x11-7

L

Family
20-0x15-7

30'-0"

Second floor

40'-0"

3-Car Garage
8' Ceiling

F

26'-0"

9'x7' Door   9'x7' Door   9'x7' Door

Up

Conc.
Stoop

First floor

2 Car Garage Apartment

Plan #710-15034

654 square feet

Price Code P13

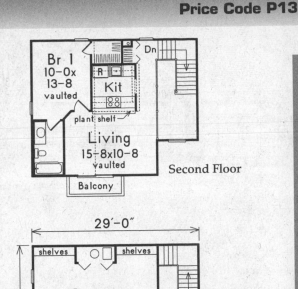

Apartment Garages

Special features

- Size - 29' x 24'
- Building height - 24'-0"
- Roof pitch - 7/12
- Ceiling height - 8'-0"
- 16' x 7' overhead door
- 1 bedroom, 1 bath
- Vaulted living room is open to a pass-through kitchen and breakfast bar and sliding glass doors to an outdoor balcony
- Complete list of materials

2 Car Garage Apartment

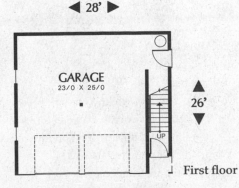

Plan #710-15510

633 square feet

Price Code P13

Special features

- Building height - 24'-0"
- Roof pitch - 9/12
- Ceiling height - 8'-0"
- 1 bedroom, 1 bath
- Two 8' x 7' overhead doors
- Lots of storage throughout including built-in shelves and a desk in the living room
- Complete list of materials

TO ORDER BLUEPRINTS USE THE FORM ON PAGE 320 OR CALL TOLL-FREE 1-877-671-6036
View thousands more home plans online at www.familyhandyman.com/homeplans

315

3 Car Garage With Storage

Plan #710-14510

Price Code P10

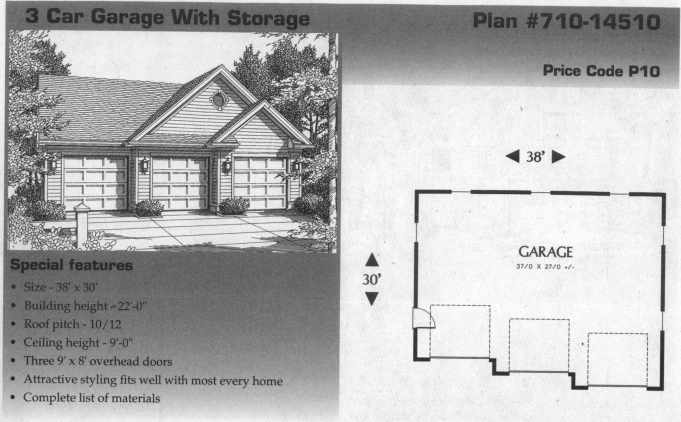

◄ **38'** ►

30'

GARAGE
37/0 X 27/0 +/-

Special features

- Size - 38' x 30'
- Building height - 22'-0"
- Roof pitch - 10/12
- Ceiling height - 9'-0"
- Three 9' x 8' overhead doors
- Attractive styling fits well with most every home
- Complete list of materials

2 Car Garage With Workshop And Loft

Plan #710-14003

Price Code P8

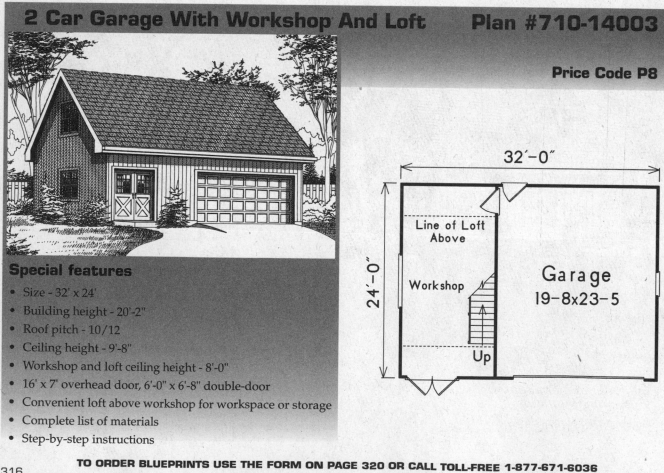

32'-0"

24'-0"

Line of Loft Above

Workshop

Garage
19-8x23-5

Up

Special features

- Size - 32' x 24'
- Building height - 20'-2"
- Roof pitch - 10/12
- Ceiling height - 9'-8"
- Workshop and loft ceiling height - 8'-0"
- 16' x 7' overhead door, 6'-0" x 6'-8" double-door
- Convenient loft above workshop for workspace or storage
- Complete list of materials
- Step-by-step instructions

2 Car Garage With Loft

Plan #710-14002

Price Code P8

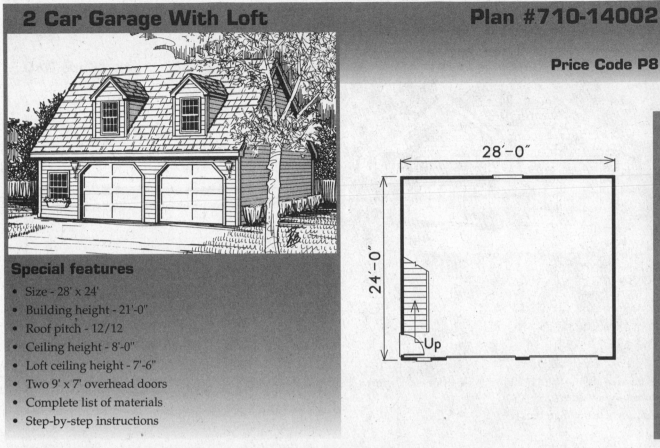

Special features

- Size - 28' x 24'
- Building height - 21'-0"
- Roof pitch - 12/12
- Ceiling height - 8'-0"
- Loft ceiling height - 7'-6"
- Two 9' x 7' overhead doors
- Complete list of materials
- Step-by-step instructions

28'-0"

24'-0"

Up

Garages

2 Car Garage With Loft - Gambrel Roof

Plan #710-14001

Price Code P8

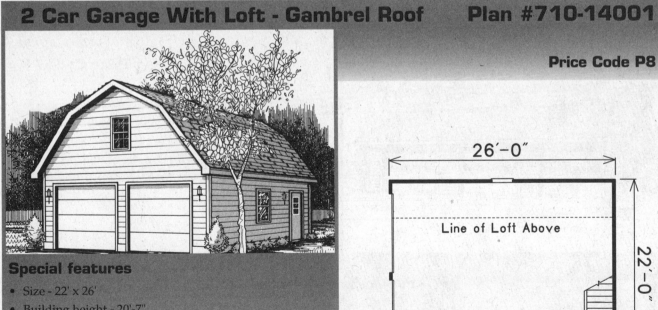

Line of Loft Above

26'-0"

22'-0"

Up

Special features

- Size - 22' x 26'
- Building height - 20'-7"
- Roof pitch - 7/12, 12/7
- Ceiling height - 8'-0"
- Loft ceiling height - 7'-4"
- Two 9' x 7' overhead doors
- Complete list of materials
- Step-by-step instructions

TO ORDER BLUEPRINTS USE THE FORM ON PAGE 320 OR CALL TOLL-FREE 1-877-671-6036
View thousands more home plans online at www.familyhandyman.com/homeplans

317

Car Garage With Storage

Plan #710-14508

Price Code P10

◄ 25' ►

▲ 26' ▼

GARAGE
24/4 X 23/4 +

Special features

- Size - 25' x 26'
- Building height - 21'-0"
- Roof pitch - 10/12
- Ceiling height - 8'-0"
- Two 9' x 7' overhead doors
- Attractive styling with double gabled front facade and decorative window
- Complete list of materials

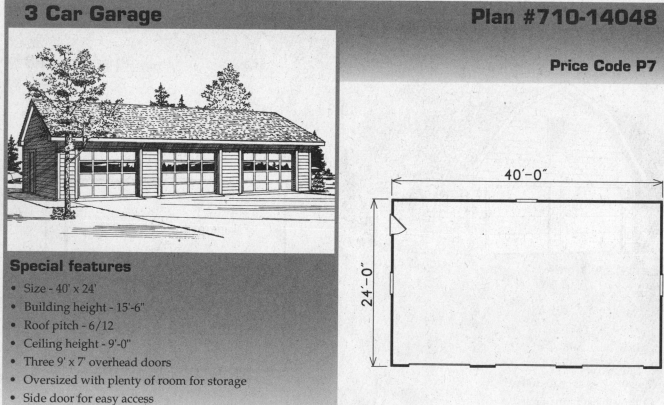

3 Car Garage

Plan #710-14048

Price Code P7

40'-0"

24'-0"

Special features

- Size - 40' x 24'
- Building height - 15'-6"
- Roof pitch - 6/12
- Ceiling height - 9'-0"
- Three 9' x 7' overhead doors
- Oversized with plenty of room for storage
- Side door for easy access
- Complete list of materials
- Step-by-step instructions

318

TO ORDER BLUEPRINTS USE THE FORM ON PAGE 320 OR CALL TOLL-FREE 1-877-671-6036
View thousands more home plans online at www.familyhandyman.com/homeplans

2 Car Garage With Loft

Plan #710-14016

Price Code P8

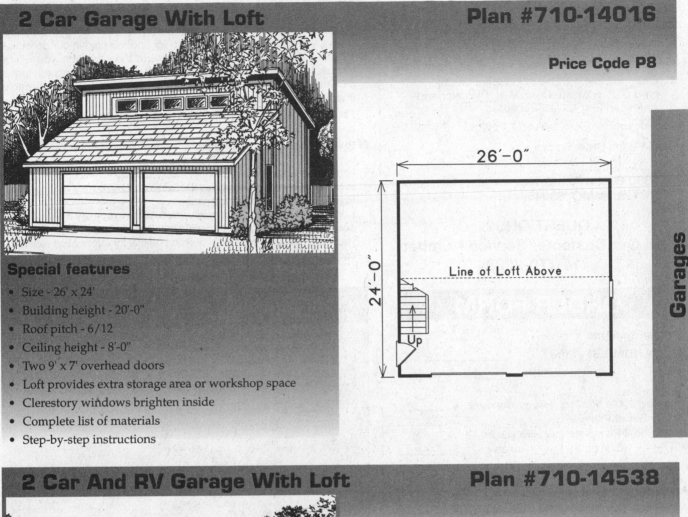

Garages

Special features

- Size - 26' x 24'
- Building height - 20'-0"
- Roof pitch - 6/12
- Ceiling height - 8'-0"
- Two 9' x 7' overhead doors
- Loft provides extra storage area or workshop space
- Clerestory windows brighten inside
- Complete list of materials
- Step-by-step instructions

2 Car And RV Garage With Loft

Plan #710-14538

Price Code P10

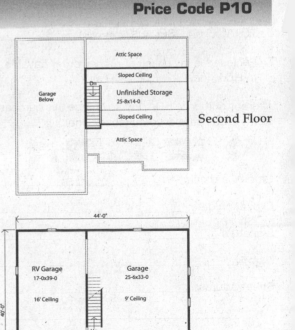

Special features

- Size - 44' x 40'
- Building height - 25'-0"
- Roof pitch - 9/12, 10/12
- Ceiling heights -
  First floor - 9'-0", 16'-0"
  Second floor - 8'-0"
- Unfinished storage is ideal for extra camping equipment
- Complete list of materials

TO ORDER BLUEPRINTS USE THE FORM ON PAGE 320 OR CALL TOLL-FREE 1-877-671-6036
View thousands more home plans online at www.familyhandyman.com/homeplans

319

For fastest service, Call Toll-Free
1-877-671-6036
24 hours a day

Three Easy Ways To Order

1. CALL toll free 1-877-671-6036 for credit card orders. MasterCard, Visa, Discover and American Express are accepted.

2. FAX your order to 1-314-770-2226.

3. MAIL the Order Form to:

   HDA, Inc.
   4390 Green Ash Drive
   St. Louis, MO 63045

QUESTIONS?
Call Our Customer Service Number
314-770-2228

ORDER FORM

Please send me -

PLAN NUMBER 710BT - _____

PRICE CODE_____ (see Plan Page)

Reproducible Masters (see chart at right) $ _____
Initial Set of Plans $ _____
Additional Plan Sets (see chart at right)
_____ (Qty) at $ _____ each $ _____

SUBTOTAL $ _____
SALES TAX (MO residents add 6%) $ _____
☐ Shipping / Handling (see chart at right) $ _____
(each additional set add $2.00 to shipping charges)

TOTAL ENCLOSED (US funds only) $ _____

☐ Enclosed is my check or money order payable to HDA, Inc. (Sorry, no COD's)

I hereby authorize HDA, Inc. to charge this purchase to my credit card account (check one):

☐ MasterCard ☐ VISA ☐ DISCOVER NOVUS ☐ AMERICAN EXPRESS Cards

Credit Card number _____

Expiration date _____

Signature _____

Name _____
(Please print or type)

Street Address _____
(Please **do not** use PO Box)

City _____

State _____ Zip _____

Daytime phone number (___) - _____

Thank you for your order!

IMPORTANT INFORMATION TO KNOW BEFORE YOU ORDER

■ **Exchange Policies** - Since blueprints are printed in response to your order, we cannot honor requests for refunds. However, if for some reason you find that the plan you have purchased does not meet your requirements, you may exchange that plan for another plan in our collection within 90 days of purchase. At the time of the exchange, you will be charged a processing fee of 25% of your original plan package price, plus the difference in price between the plan packages (if applicable) and the cost to ship the new plans to you.

Please note: Reproducible drawings can only be exchanged if the package is unopened.

■ **Building Codes & Requirements** - At the time the construction drawings were prepared, every effort was made to ensure that these plans and specifications meet nationally recognized codes. Our plans conform to most national building codes. Because building codes vary from area to area, some drawing modifications and/or the assistance of a professional designer or architect may be necessary to comply with your local codes or to accommodate specific building site conditions. We advise you to consult with your local building official for information regarding codes governing your area.

BLUEPRINT PRICE SCHEDULE

Price Code	1-Set	Additional Sets	Reproducible Masters
P4	$20.00	$10.00	$70.00
P5	$25.00	$10.00	$75.00
P6	$30.00	$10.00	$80.00
P7	$50.00	$10.00	$100.00
P8	$75.00	$10.00	$125.00
P9	$125.00	$20.00	$200.00
P10	$150.00	$20.00	$225.00
P11	$175.00	$20.00	$250.00
P12	$200.00	$20.00	$275.00
P13	$225.00	$45.00	$300.00

Plan prices guaranteed through March 31, 2005. Please note that plans are not refundable.

SHIPPING & HANDLING CHARGES
EACH ADDITIONAL SET ADD $2.00 TO SHIPPING CHARGES

U.S. SHIPPING

Regular *(allow 7-10 business days)* $5.95
Priority *(allow 3-5 business days)* $15.00
Express* *(allow 1-2 business days)* $25.00

CANADA SHIPPING

Standard *(allow 8-12 business days)* $15.00
Express* *(allow 3-5 business days)* $40.00

OVERSEAS SHIPPING/INTERNATIONAL
Call, fax, or e-mail (plans@hdainc.com) for shipping costs.

* For express delivery please call us by 11:00 a.m. Monday-Friday CST